F. Daniel Morales Hernández
Latin Americans in London

Language and Social Life

———

Edited by
David Britain
Crispin Thurlow

Volume 29

F. Daniel Morales Hernández

Latin Americans in London

Language Ideologies and Discourses of Migration

ISBN 978-3-11-221484-8
e-ISBN (PDF) 978-3-11-098797-3
e-ISBN (EPUB) 978-3-11-098820-8
ISSN 2364-4303

Library of Congress Control Number: 2023940861

Bibliographic information published by the Deutsche Nationalbibliothek
The Deutsche Nationalbibliothek lists this publication in the Deutsche Nationalbibliografie;
detailed bibliographic data are available on the internet at http://dnb.dnb.de.

© 2025 Walter de Gruyter GmbH, Berlin/Boston Cover
This volume is text- and page-identical with the hardback published in 2023.
image: Tim Perdue/Moment Open/Getty Images
Typesetting: Integra Software Services Pvt. Ltd.
Printing and binding: CPI books GmbH, Leck
www.degruyter.com

Contents

Prologue —— VII

Introduction —— 1

Chapter 1
Latin Americans in the UK —— 27
1.1 Introduction —— 27
1.2 History of Latin America —— 30
1.3 Diaspora —— 43
1.4 Latin American migration to the UK —— 47
1.5 Community formation —— 53
1.6 Social class —— 58
1.7 Neoliberalism —— 63

Chapter 2
Language, identity and society —— 71
2.1 Introduction —— 71
2.2 Identity —— 72
2.3 Ideology —— 80
2.4 Language ideologies —— 84
2.5 Critical Discourse Studies (CDS) and society —— 89

Chapter 3
Latin American immigrants' voices of immigration —— 99
3.1 Introduction —— 99
3.2 Who is an immigrant? Social class and immigration —— 100
3.3 Being "illegal"; deportation or removal? —— 114

Chapter 4
Work and social interactions of Latin American immigrants in a neoliberal context —— 123
4.1 Introduction —— 123
4.2 Assumptions and ideologies of Latin Americans in the service sector —— 124
4.3 Social categorisations among Latin Americans —— 144

Chapter 5
Latin Americans' multi-sited ideologies —— 161
5.1 Introduction —— **161**
5.2 Assimilation, authenticity and superiority —— **161**
5.3 Socieoconomic mobility —— **176**
5.4 Language ideology in institutional sites —— **184**

Chapter 6
Conclusion —— 197

Appendix A —— 205

Appendix B —— 207

References —— 211

Index —— 241

Prologue

This prologue serves two main purposes. The first one is to offer some clarification as to the use of important terminology that appears both in the title of this book and the political and cultural history of the social actors on whom it concentrates. The second one is to acknowledge family, friends, colleagues and institutions for their support so this work could come to fruition.

Some notes on terminology

A term that is employed throughout the book is Latin American. This is used to refer to the geographical origin of the people whose stories constitute the main voices of this work. Such term also applies to the author of this book whose place of birth and living is also situated within the same region. The focus on Latin America as a geographic territory intends to draw attention to the migration trajectories that people have travelled at a particular moment in history. This is crucial for our understanding of the political, cultural and economic transformations that the region has experienced and that have influenced people's identities and decisions to move to another country or another continent. This last idea is to suggest that Latin American people are neither homogenous nor have they had the same social or migration experiences; it rather intends to emphasise the structural differences from which migration occurs.

Other terms such as Hispanic, Latinx, Latino, Latina are not entirely avoided. They are included as a way of reporting what other studies in the United States and the participants in this study describe. In section, 1.2, Hispanic and Latinx, for instance, are used to report a macro racial term and identity politics category used by censuses and people in the US respectively. Although the book does not focus on identity politics, such terms are problematised in the corresponding section to avoid the reification and top-down attribution of identities. The US is not a context on which this book concentrates either, but this work refers to it as a way of both recognising the political relevance of a term such as Latino and understanding migration flows from Latin American countries to other parts of the world. The term Latino/a is also used in a descriptive manner as the participants in this study reproduce it when narrating their experiences with other co-ethnics.

Given that this work is situated in a complex context in which various discourses of migration have circulated historically, terms such as migrant and "illegal" deserve clarification. I use the term migrant interchangably with immigrant to refer to a person's change of residence across administrative borders. In this sense, this book attempts to take on an inclusivist view in which migrants are regarded as people who have moved to another country irrespective of their motivations. By delimiting this interpretation, this book also attempts to show awareness of debates about the lack of terminological consensus of who may be a migrant. Its meaning transcends dictionary definitions due to its political overtones and could have legal and social implications for people in a destination society. The term migrant is many times conflated with other categories such as illegal, which must not escape scrutiny for its potential dehumanising effects. The label "illegal" has undeniably become a social fact across many societies that designate the moral worthiness of some people to be in a country. Such label, nevertheless, should not be dehistoricised since migration policies have been changing throughout the years in a number of countries. As Dauvergne (2009) states:

> Since the early 1990 prosperous western states have been engaged in a worldwide crackdown on illegal immigration. This has included institutional changes in Germany, a range of restrictions in France by the notorious Pasqua laws, extensive reduction of asylum seeker rights in Britain. . .the United States has increased border and inland security (Dauvergne 2009:14–15)

In other words, illegality does not emerge by itself but as a construct created by tougher migration rules. In fact, the concept "illegal" was nonexistent in UK political debate until the mid-1960s, and even clandestine landing by Commonwealth citizens was not regarded as illegal (Slaven and Boswell 2018). This book avoids its use to define either a type of migration or people's migration status. It does not draw on it to refer to people either due to its criminalisation overtones that may even be used to justify violent actions against migrants. However, the term is used as a descriptive category when some of the participants employ it as a way of narrating their experiences of marginalisation and social disqualification. It thus appears as a claim for a more reflective use of language that allows to account for the creation of social identities and that may also conceal important distinctions about people's social realities and rights that we will see in chapter 3.

Clarification of how the label "illegal" is to be treated in this book is also concomitant with the elucidation of such terms as undocumented and irregular. This book uses the term undocumented to refer to a migration status rather than a person. It also refers to irregular as a temporary migration status; that is, people may enter a country with a tourist visa that eventually expires and leads them to an irregular status that, nonetheless, could be regularised again. This decision rests upon the intent to recognise the shifting nature of many people's migration status and should not be interpreted as an attempt to offer a reductionist view of the intricacies of migration policies that may regulate people's movement and prerogatives. As some scholars have pertinently observed, demarcating the meaning of "illegal", undocumented or irregular is a painstaking process since there could be different forms of irregularity. Documented migrants with a temporary work permit may become irregular if they violate their terms of employment and thus they may be liable to expulsion of the destination country (Triandafyllidou 2010). There are also those people who conduct irregular work on a tourist visa (Vollmer 2010). This book neither assumes that terms are neutral nor does it suggest that they mean the same for different people.

Finally an important construct that informs the analyses in this book is social class. The latter is the preferred and more consistently employed term in the book although the reader will also find it used interchangeably with class. Such use responds to stylistic decisions and does not intend to refer to a different conceptualisation of such a complex term.

Acknowledgements

I would like to thank the many people who have helped me bring this book to completion throughout the many years involved in its research and writing process.

I thank my parents and wife for their understanding and long-lasting support. Thank you, Angel and Cecilia, for the work that you generously do to help the elderly, the sick, the poor, the unemployed, and the migrant in our *pueblo* as well as the youth in our *barrio* in Queretaro. Your work has been a a daily incentive and a good example of humanist values that constantly remind me of the empathy needed in the society in which we live. Thank you Lilia for your genuine support, patience and constant availability to listen to my reflections and frustrations in all the stages of writing this book.

Clare Mar-Molinero, Darren Paffey, Laura Lewis, Gabrielle Budach, Heidi Ambruster, Adriana Patiño-Santos, Patrick Stevenson and Dick Vigers also deserve my gratitude. Your questions, academic encouragement and both our formal and informal conversations have been crucial for the development of this work over the past several years. I also thank David Block for suggesting and encouraging the writing of this book.

I am also very grateful to Natalie Fecher for showing interest in the issues discussed here. I cannot thank her enough as well as the editors of the Language in Social Life series and all the team at De Gruyter for their patience and work for this book to come to fruition.

A great deal of inspiration for the genesis of this book also comes from my experiences with former US, Salvadorean, Guatemalan, Honduran, Mexican students in the US and Mexico. My academic interests and personal motivations have been greatly shaped by their social and migration trajectories.

I also thank all those people in my *barrio* whose defence of public places has not only made them spaces of socialisation but recreation and freedom. Their activism has benefitted many generations like mine.

Finally, I would like to thank all the participants in this book. Without their experiences and stories of migration this book could not have been written. It is my intent to treat their experiences respectfully, and it is my hope that they give voice to their needs and serve as a window to mutual understanding.

Publication acknowledgements

Some of the ideas presented in this book have been included in previous publications. Parts of Chapter 5 are based upon the articles:

Morales, F. Daniel. 2018. "Si me quedo aquí toda la noche, seguiré hablando español". Ideologías lingüísticas en inmigrantes latinoamericanos en Londres ["If I stay here all night, I'll continue speaking Spanish". Linguistic ideologies in Latin American immigrants in London]. In Gugenberger Eva & Clare Mar-Molinero (Coords.), Sección temática: El impacto lingüístico de la migración transnacional y la migración de retorno en, desde y hacia el espacio iberorromanico [Thematic section: the liguistic impact of transnational and return migration in, from and to the Iberoromanic space]. *Revista Internacional de Lingüística Iberoamericana*, 16(1). 99–122.

Morales Hernández, F. Daniel. 2022. Una lengua, una nación. Fronteras lingüísticas sociales y políticas en dos casos de la migración latinoamericana al Reino Unido [One Language-One Nation. Linguistic, Social, and Political Borders in Two Cases of Latin American Migration to the United Kingdom], *Migraciones Internacionales*, 3:5, 1–21. https://doi.org/10.33679/rmi.v1i1.2311

Part of Chapter 4 was published as Morales Hernández F. Daniel. 2021. "'You know what we Latinos are like': intragroup evaluations and relations among outsourced Latin American workers in London" (2021), *Language and Intercultural Communication*, 21:5, 558–571. https://doi.org/10.1080/14708477.2021.1920970

Part of chapter 5 was published as Morales Hernández, F. Daniel. 2023. Language Experiences in Diaspora across time: Two Spanish-Speaking Latin Americans in London. In Márquez-Reiter, Rosina & Adriana Patiño-Santos (eds.), *Language Practices and Processes Among Latin Americans in Europe*, 208–229. London: Routledge.

Introduction

My motivations to understand sociolinguistic events in contexts of migration have been informed by my social trajectory that I have not travelled alone. I cannot ignore friends, families, local and larger sociocultural as well as political events that have relationally and empirically transformed my ways of seeing and being in the world. As Marx (1973: 265) put it, "society does not consist of individuals, but expresses the sum of interrelations, the relations within which these individuals stand". How I make sense of these historical interrelations will be a subjective exercise that encompasses the individual and the collective. The following accounts only become meaningful insofar they express the stories of those people who have made an imprint on my social identity.

The working-class *barrio* in which I grew up is located in a small town in the state of Queretaro, Mexico and where a European textile factory, *El Hercules*, was founded in the 1840s. It was indeed one of the first textile factories founded in Mexico. My paternal and maternal grandfathers, relatives, older friends and my father, for a short time in the 1960s, were factory workers who often rotated or doubled long shifts for extra pay in such an industrial site. This was often dubbed "Alcatraz" by local people and friends in reference to the former American prison and its incarceration-like work conditions in which many workers found themselves. As I recall my father telling me, "It was like torture working there, it was unbearably hot and noisy because of the machines that were in poorly ventilated rooms, the work was strenous and the salary was low". His description, in conversations with some of my friends' fathers in the early 1990s, was not only confirmed but was explained as a price to pay for not studying past elementary school; a type of self-blame that was intended to be passed on as a lesson from which close friends and I should learn. Studying was thus the recurrent advice as a way out of textile-factory work and into, allegedly, a better job, salary and lifestyle. Indeed, some of us were able to follow through our studies and got into higher education in the public education system, but one could wonder: how could people have continued their studies since many of them had to help parents and older brothers provide for their families at a young age?

A working-class *barrio* is not homogenous in that economic inequality affected some families more than others for whom education was a type of luxury they could not afford. Many friends of mine, like their parents, older brothers and sisters, had to support their families. At the age of 15, they had to find employment in construction, local carpentry workshops and paint and body shops or, as soon as they turned 18, in other factories that were beginning to operate in the state of Queretaro in the 1990s. The North American Free Trade Agreement

(NAFTA) had already been implemented in 1994 and transnational industries were drawing labour from various local regions. In fact, the state of Queretaro had received Foreign Direct Investment (see Micheli-Thirión 2020), which boosted the automotive, rubber and plastic industries where some friends began and continue to work to this day.

For many friends, working in a factory was not only draining but tedious and discouraging due to the repetitive nature of poorly-paid jobs. They decided to "try their luck" in the US. Before I got into University, I often heard: "why don't we go to *el gabacho* (the US)? My cousins are in Arizona already and they can help us get a job there". I had no idea where Arizona was and what sort of job could have been in store. My ignorance was even more accentuated with questions like "how are you supposed to cross the border? Will you cross on your own or will there be someone to help you cross?". The usual answer was that my friends' relatives knew a *pollero*, a smuggler who would guide them accross the dessert and took them to the US city where their contacts would pick them up. After a number of discouraging factory work experiences and poor salaries, some friends and relatives were attracted by the prospect of migration even though they said they did not like *gringos* (Americans), "They are boastful and think they rule the world", I remember them saying. One of my cousins with whom I was very close made it to Arizona after four days in the dessert where he nearly died of dehydration. He lived to tell the tale and soon found a job and began to remit money back to his family. Through similar channels of migration and after having been dissatisfied with factory jobs, other friends moved to North Carolina where acquaintances from other *barrios* had established and found them jobs in the construction industry.

In hindsight, the emigration of friends and close relatives shows me what scholars have called "social capital" (Putnam 2000), the connnections developed by families, friends or acquaintances fed up with economic precarity and uncertainty back in the late 1990s. Social capital developed out of a need to leave a poorly paid job rather than a sole motivation to migrate to the US where the jobs available to friends and relatives were still located at the lower end of the pay scale. They thus weighed up income opportunities in both sending and destination societies despite the fact that they risked their lives. More importantly, my friends' and relatives' realities instruct me that the experience of migration may involve both those who move to another country and those who stay in the place of origin where social and family relations are restructured and, when they are not fractured by violence or family separation, fraternal ties may transcend local boundaries.

As suggested above, I got into a Mexican public university and obtained a degree in English. I worked in higher education as an English teacher for three years while I was getting an hourly-rate salary of 50 mexican pesos (£2.5 approximately). With no guarantee of obtaining a steady job nor benefits, I sought opportunities to advance professionally and improve my economic situation abroad. A US-sponsored scholarship was my ticket to teach Spanish for one academic year in an American public high school in 2010. This was indeed a multicultural environment that enriched my teaching and that provided me with social experiences that destabilised my naive views of education; it put an emphasis on people's material living conditions and circusmtances that influenced their education opportunities. Although many of my students were US-born, some others had been born in El Salvador, Honduras, Guatemala and Mexico who had arrived in the US either as refugees who reunited with their families or through alternate routes. I still remember one of my students whose pseudonym is Carlos. He had been in the US for three years and had arrived as an unacompannied minor from El Salvador. When I asked him why he was enrolled in my course since he was a Spanish speaker, he said he wanted to practice it to not lose it and to obtain a hig mark. This could allow him to build a good academic record that proved his moral standing as a responsible individual who was trying to regularise his migration status and who wanted to pursue higher education studies in the United States. In class, he was indeed participative, but at times he dozed off. As he later told me, Carlos worked in a restaurant where he would end his shift late at night. He would then go to the house where he was renting a room and got some sleep before going to school. He said that he had to work since he needed the money to pay for rent, buy food and dress as well as, whenever he could, remit back money to his family in El Salvador. His socioeconomic reality and motivation to leave his home country and get an education brought me to the realisation that my workplace and my role as a teacher were embedded in larger unequal political and economic structures that he had been navigating with social agency.

In 2011, I returned to Mexico and attempted to reconnect with close friends. I would go to gatherings and family celebrations where we would talk about what we had been up to. As our conversations and meetings became more frequent, they said I had become a *"gringo"* and that I behaved like one. They never said why or how a *"gringo"* behaves, but they said it with animosity as though I had committed an act of betrayal. "You no longer belong to the *barrio*", they added. As I tried to make sense of their words, it became clear that I had been attributed traits that they found foreign and that gradually made me feel out of place and insecure about my ways of speaking to and interacting with them. My being othered was further exposed when friends and close relatives talked about break ins and crime afflicting our *barrio*. They said that burglars had to be lynched to deter others from commiting a crime, but I suggested that they should be reported to the police so violence could not lead to more violence. "You don't know anything about these problems and how we should deal with them since you haven't been here", "you haven't got the slighlest clue of what is going on" they answered. I still remember the abrupt discomfort I sensed by being placed outside a social circle whose realities I assumed I knew. In this respect, I still wonder whether my interactions and opinions could be explained not only by what I regarded a short absence, but as a product of my social trajectory altered by one of geographic mobility to a place historically viewed as a rival. The US and Mexico have had a historical relationship of tensions and contradictions that, for example, date back to the 1848 Treaty of Guadalupe Hidalgo whereby Mexico ceded 55 percent of its territory to the US. This is an event that remains in the collective memory that unites many Mexicans socio-politically and that may account for the label I was put.

The social dynamics in my *barrio* had not only changed but had become more complex in 2014. Emigration continued as other friends had left for the USA where they had connections that they had developed through acquaintances from other "*barrios*" that knew how to cross the border. Some were already established in North Carolina while others went to Chicago where they had construction jobs awaiting them. Furthermore, migrants from Central America and southern Mexico on their way to USA were arriving in my *barrio* and neighbouring ones after getting off "*la bestia*", a freight train that runs through many towns and states in Mexico and that is used by many Central American migrants to travel to the Mexico-US border. They were on the street or on public buses begging for change or food to eat while holding out a Honduran lempira note. This was meant to serve as some kind of proof of their national identity that could dissipate any doubts about their geographic origin that some sectors of society often questioned. Some locals gave them food and shelter where they could shower and rest, and those who were badly injured after having fallen or having been pushed off the train were provided with first aid before they could get on the train again to continue their journey to the US. Travelling on freight trains has become even more dangerous given that they have been running at higher speeds as a deterrent practice designed by the private companies that own them. As Central Americans' presence was increasing, a group of young local lawyers, accountants, other professionals and I met to discuss the opening of a migrant shelter in our town. The migrant shelter was to be a house close to the railroad tracks and was to be donated by the local parish. However, the idea was received with antipathy and xenophobic attitudes by some locals who said that those migrants would bring problems and crime to our *barrios*; a widely promoted stereotypical depiction of migration that is not uncommon in other large, global cities that gained local support that prevented the migrant shelter from opening.

A place like the one in which I grew up finds itself in larger historical processes of globalisation, migration, socioeconomic inequality and marginalisation. Many central Americans still travel on top of the freight trains that run through my town where they, despite conflicting attitudes from locals, continue to find a helping hand. This often materialises in food, money, clothing, shoeware or medicine given by a local self-funded dispensary run by women. As in the case of the UK, civil society organisations have also played a role in addressing Central American migrants' material and psychological needs in neighbouring towns. Other friends and relatives have returned from the US to their places of origin where some have reunited with their families as they try to adapt to a new pace of life. Some remain in the US where they have made a home and a family despite discrimination while others still try to get their "papers" and have to go unnoticed so they are not deported.

London experiences

The sociohistorical experiences that have shaped my views and ways of being in the world have indeed become more meaningful as I set out to explore and understand people's migration trajectories in a city such as London. Being a Latin American myself and being outside my own country are common characteristics that I share with other Latin Americans. Speaking Spanish is also a commonality that could allegedly ease access to social spaces and interaction opportunities with other Latin Americans. Indeed, speaking a common language was in many cases an important constituent of social relations with co-ethnics in London.

However, I was brought to the realisation that my male identity was problematic. In a migrants' rights workshop, I met the Director of a Latin American-oriented NGO and told her I was interested in meeting more Latin Americans to understand their realities and, if needed, offer help. She said she needed to know more about me and my interests and I was thus invited to the NGO's headquarters. In our meeting, she explained that most of the people she knew were Latin American women who had experienced gender-based violence, which had had an effect on their mental health and social relations that many of them were finding difficult to reconstruct. Their partners would often hide their passports so they did not go out and look for a job. My presence and possible interactions with some of them could be not only difficult to trust but threatening, she said. This was later confirmed by other volunteers in subsequent conversations where they said they needed to know me better and know who I was. I was thus ascribed identities that cannot go unchecked in a context where direct interaction with people is sought as a way of understanding their realities, needs and trajectories.

Being a male Latin American researcher entailed being confronted with my own privileges as well as being positioned as an interviewee whose presence raised suspicion that needed to be dissipated. As noted by some other scholars, the researcher cannot escape the implications of gender as, in some contexts, their gender bars them from some situations and activities (Westmarland 2000; Hammersley and Atkinson 207). Although I was granted access to people's stories after a series of interviews by volunteers, the effect of gender informed both my encounters with and inflected my questions to some of the participants; my presence was not innocuous, and thinking of what questions could be posed to them was not necessarily a methodological decision that could lead me to explore their stories in more depth. Some questions were left unasked and some others softened and, perhaps, unecessarily convoluted to avoid opening injuries or sounding patronising. Interviews are neither neutral nor a mere tool to "collect" data in a situation where the interviewer is allegedly in control and can dictate the direction of the narrative event. Interviews take place in a particular context in which the meaning that emerges from them can construct or reinforce more complex, power relations in real life.

As I attempted to become familiar with places where I could meet more Latin Americans, I frequently visited the Elephant and Castle shopping centre located in the borough of Southwark. There were a number of shops, cafes and restaurants owned and run by many Latin Americans who also socialised and found information about jobs and places to rent. The Elephant and Castle shopping centre had become one of the iconic Latin American places since the 1990s up to 2021 when it was demolished by developers after a gentrification project that started in 1999 (see Román-Velázquez 2014; 2022). In the hope of meeting and learning of the realities that Latin Americans experienced, one of my visits entailed observing and participating in a migrants' rights demonstration. It was organised by Latin American-oriented NGOS and organisations as a way of challenging the anti-immigrant attitudes and discourses that circulated in 2015 when the conservative party made a pledge to hold an in-out referendum on membership to the EU.

The demonstration started with a number of dance and music performances inside the shopping centre where divergent attitudes caught my attention. One of the attendees that I struck a conversation with said that the demonstration should have taken place somewhere else; "this place is ugly and makes us look poor", "we should have chosen a more modern place". Other people such as families and their kids were engaged in drawing flags of Colombia, Ecuador, Chile, Mexico, Peru among others on a large piece of cardboard. They also drew the Union Flag accompanied by the word "home". In a procession, they eventually headed to an adjacent theatre where they would end the demonstration with a concert as a celebration of diversity. I could not distance from the emotive and political elements of the demonstration but rather identified with them since, in one way or another, I was also a migrant. I may have had a different and, perhaps, privileged migration experience from that of many Latin Americans, but it was not exempt from othering practices implemented by migration policies. They asked Universities to monitor overseas students' attendance and, in some cases, share emails with the UK Visas and Immigration office (see Topping 2014). My attendance to the demonstration was not an inconsequential personal experience, but one that brought about my emotions. These should indeed be acknowledged as they influenced both what I saw (see Kleinman 1991) and my own social position whereby I related to the voice that migrants contribute (see Figure 1).

Figure 1: Migrants contribute flyer (Photo taken by Daniel Morales).

The Elephant and Castle shopping centre became a more familiar place as I continued to visit it. On another occasion, I went into a small restaurant behind a small coffee shop named "La bodeguita cafe" and sat down next to a couple, a man and a woman, who were having a conversation in Spanish. Their conversation seemed to be about finding ways of financing the man's personal business. After their conversation ended, the man left and the woman remained seated while putting her notebook and diary away. I told her I could not help hearing they were having a conversation in Spanish. Indeed, I used Spanish as a commonality whereby I could approach her. I introduced myself and asked her if I could sit with her. She agreed. Her pseudonym is Sonia and she was born in Ecuador although she lived in Spain for more than ten years and obtained EU citizenship. She had been in England with her Spanish husband for four years. She asked me about the reason why I was in the UK but particularly about my visit to Elephant and Castle. After hearing my reasons to be in the shopping centre, she offered to help me contact Latin American people who she said she knew very well through the network marketing company for which she worked.

On various ocassions, Sonia and I would have conversations about Spanish being a bond among many Latin Americans as well as personality traits of affability and warmth that allegedly characterise all of us. However, Sonia often distanced herself from Latin Americans when she said that "we" Europeans are more direct and blunter compared to other Latin Americans who are shy and insecure. At this point I wondered if I fell into that category or how she would position me during and after our conversations since I do not have an EU passport. She went on and said that the Latin Americans in the Elephant and Castle are either homeless, jobless or drunkards due to their conformity and low aspirations to improve their living conditions, they either settle for a menial cleaning job or rely on government welfare. She added that they do not know anything about English culture and have no interest in learning English, which she reinforced by saying "if people decide to stay in their ghetto, they do not make any effort to improve their life opportunities, and England is a land of opportunities". Her words not only attributed identities to other Latin Americans like me but began to resonate with larger discourses of migration and Hayekian economics; a neoliberal entrepreneurship mindset that, as we will see in later chapters, tends to ignore people's social trajectory and promotes financial self-responsibility as the vehicle to economic success.

Sonia's evaluative attitude to other Latin Americans' alleged conformism was, nevertheless, inconsistent with the various shops that Latin Americans run in and outside the shopping centre. Just across the Elephant and Castle shopping centre was an area known as the arches where there were also Latin American-run shops (see Figure 2).

Figure 2: Restaurant, shipping services and a dentist's office in arch 147 in the Elephant and Castle area (Photo taken by Daniel Morales).

As the picture above shows, arch 147 could house different types of businesses that offered socialisation and income-making opportunities, which challenge ideas of alleged conformity by foregrounding creativity. It also attested to people's agency to transform physical spaces symbolically. Arch 147 offered an interesting semiotic landscape that, on the one hand, indexes its transnational nature by recreating images of places of origin that dialogically transform the social texture of the site where people interact, socialise and address their (trans)local needs. Colours of national flags and food evocative of Colombia, shipping services to Ecuador and the use of Spanish reflect migrants' practices and creation of support networks. These are, indeed, important for vulnerable groups attempting to make their ends meet. On the other hand, the symbolic character of this site interacts with wider historical and economic forces that impact people's material living conditions. As mentioned above, the Elephant and Castle area was facing a gentrification process that threatened many Latin American-run shops and was feeding individualistic attitudes among Latin Americans retailers who drew a dichotomy of winners and losers (see Patiño-Santos and Márquez-Reiter 2019). At the time of research, Arch 147 was behind the Strata Tower, a skyscraper also known as "the Razor" built in 2005 and regarded an emblematic building of a larger developer-led gentrification project in Southwark (Román-Velázquez and Hill 2016). As I was able to observe, the symbolic resources that may encourage people to cohabitate physical spaces are in tension with material ones with which they may claim and appropriate them in such a global city as London. As gentrifying projects continue to date, occupying and transforming urban space index "the right to the city" (Lefebvre 1996) as a form of grass-roots resistance that, at the time of writing, Latin Americans were still undertaking against global capital (see Román-Velazquez 2022). Cities are always in the making and, as Sassen (2017: 124) put it, they are complex but incomplete systems where lies the possibility for those disadvantaged to assert "we are here" and "this is also our city".

My interactions with other latin Americans were often accompanied with unquestioned views of social interactions. These were festivals that I also attended in various London boroughs and that were organised by Latin American-oriented NGOs to make their presence and needs culturally and politically visible (see Figure 3). I have discussed this elsewhere (Morales Hernández 2021) but would like to emphasise the discrepancy between my presence as a Latin American researcher and people's immediate economic needs that I overlooked. In a conversation with a Colombian woman who was selling shirts, jeans and handbags in Southwark, I was shown my lack of sensitivity since after three or so minutes into the conversation, she asked me: "are you going to buy something? Because if you aren't, I haven't got time to talk to you". I could not help feeling uncomfortable and as an outsider because of my miopic view of her motivations to be in the festival. This experience reminded me that I needed to keep in mind people's varied socioeconomic conditions and social circumstances in which I could also be positioned not merely as an attendee to the festival but as a person that could contribute to people's income.

Figure 3: Mariachi band performing in a Latin American festival in Southwark (Photo taken by Daniel Morales).

As I arrived at another so called Latin American festival in a public park in Newham, my conception of what seemed familiar places and events continued to be abruptly transformed. There were dance and music performances displayed by a number of folklore groups that recreated cultural symbols of their homeland. There were also stalls that offered "authentic" Latin American food and facepainting for kids. However, there was a purple flag and a big green sign that read "BRING US IN HOUSE" in capital letters. I could not make any sense of the phrase even by looking at the initials of what seemed to be the name of a London-based university (see Figure 4 below). What does "BRING US IN HOUSE" mean? I then saw a man hand out leaflets as he said "la lucha continua" (the struggle goes on). He spotted me and asked: "Latino"? "Yes" I said, "acércese para explicarle sus derechos" (come and I'll explain your rights). He showed and handed me one of the leaflets whose content was about labour rights for outsourced cleaners working in universities and that he vigourously explained to me. When he asked at what university I was working, he found out I was not a cleaner and "we also need the support of students to carry our voice and demonstrate against the injustices that we suffer" he said. As he explained that he and his co-workers were also facing an intimidation campaign by the company that hired them, my ignorance about Latin American cleaners' demands and sense of inadequacy set in. I did not anticipate a political claim in what I unquestionably imagined to be a festive space. Also, being positioned as an outsourced cleaner brought me to the realisation that my geographical origin and my brown-skinned appearance may have been a trait embodied in an economic and political system of exploitation rather than a mere ethnic commonality with him. I do not mean to suggest that I discovered a new practice in a public park since

Figure 4: "Bring us in House" sign in Newham, London (Photo taken by Daniel Morales).

sites are historical places constituted by people's practices that precede my presence. Rather, I intend to emphasise my own lack of knowledge and familiarity with people's struggles that did not figure in my assumptions of what a festival was. It is thus important not to mistake places for contexts since places do not determine practices and behaviours that could also occur somewhere else (Goffman 1963; Hammersley and Atkinson 2007). A festival was indeed resignified by the political claims that trascended the physical locality where they were seemingly contained.

As I began to learn of Latin American's dispersed presence across London, I also visited the borough of Tottenham where there was a community centre that housed the so called Latin American kitchen every Tuesday (see Figure 5). As I entered the place, salsa music was being played, a man was taking some dishes to what appeared to be the kitchen and three women were busily serving food behind the counter. They were talking to each other in both English and Spanish. I greeted them and ordered something to eat, and made my way to the only available table in the hall room. I was then approached by a man in his mid forties and asked me, in Spanish, whether he could join me. He sat across the table and began to make conversation with me. He asked me where I was from and how long I had been in England. He said that he had been England for two months. Like Sonia, he then asked me what I was doing in this country. After I told him that I was attempting to meet people from Latin America to understand their migration experiences, he said "es un inicio de cero, migrar" (to migrate is a start from scratch) and told me "I have been on the road for more than 15 years and my clothes and my life are in a suitcase". He said that he had left Colombia due to "la violencia" in the 1990s; car bombs would blow up on the streets and threatened his life when he was much younger. He said that he slept in a sofa and had no home although he planned to bring his wife and two sons from Spain to the UK where there were better life prospects and where they could move away from racism against Latin Americans. He regarded himself lucky because he had received support from other Latin Americans upon his arrival in the UK where he felt lonely and disoriented due to his inability to speak and understand English.

I did want to ask him what he was doing to learn English but I had to dispense of such a thought. We had just met and I felt that asking questions could be both an intrusion to the reality of a person who suggested he trusted me to tell me about his life and whose economic needs I did not know. As some scholars remind us, we should critically examine the ethical implications of imposing our positions and ask ourselves whether we are the ones entitled to ask questions (Fitzpatrick and May 2022). I thought it best to continue to listen as he told me that he tried to attend the community centre on Thursdays when English classes were taught for Latin Americans and people from other nationalities. What he wanted was to get his ideas across in English and be able to widen his social circle. I also told him about my experience in the US and some of the language and work-related difficulties that I encountered whilst living there. Our migration experiences did not occur under the same circumstances but talking about them provided us with some common ground on which we continued our conversation. It went on for about two hours until we walked out of the community centre together. We exchanged phone numbers and agreed to meet again the following week in either the Latin American kitchen or a nearby area like Seven sisters. We never met again due to his work. Through people that he met in the community centre, he found a job as a cleaner and worked shifts and unsociable hours like many other Latin Americans in London. Meeting him showed me the value of listening to people as it can mitigate assumptions that often emerge as one may impertinently rush to ask questions that could impinge upon their lives.

Figure 5: Sign of the Latin American kitchen in a community centre in Tottenham (Photo taken by Daniel Morales).

Other places that attempt to address Latin American's needs such as obtaining a job and information about school for their kids have a history. An NGO located in the borough of Lambeth is a case in point as it is a place whose opening indexes political instability in Latin America and the formation of transnational ties in London. The Latin American-oriented NGO's name was *Chile Democrático*, Democratic Chile. It was founded in 1982 as a response to the needs of Chilean refugees that arrived in the UK between 1974 and 1979 after Pinochet's 1973 dictatorship (IRMO 2020). *Chile Democratico* supported refugees and their families by not only providing them with English classes, welfare, Saturday classes for children but by advocating political change in Chile from the UK. In 2000, *Chile Democratico* was renamed Indo American Refugee Migrant Organisation (IRMO) (see Figure 6) as a more encompassing term that could recognise the diversity of people of Latin American origin in London (IRMO 2022).

Figure 6: Indoamerican Refugee Migrant Organisation (IRMO) (Photo taken by Daniel Morales).

IRMO's presence and work has been valuable to people who need information in Spanish. In one of my visits, an Ecuadorian woman who had been in England for six months was looking for assisstance and advice to enroll her ten-year old in elementary school. She said she neither spoke nor understood English and was having difficulties understanding the UK education system. She looked stressed and was worried that her son would miss a school year. She asked me if I spoke English and if I knew how she could have her kid enrolled, but my limited knowledge of the school system and how the NGO worked at the time forced me to say I was unable to help her. I accompanied her to reception where she was helped by one of the volunteers as I felt that my ignorance of her needs was far greater than I had anticipated. I had to put myself in the position of being an acceptable incompetent (Lofland 1971) and had to ask questions, observe and listen to try to acquire a better sense of the structure of the NGO and perhaps began to understand people's social needs (Hammersley and Atkinson 2007). Being willing to help could have interfered with the types of services that the NGO offers and that it has in place through volunteers who many times not only guide migrants as to school-enrolling processes but also make phone calls on their behalf to learn about their kids' school needs and progress (see Figure 7). In other words, one's limitations should be openly acknowledged so they do not disrupt the social order in which people may find solution to the challenges that they face and that could leave them out of or thwart their integration opportunities.

Figure 7: Services offered by IRMO (Photo taken by Daniel Morales).

London markets are also places where Latin Americans find sources of employment by opening restaurants or selling produce they make (see Figure 8). In one of my frequent visits to Brixton market also located in Lambeth, I met Don Luis, a Colombian-Spanish man in his mid sixties who tried to sell home-made cheese to passers by. He carried it in a small trolley through the aisles of the market and, whenever I bumped into him, I contributed to his bussiness. He had been in England for five years where he was trying to get back on his feet and where his wife would join him. In Spain, he used to ran his own restaurant but he, like many other people, lost it along with his house in the 2008 financial crisis. In our conversations, he often ranted about bankers and politicians who he called thieves and he said he had many stories to tell about his life in both Spain and England. His voice could not be included in this work since he was often on the move from a market to wherever he could sell his cheese. At the time, he was trying to set everything up for the arrival of his wife; Don Luis rented a room that he shared with three more people and was looking for an apartment where he and his wife could live. Don Luis was one of the many onward migrants who relocated their lives as a reaction to adverse socioeconomic problems that they did not create.

Figure 8: Façade of Latin American-run butcher's in Lambeth market, London (Photo taken by Daniel Morales).

The same market was a place of job opportunities for other people such as Miguel who also arrived in the UK from Spain. Miguel, a Venezuelan-Spanish immigrant, worked in a Mexican restaurant. He said he did not know anyone upon his arrival in London but someone told him that he should go to Brixton where he would meet other Latin Americans. He met a Colombian woman who ran an *arepas* stall inside a butcher's shop and who had been in England for several years. Miguel said she was very kind and understanding and put him in touch with other Colombians and Venezuelans in the area where he could find a job. Miguel did all sorts of jobs in Barcelona and had been looking for any kind of decent job in England that allowed him to earn and remit money to her daughter in Venezuela. In London, he had two jobs, one of which, as he said, was a "taco man" who would offer "chicken, pork or beef tacos", "the best tacos in the world" to market goers from his stall outside a Mexican restaurant owned by a fellow Venezuelan. Miguel said that the restaurant originally served Venezuelan food but it was so close to going bankrupt that the owner, a man in his thirties and Miguel's boss, decided to change the name. It was then called Jalisco, the name of a western Mexican state regarded the home of *mariachis* and *tequila*, and its printed letters featured a jalapeño pepper that stood for the letter *J* (see Figure 9). "Everyone knows Mexico and Mexico sells, my friend", Miguel said. His story of migration and job insertion in London illustrates the social networks that migrants develop once they are in a destination society, which, according to Miguel and as we will see in chapter 3, welcomes vulnerable migrants.

Figure 9: Mexican restaurant called Jalisco in Lambeth market, London (Photo taken by Daniel Morales).

After many visits to and ethnographic observations in various London boroughs where Latin Americans socialise and work, more than thirty people were invited to this study. Although they accepted, their economic needs and fragmented work schedules often prevented them from meeting with me, and only sixteen people could find the time to tell me their life stories. The complexities that accompanied the interactions that I had with the ten female and six male Latin American immigrants whose voices are included in this book presented me with both opportunities and challenges to understand complex migration experiences. These are neither linear nor stable since some of them have lived and worked in Spain before coming to the UK and others have been in an irregular migration status. In this sense, sharing one's life story may generate social problems of which I believed I was conscious. As we will see in chapter 4, one of the participants from Ecuador lowered his voice as he recounted his experiences as an undocumented migrant and working with other Latin Americans in an exploitative environment in the service sector as a cleaner. His as well as other stories made me aware of the social responsibilities that I was to be entrusted. Being a Latin American researcher entails being confronted with personal biases, assumed knowledge and social imaginations that are repetitively destabilised by the multi-layered realities that people's stories disclose.

Life stories

Our human-created societies exhibit salient complex interrelationships and disparities. The flow of Latin American people into the UK and into new societies is multidirectional and it evokes inequalities across the globe (Blommaert 2003). This observation leads us to reflect upon and question general assumptions about what is meant by the national, ethnic, regional or cultural characteristics of particular groups of people (Blommaert 2010) and casts light on immigration statuses, locality, economic mobility, social class, etc. (Creese and Blackledge 2012, p. 552). To capture this complexity, as a late scholar put it, it has been necessary to "put forward an approach through which the interpretation of local events takes into account the translocal and is framed in terms of flows and movements" (Blommaert 2003: 612; see also Blommaert 2010).

In recent times the study of narrative and identities has become more prominent in sociolinguistics (Georgakopoulou 2011; Patiño-Santos 2020); however, it must be said that essentially its study is not new at all. Labov and Waletsky's (1967) work on oral narratives as part of a sociolinguistic project that concentrated on vernacular language variation is regarded as an influential approach to narrative structure and one of the initial studies to focus on personal narratives (De Fina and Georgakopoulou 2012). Labov and Waletsky defined narrative as "one verbal technique for recapitulating past experience, in particular a technique of constructing narrative units which match the temporal sequence of that experience" (1967: 13) They were interested in capturing spontaneous vernacular speech forms and asked the participants of their study whether they had been in a situation where they were in danger of dying. Most of the narratives elicited were designed to emphasise the strange and unusual character of the situation narrated and put the narrator in a function called "self-aggrandizement"; that is, the narrator placed in the most favourable possible light (Labov and Waletsky 1967: 34).

A defining feature of the Labovian model, as it is commonly known, is its concentration on the inner structure of the narrative itself (Labov and Waletsky 1967). This model is constituted by six basic narrative components: abstract, orientation, complicating action, resolution, evaluation and coda. The abstract is an initial clause that reports the entire sequence of events of the narrative while the orientation element of narrative serves to orient the listener in respect to person, place, time and behavioural situation (Labov and Waletsky 1967); that is, what the actors are doing (Labov 2010). The complicating action stands for the referential function of the narrative reporting a next event in response to the potential question "what happened (then)?" (Labov 1997: 402). For Labov, there is no narrative without the complicating action, which is terminated by a resolution; the set of complicating actions that follow the most reportable event (Labov 1967: 414). In addition to these structural elements, Labov refers to evaluation. This is "the means used by the narrator to indicate the point of the narrative; why it was told and the point the narrator was getting at" (Labov 1972: 366). Finally, the coda refers to a "functional device for returning the verbal perspective to the present moment" (Labov and Waletsky 1967:39) as in "that was it. That was me getting arrested for fraud" (Smith 2006: 474).

As observed above, Labov's model follows a linear structure in which narrative has "a beginning, a middle and an end" (1997: 396). Nonetheless, Labov's model has been criticised for a lack of attention to the sociocultural context of narrative production. That is, for "seeing narrative as a detached, autonomous and self-contained unit with clearly identifiable parts", and by its treatment of stories as monologic in which no attention to the co-construction of the story between teller and audience is paid (De Fina and Georgakopoulou 2012: 35). The absence of context in Labov's model also suggested an a priori and universal treatment of narrative, which overlooked that a good part of the meaning of narrative is found in the occasion of their production (Antaki and Widdicombe 1998). Despite these criticisms, his work continues to be valuable as it has stimulated other scholars to expand on some of the components of his approach. Patiño-Santos (2020), for instance, discussed evaluation in relation to reflexivity. She argued that evaluation as a narrative component allows tellers to stop the narrative event to express a point of view or a moral stance about what is narrated; the possibility to discursively construct a rational way of accounting for our actions. As other scholars have stated, Labov's model has had an extensive use for varied aims by researchers in a very wide range of disciplines, and thus, to some extent has informed the conceptual work on which narrative analysis is based (Bruner 1991; Holmes 1997; De Fina and Georgakopoulou 2012).

As I suggested above, new theorisations and methods in the study of narrative have also emerged and have been signalled by a paradigmatic shift. The narrative turn that began to gain prominence in various disciplines such as sociology and anthropology in the 1980s was an important turning point in the understanding of social events (De Fina and Georgakopoulou 2012). It arose as a response against quantitative- oriented studies in which it was ignored how people make sense of their social experiences and also against extractivist ethnographic approaches that treated participants merely as a vehicle to get information (Narajan and George 2001). The narrative turn put an emphasis on and takes into account individuals' every day experiences, the content of what they say, how they express it and the sociocultural context where they produce language (Narajan and George 2001). Thus, the narrative turn is characterised by its experience-centred approach that is also interpretative, subjective and particularistic that seeks to bring to the fore individuals' voices to be heard (De Fina and Georgakopolou 2012; Andrews et al. 2008). Furthermore, the narrative turn has also meant the use of narrative for the analysis of people's experiences such as those of migration that we will see in this study or in the context of medicine (see Kalitzkus and Matthiessen 2009; Greenhalgh and Hurwits 1998).

In the context of asylum-seeking interviews, the use of narrative has also gained political relevance. Shuman and Bohmer (2020) discuss the ways in which larger, cultural narratives inform how individuals' stories are assessed in legal settings. Narratives are complex modes of communication that depends on cultural conventions relevant for asylum seekers who attempt to "narrate horrific and traumatizing experiences" (Shuman and Bohmer 2020: 549). Asylum narratives are told by people who have suffered "atrocities unimaginable to others and may not seem coherent at first" (Shuman and Bohmer 2020: 550). As Shuman and Bohmer argue, the complexity of narrative is rarely taken into account by officials who may "dictate the direction of the narrative event" (Shuman and Bohmer 2020: 559) and whose assumptions often influence the plausibility, credibility or consistency of people's stories (Millbank, 2009). The study of narrative in legal settings has underscored the need to integrate research and policy to help asylum seekers and their lawyers to gain a better insight into the intricacies of producing a coherent, credible narrative (Shuman and Bohmer, 2020).

It must be added that the narrative turn is not a shift that stands for one specific and single approach to narrative. Rather, there are varied approaches that have led to what some authors have also termed the "new" narrative turn (Georgakopoulou 2011) in which we find the conceptualisation of small stories (Bamberg and Georgakopoulou 2008; Georgakopoulou 2006; Bamberg 2006) and big stories (Freeman 2006). Small stories consist of:

a gamut of under-represented and "a-typical" narrative activities, such as tellings of ongoing events, future or hypothetical events, shared (known) events, but also allusions to tellings, deferrals of tellings, and refusals to tell (Georgakopoulou 2006:130).

This approach both has originated as a critique to rigid canonical models of narratives in which a narrative is defined on the basis of vital constituents of "narrativity" and is characterised by its treatment of ongoing, immediate and often unreflective stories since they are told as the events unfold (Georgakopoulou 2015: 259–262 inverted commas in original). Big stories refer to narratives that are "often derived from interviews, clinical encounters, and other such interrogative venues, that entail a significant measure of reflection on either an event or experience, a significant portion of a life, or the whole of it" (Freeman 2006: 132). It is within big stories that this study is initially situated given that it allows it to distance from a proclivity to view narrative structurally and aesthetically to focus on a more human-centred aspect of it that is relevant in migration trajectories such as retrospection. Freeman (2015: 27) states "narratives always and necessarily entail looking backward, from some present moment, and seeing in the movement of events episodes that are part of some larger whole". That is, narrative is interwoven in the fabric of human experience, in this case the migration experience, since it involves a retrospective element that allows individuals to reflect and make sense of past experiences in the here and now (Freeman 2015; see also Morales-Hernández 2023).

As Freeman goes on to stress, the retrospective dimension of narrative is important because it both embraces "the historical nature of people's reality and serves as a pathway into dimensions of meaning" (2015: 28). This is consonant with what other researchers state and that allows us to better grasp what the study of narrative involves for the analytical purposes of this study: "narrative roots itself in the lived, felt experience of human agents in an ongoing way with their cohorts and surrounding environment" (Herman 2009: 21). In this vein, an additional characteristic comes to the fore, which is the cultural situatedness of human lives and narrative production. This feature, as criticised in the Labovian perspective, should not be ignored and we should thus take it as an invitation through which we as researchers and readers become sympathetic and "better attuned to cultural context" in order to capture and understand how "it has been woven into the fabric of both living and telling" (Freeman 2015: 29). In the context of Latin American migration, such an invitation is hard to turn down since the participants' stories do not occur in a sociocultural vacuum.

In addition, an approach to narrative that also concerns us and that is located within a biographical paradigm is that of the life story. It is biographical in the sense that the individual narrator is both the source of data and the target of analysis (De Fina 2015). As one of its main proponents argue:

> A life story consists of all the stories and associated discourse units, such as explanations and chronicles, and the connections between them, told by an individual during the course of his/her lifetime that satisfy the following two criteria: 1 the stories and associated discourse units contained in the life story have as their primary evaluation a point about the speaker, not a general point about the way the world is. The stories and associated discourse units have extended reportability; that is, they are tellable and are told and retold over the course of a long period of time (Linde 1983: p. 21).

Such a definition allows us to explore the tellers' social identities and to show I am such and such a kind of person since I acted in this way (Atkinson 2002). That is, life stories enable us to see social identities as a social unit in that the individual relates to a larger social group to which they may belong contextually. Nonetheless, this definition still begs clarification in order to avoid reducing a life story as any kind of story (see Abrams 2016):

> the life story is not simply a collection of stories, explanations, and so on, instead it involves all the relations among them. Thus, when any new story is added to the repertoire of the life story, it must be related in some way to the themes of the other stories included in the life story (Linde 1983: 25).

In other words, a life story is a narrative device that connects seemingly discrete, digressive accounts into a coherent whole within which an individual's life trajectory evolves (Abrams 2016). In addition, it proves to be a highly interdisciplinary tool for both the analysis of sociological issues and for the examination of language and social practice since various discourse units surface as people tell stories about their lives (Atkinson 2002; Mkhonza 1995). That is, a life story has been instrumentalized to capture Latin Americans' migration experiences in situ and, thus, the manner in which they use language to describe them is a major focus in this book since it is reflective of the social circumstances in which they speak and which are interconnected to meso and macro levels such as political, historical and economic aspects that influence how they voice their experiences (Pavlenko 2007). Treating narrative this way within the context of this study can help us understand the flows of people into new societies and how people attribute meaning to their new social realities.

Additionally, paying attention to people's stories has become instrumental for our understanding and questioning of the stratifying mechanism that characterise present-day societies. People traverse spaces and places in which there are norms, expectations, rules and conventions and thus their trajectories involve "processes of localisation, delocalisation, relocalisations of resources" (Blommaert 2010: 80) as well as declassing and reclassing processes. I will say more about these two last processes in chapter 1.3. In this light, the study of people's narratives within sociolinguistics goes beyond the confine of its structure since it can enable us to cast light on various domains of social life in which migrants live and how they experience them as they interact with others and attempt to both make sense of their reality and integrate into a new society.

Sociolinguists have continued to explore new ways of explaining current society-related phenomena affected by globalisation processes. The latter have created the need for a "critical science of language" and, as it has been stressed, pose theoretical challenges to present-day analysis and understanding of the development of language use and change (Blommaert 2010: 3). In this context of complex and unequal globalisation processes, there has been a reorientation of focus. As Slembrouck (2011: 155) has argued that "central to sociolinguistic enquiry here are questions of the representations of (trans) locality, as spatialized and as inserted in time, and struggled over realities of person, place, group, object, etc." In this vein, a sociolinguistic approach to people's stories finds itself in a position from which it can unveil how language echoes the difficulties and challenges of people in a globalising world (Blommaert 2010: 198). Therefore, it could be argued that the communicative value of language centres individuals in their contextualised social realities; discursive events through which speakers disclose the stratifying mechanisms that characterise present day human-created societies.

Although nation-states still remain an influential social, political entity that may regulate migrants' trajectories, it is necessary to stress that people move not only locally or nationally but internationally. A good instance of an intercontinental movement of people is that originated in Latin America. The presence of Latin American immigrants in the UK dates back to the 1970s and has recently increased. According to demographic data, there are around 250,000 people from Latin America of whom 145, 000 people live in London. This sociocultural group has been referred to as a community, a notion that seems to function as a reality sense-making strategy for many Latin Americans (Block 2006) and that has been importantly mobilised to obtain political recognition as an ethnic group in various London boroughs. Their presence exhibits migration patterns, channels and status which are multidirectional and varied since many have lived in other European countries before arriving in the UK while many have emigrated from Latin American countries, which has materialised in their dual nationalities.

In addition, while many have emigrated due to economic motivations, many others are in search of professional development that is also linked to different levels of language proficiency and knowledge. This is also linked to both a socioeconomic stratifying effect that becomes manifest in their experiences of declassing and a socioeconomic mobility aspiration associated with the perceived economic and academic progress English can offer. Furthermore, their heterogeneous national composition as well as the undocumented migration status in which many find themselves intimate that there might be sociocultural forces and socioeconomic differences that question the notion of a uniform community within the same group of people.

In light of the above, *Latin Americans in London: Language Ideologies and Discourses of migration*, stems from two interrelated needs. One is the need to examine the inter-relationships of a cultural group that has remained largely understudied by sociolinguists (Block 2006; 2008; Marquez-Reiter and Martin-Rojo 2015; Patiño Santos and Marquez-Reiter 2019; Patiño-Santos, 2023). That is, the social identity construction of Latin American immigrants is a process that demands attention as they bring with them a manifold array of interests and leave their localities with cultural and economic resources specific of their social trajectories. The social identities that reflect and constitute who people are might reveal how they associate with or disassociate themselves from other Latin American people in the various social spaces in which they have interacted. The second is the need to study the little explored production of language ideologies in this population. English, as stated above, figures as both an incentive and obstacle for many Latin Americans in London but their perceptions and knowledge about the language and how they may influence their social relations and realities have been little explored from an in-depth emic perspective. Furthermore, the study of language ideologies also enables us to gain insight into extralinguistic phenomena in the sense that their social relations, interests and realities are reflective of differentiated social class positions. These do not disappear once they have relocated their lives to a new society such as London that is not impregnable from a neoliberal economic model and ideology in which Latin Americans' lives and relations develop and where their jobs are also situated.

Neoliberal economic models have also had an impact on local populations and have triggered emigration from Latin America. At the same time that neoliberal ecomomic models have contributed to the creation of more desirable and self-disciplined skilled workers in both sending and receiving societies (Munck 2012; Urciuoli and LaDousa 2013). In this context, the social texture of local environments has not only changed but it can evidence re- stratification processes in a larger scale (Bauman, 1998). Both social class and neoliberalism have also been understudied in the Latin American community from a sociolinguistic lens, and they are necessary to examine due to the stratified and unequal social realities and relations that we witness in our societies. Thus, the questions that this book seeks to answer are: How do Latin American immigrants in London self-present in the social spaces that they have inhabited in a destination society? What insights into the social interactions of Latin Americans in London can we gain by looking at the social values and ideologies emergent in their discourses? And, to what extent can the emergent language ideologies enable us to gain insight into the constitution of Latin American immigrants' social relations and experiences when such ideologies intersect with social class? These questions will allow us to understand the language-mediated social experiences and interactions of the participants included in this work and they will bring to the fore their social identities who as members of a larger social group negotiate as they pursue their interests in a destination society.

This book comprises 6 chapters. Chapter 1 will refer to the history of Latin America that does not intend to be exhaustive but a canvas against which we can understand historical inequalities and differences in the region. Thus, processes of industrialisation, rural to urban migration as well as intraregional and extraregional migration in Latin America will be discussed. Such an account will also enable us to gain insight into historical unequal socioeconomic structures that affect people's everyday lives and influence their migration motivations, their social capital and ideologies that they may have and where they relocate their lives. In this respect the concept of diaspora is key and will also be discussed to frame the description of migration of Latin Americans to the United Kingdom. A discussion of social class and neoliberalism will ensue and close this chapter. Both social class and neoliberalism are relevant constructs that cast light on the variability that makes up the population under study as well as the economic logic and values that have permeated the various social domains and spaces that Latin Americans have cohabited in a destination society.

Chapter 2 concentrates on how language, identity and society are understood and what disciplines inform such an interpretation. Gender, race and ethnicity are also discussed since they are closely related to identity and crucial to account for how the participants verbalise their sociolinguistic experiences. The concept of ideology will also be included and its historical origin and development will be explored before stating how this book defines it. The definition offers an understanding of knowledge and attitudes of social-class based and neoliberal-oriented groups as well as those emerging in the participants' discourses. It will also be linked to the field of Linguistic Anthropology in order to introduce language ideologies and locate them outside a cognitive realm to emphasise their sociopolitical influence. This chapter concludes with a discussion on the relationship between language and society informed by Critical Discourse studies.

Chapter 3, 4 and 5 contain individual accounts of sixteen Latin American immigrants who narrate their social, work and linguistic experiences in different domains in London. Chapter 3 focuses on negative representations of immigration that three of the participants in this book reproduce and that can be found in other sectors of society as well as other immigration countries. Participants' discourses of "illegal" migration are also examined to explore the social consequentiality of such language use. As we will see, discourses of illegality blur transcendental distinctions such as deportation and removal that could determine the conditions in which people can stay and re-enter the country. Chapter 4 concentrates on the interactions of Latin Americans in various social domains such as the service sector, domestic work among others that will be specified later on in sections 4.3. Practices of exploitation, manipulation in outsourced work environments as well as ideologies of neoliberalism and social class are contextually examined as they intersect in the discourses of the participants who account for their experiences with other Latin Americans.

Chapter 5 deals with language ideologies in various sites in London. Ideologies of linguistic assimilation, accent, authenticity as well as the standard language and language superiority are under scrutiny. As we will see, such language ideologies contextually interact with social class and neoliberal ideologies of language as an added value to socioeconomic mobility and the desired skill whose absence leads to self-disqualification. Furthermore, the one nation one-language ideology in institutional sites such as hospitals, a town hall and the court points to the power of language associated with the social positions of the participants that will be dealt with in section 5.4. In all these accounts, I take into account material and symbolic characteristics of social class such as the role of social capital as I explore the participants' discourses and see how relevant the language ideologies mentioned above are when people along with their language and economic capitals traverse national boundaries motivated by specific circumstances. Finally, chapter 6 will include concluding comments and reflections upon the discourses analysed in this book at the same time that it will refer to constructs, approaches and attitudes that could benefit sociolinguistic studies.

Chapter 1
Latin Americans in the UK

1.1 Introduction

As stated in the introduction to this book, this chapter will open up with a history of Latin America. It will firstly refer to the origin of the term Latin America before moving on to the colonisation period that is to be followed by a discussion of independence movements. These will allow us to understand nation-state formation processes in the region. Subsequently, the chapter will refer to Latin American oligarchies' role in controlling political and economic affairs as well as encouraging European immigration. Furthermore, processes of industrialisation during the post-war period (1945–1970) will also be discussed to explain rural to urban migration and introduce the process of intrarregional migration in Latin America (Castles et al. 2009). Intraregional migration often refers to migration from and to Latin American countries, but migration patterns are not merely containted in one single geographical region. In this sense, so called extraregional migration that involves migration to the US and Europe (See Masferrer and Prieto 2019) is also crucial to our understanding of historical unequal socioeconomic structures as well as arbitrary political decisions that continue to shape the social texture of localities. In other words, migration from Latin American countries to the US, return migration from the US to Mexico as well as migration to European and Asian countries deserve attention since many Latin Americans have European and Asian ancestry and have relocated their lives outside the region to seek better job opportunities. This description will not only point to where people move, their social capital and ideologies that they may have (Mignolo 2007; Keen and Heynes 2013; Munck 2012; Block 2017; Téllez and Martínez-Casas 2019), but it will foreground the diasporic character of these migrations.

In light of the above, a discussion of the concept of diaspora will ensue. Since diaspora was originally associated with the Jews and the prospect of no return, the term has shifted over the decades and has been adapted to various scholarly traditions to which I will refer. The changeable and variegated treatments and contexts in which diaspora has been conceptualised has also raised criticisms and caveats that I will also discuss before it is defined for the purposes of this study. I will thus refer to three main features of the concept; dispersion, homeland orientation and boundary maintenance (Brubaker 2005). This, on the one hand, will allow me to account for cultural practices and imaginaries that the population under study perform and recreate away from the homeland in London. On the other hand, this discussion of diaspora, will draw attention to Latin American migration patterns within the region and, as a reminder to the reader, to various parts of the world such as the US and Europe; a discussion that will conceptually frame Latin American migration to the UK. Here I state that Latin American migration is a South to North migration that evidences the structural inequalities from which many migrants attempt to escape. I will then refer to the demographic presence of Latin Americans in the UK before I discuss its historical origins by locating it within political phenomena such as dictatorships in Chile and Argentina in the 1970s. Subsequently, I draw the reader's attention to the 1990s as a decade in which globally interconnected factors and neoliberal practices influenced Latin American emigration (García Canclini 2002).

Thirdly, I refer to migration routes such as Spain that recent Latin American migrants have travelled and that both has been a gateway to the UK and has had an impact on their identities. The latter will bring about their transnational character, which will be linked to a subsequent discussion of identity in section 2.2 and that will precede a discussion of the profile of Latin American immigrants. Such a discusssion will allow us to highlight their highly diversified background and motivations to be in the UK. Furthermore, I describe where many Latin Americans live by pointing to London boroughs where they are geographically concentrated and that can allow us to shed light on their varied social class differences. Here I will include views of the processes and consequences of migration such as declassing and reclassing, which continuously motivates us to keep in sight important distinctions that affect the participants' experiences and relations.

As to the section that addresses the concept of community, I firstly offer a definition of it before I move on to community formation processes of which Latin Americans in London have actively generated. In this section, I will refer to two important sites, The Latin American House and The Elephant and Castle Shopping Centre, associated with political and economic factors that help us explain and understand both why Latin Americans are mostly geographically located where they are and how they have come to be regarded as a community. I additionally mention other organisations they have formed as well as their role and usefulness for Latin Americans in London. I then move on to and problematise the assumed homogeneity that the concept of community may conjure up since both historical and globalisation-associated processes such as different types of migrations result in different economic resources, migration status and contrasting social attitudes among fellow citizens. To back this up, I will refer back to historical political processes and the construct of social class as well as the variability that makes up the population under study. That is, reference to a neoliberal ideology that does not reflect values evoked by the concept of community will also be made.

Subsequently, I will develop the notion of social class. I will refer to my initial understanding of it, as having an economic element, although not necessarily the only class marker. This will be subsequently linked to an interpretation of social class from a Bourdieusian perspective. His interpretation of other class markers such as cultural and social capital as well as habitus and field will allow us to consider and conceptualise social class not only as economic but also as culturally constructed. I will then move on to how these materially and culturally-based interpretation and examination of class have been taken by sociolinguists in the context of migration and how they can offer us a window into how class influences both how migrants experience the realities they narrate as well as how they talk about them.

Finally, I will also offer two definitions of neoliberalism, which come with a caveat. The decision to draw on the definitions presented in section 1.5 is neither to suggest that I will offer all-encompassing meanings of such a complex phenomenon, nor assume that they stand for the same effects in every single society. Neoliberalism is indeed a varied phenomenon whose effects and consequences hinge upon the structural differences of the societies it penetrates (Peck and Theodore 2007). In addition, I am aware that the term neoliberalism is hardly used by those who advocate it and who may not call themselves neoliberals (Aalbers 2013). Still, as Jessop (2013) states, the term lends itself to framing criticism that can guide research and attempt to shed light on the processes that influence the social organisation of life. The definitions provided thus attempt to identify the intersecting domains in which neoliberalism has become manifest and which will help us delimit it to gain insight into its tenets that are relevant for the social realities and relations of the participants of this study.

I will then refer to the origins of the term neoliberalism by mentioning the thinkers and the institutions through which they spread their ideas for one main reason, which is the fact that neoliberalism is a historical and deliberate economic project that along with other factors that we will see in section 1.4 is associated with and forced one of the first Latin American migrations to the UK. I will then draw on the ideas of a scholar of neoliberalism, Harvey, to offer a brief contextualisation of the socioeconomic environment that also contributed to the development of neoliberalism as well as its resulting effects on labour rights. These are important to mention as they are also linked to present job conditions and hiring practices such as outsourcing in which many Latin American immigrants work and to which I will then move on. Towards the end of this section, I will touch upon the figure of the entrepreneur and provide examples where such a figure was referred to and thus underscore the values it sought to mobilise. I will move on to contexts such as that of migration and language learning to exemplify that entrepreneurial values have entered people's subjectivities and which carry negative implications such as a process of exclusion and self-disqualification that we will see in chapter 5. Finally, I will refer to the notion of language as a commodity and as a skill in which people attempt to invest and which is equated with neoliberal ideas of economic mobility. However, socioeconomic constraints and conditions, like those in which some of the participants find themselves, also play a role in the acquisition of such a commodity, which I will discuss before concluding this section.

1.2 History of Latin America

Latin America is a large, culturally diverse geographical area that comprises the regions of South America, the islands of the Caribbean, Central America and Mexico. However, the term Latin America should not be dehistoricised as it is not devoid of foreign political connotations or interests. As noted by Phelan (1968: 279), the name *l'Amérique latine* "was conceived in France during the 1860s as a program of action embodying the role and the aspirations of France toward the Hispanic peoples of the New World". That is, France was assumed to be the natural, catholic leader and defender of Latin people against the protestant, Anglo-Saxon influence and domination that the US represented (Bethell 2018). In this vein, Latin America is not merely a geographical region in which many nation-states and cultures are seemingly contained. Latin America may be conceived of as a historical political project in which diversity, complexity and inequality among other factors intricately intertwine and inflect the ongoing transformation of its societies. These are multidimensional and interrelated to various scales that encompass the individual, the institutional and political forces and interests such as colonisation as an ineludible fact to explore the current complexity of Latin America.

Modern-day Latin American nations experienced European colonisation. This is understood as a structure of domination and exploitation in which the control of resources and authority over a population was upheld by a foreign power (Quijano 2014). Colonisation was perpetrated by the Spaniards and the Portuguese who arrived in the late 15th Century and who maintained their power through to the 18th century. Also, the French imposed their rule in Haiti in the 17th century until the beginning of the 19th century when an independence movement became successful. Portugal imposed its rule on present-day Brazil while Spain invaded the rest of the Latin American continent. As suggested above, the colonisation of the region is a historical process that involved the exploitation of indigenous populations and their land as well as the imposition of political institutions. For instance, the Spanish colonisers sought to secure government and obtain economic profits through the council of the Indies and viceroyalties from the XVI to the XVIII century. Although it was subordinate to the King of Spain, the council of Indies was the highest legislative, judicial and executive body that nominated high colonial officials to the king (Keen and Heynes 2013). It was mainly made up by lawyers, but it also incorporated people with military training and little knowledge of the law (Andujar-Castillo 2017).

Spanish-dominated local areas were governed by such royal agents as viceroys. They served as administrators that imposed royal authority and were responsible for the maintenance and increase of the prime source of royal revenue such as mining in politically delimited areas called viceroyalties. These were economically structured around silver mining in areas such as Zacatecas (Mexico) and Potosí (Peru) that opened in 1540 and that concentrated major commercial and political power in 1770 (Chasteen 2001). Furthermore, the viceroyalties of New Granada (Colombia) and Rio de la Plata (Argentina) were established in 1717 and 1770 and were created to mine gold and stop Potosi silver from being untaxed respectively (Chasteen 2001). Viceroyalties were indeed important political jurisdictions, but they also inflicted exploitation. For instance, the viceroy Francisco de Toledo in Peru created the *mita*; a system of forced labour in silver mines that disarticulated indigenous people's social organisation and led to a large number of deaths (Keen and Heynes 2013).

In Brazil, Portuguese settlers' colonial power and economic profit were not based on mining but sugar. The soil and climate of the northeast coast offered the right conditions for the cultivation of sugar cane and, by 1560, sugar growing and processing had become the dominant economic activities in present-day Bahía, Pernambuco, Alagoas and Sergipe (Taylor 1970). That is, sugar plantations were the main generators of export production and, by 1650, Brazil was the world's major supplier of sugar (Taylor 1970; Chasteen 2001). This, nonetheless, involved practices of exploitation. For instance, conservative estimates refer to 350, 000 enslaved people that were imported to work in the sugar plantations in Brazil in the XVII century alone (Simonsen 1957). In addition, sugar cultivation also led to a type of monoculture agriculture whose legacies are still felt in a highly stratified society, concentrated land ownership and unequal income distribution (Munck 2012).

In addition to the political and economic impositions that benefited a small elite, colonial authorities established the caste system. As a hierarchical, race-based ideology that classified people's worth and status according to their "purity of blood", the caste system allowed white Europeans to position themselves at the top of the colonial social structure (Keen and Haynes 2013; Chasteen 2001). The white ruling class was, nonetheless, divided by creoles, Spaniards born in the colonies, and peninsulars, European-born Spaniards. Both groups were legally equal but there were important distinctions between them. Although they were often owners of mines and ranches, creoles were usually excluded from high office in church and government (Chasteen 2001). They were deemed as indolent, incompetent and frivolous due to the American climate by the peninsulars who in turn were deemed mean by creoles but who filled out office posts and enjoyed greater access to the courts (Keen and Haynes 2013). The lower middle-class was made up by mestizos, individuals of mixed European and indigenous ancestry. Many of them often occupied such jobs as small farmers, shopkeepers, and artisans and many others were peons or enrolled the colonial militia (Keen and Hayness, 2013; Quijano 2019). Blacks, Mulattos, those of mixed European and African ancestry, and Zambos, people with African and indigenous ancestry, were at the bottom of the social ladder (Keen and Haynes 2013).

However, the caste system was not racially fixed since agreements between elite groups and economic power could serve as vehicles to social ascent. On the one hand, descendants of the indigenous nobility enjoyed privileges such as carrying arms, land ownership, tribute exemption and, in some cases, they were recipients of tributes (Romero-Galvan 2003). On the other hand, mestizos or mulattos could become part of the colonial aristocracy if they were descendants of a wealthy landowner who made them their legal heir or if they could purchase a document from the Spanish crown that established their legal whiteness (Keen and Haynes 2013; Twinam 2016). It is worth mentioning that there were poor whites who did not have economic privileges and many of them lived in poverty (Keen and Haynes 2013). Nonetheless, ideas on white superiority structured social relations. Some families could move up the social ladder and could enjoy a higher social status by marrying a partner whose skin was lighter than theirs (Chasteen 2001; Navarrete 2016). Indeed, a phrase such as *hay que mejorar la raza*, (let's improve the race by marrying a white-skinned person), exemplifies a race-based ideology of social advancement that is still reproduced in many Latin American societies today (see, Telles and Martinez Casas 2019).

Colonial rule continued its influence, but it began to face discontent from various sectors from the second half of the eigtheenth century on. In 1780, Tupac Amaru II, a descendent of the last Inca ruler, led a rebellion in the viceroyalty of Peru. His struggle for the abolition of slavery and independence extended to several areas of Peru, but he was captured and executed after three months of battle (Walker 2019). Other Spanish-controlled areas such as New Granada began to deal with the the Communero protests. In 1781, Manuela Beltran led the rebels who demanded the cancellation of tax increases on tobacco imposed by the Spanish Government, which met their demands. Later on, the concessions were made invalid by the Spanish viceroy and many of the rebels were either imprisoned or executed (McFarlane 1995). Despite these setbacks, the anti-colonial spirit was successful in the caribbean. In 1791, revolutionaries such as Toussaint L'Overture, Jean Jacques Dessalines, Henri Christophe and Alexandre Petión led an uprising against French colonists who, as stated above, had occupied the island of Haiti in the sixteenth century. After a series of struggles, these revolutionaries ended slavery and defeated the French in 1804 and thus established the first independent nation in Latin America (Keen and Haynes 2013).

In addition to internal uprisings, external factors also undermined the political sway of the Spanish crown in the colonies. On the one hand, Napoleon's invasion of Portugal was crucial for the destabilisation of Spanish rule. Since Portugal had refused to close its ports to English shipping, Napoleon's army headed to Lisbon after obtaining Charles IV's consent to march through Spain in 1807. Consequently, Napoleon's army swept across Spain as the Portuguese royal family escaped to Brazil (Keyne and Haynes 2013). A year later, the Spanish King was captured in Madrid and, according to some scholars, this was an indication for creoles in America to begin a struggle for independence (Munck 2012). On the other hand, subvervise ideas exerted a great deal of influence on other sectors of the creole elite. That is, the ideas of the American revolution and the Enlightment expressed by the French revolution resonated in some groups in the American colonies since both events intimated that colonial rule could be ended (Chasteen 2001; Quijano 2014). Nevertheless, the road to independence would be a long one; some sectors of the creole elite had a great interest in keeping their rule over the oppressed groups whose role in the movement to Independence was minimal at first (Keen and Hayness 2013).

In light of the above, well-educated figures, mostly creoles, played a major role in the liberation of the Americas in various parts of the continent. Simon Bolivar, for instance, fought and led battles for the Independence of Venezuela (1811), Colombia (1810), Ecuador (1822), Peru (1824) and Bolivia (1825). In 1810 and 1815, Miguel Hidalgo and Jose Maria Morelos were the precursors of Mexico's Independence movement that, under the leadership of Agustin de Iturbide and Vicente Guerrero, was accomplished in 1821. By 1826, most of Latin America had become independent except for Cuba, which had defeated Spanish rule in 1898 but obtained independence in 1902 when US military forces withdrew from the territory (Chasteen 2001). Brazil obtained its independence in 1822 when Dom Pedro, son of the portuguese King Joao VI, refused to obey his father's command to return to Portugal and proclaimed a monarchy (Schultz 2017).

After Independence, Latin American nations followed a Europe-based model of nation building process that did not uproot colonial ideologies. Newly formed Latin American nations emulated the French republic and American models that the ruling class admired (Chasteen 2001). Independence did not bring about equality and opportunities of social ascent for the opressed population neither. In fact, the end of colonialisation brought about the emergence of local oligarchies; power changed hands in that the creoles became the elite who controlled the economy and the state (Mignolo 2005). They had indeed control over political and economic affairs such as mining despite the fact that "they represented a minority in the newly independent Latin American nations" (Munck 2012: 41). Local oligarchies did not intend to incorporate the lower classes as it became evident in the lack of redistribution of land and income among them since wealth, power and prestige continued to be concentrated in the hands of a ruling class (Munck 2012; Quijano 2014; Tellez and Martínez-Casas 2019).

In the first half of the XIX century, Latin American elites insisted upon building their modern nation-states on Eurocentric views that endured until the end of the twentieth century. Such views are still palpable today in a system of pigmentocracy to which I will return below. Elite thinkers believed that the non-white population represented an obstacle to their nations' progress and that they would condemn their societies to a second-class status (Telles and Martínez Casas 2019). In other words, non-white people were associated with backwardness, a "barbarism" that needed to be uprooted (Munck, 2012:40). For instance, Mexican thinker José María Luis Mora stated:

> Through good administration, these indigenous people could give up idle life and form peaceful colonies by mixing and civilising them through the settlement of European families that at the same time could instruct them in religious duties and inculcate in them the arts and foster the habit of hard and laborious work (Mora, 1986 cited in Martínez Rodríguez 2010: 107).

Indeed, European migration was desired over other groups such as Jewish, Turkish and Chinese who some sectors of the Mexican press labeled "undesirables" later in the second half of the XIX century (see Pérez Vejo 2015:99). In Brazil, the elites thought of European immigration as a solution to Brazilians' inferiority. Between 1884 and 1913, about 2.7 million white European migrants who received state-sponsored ship tickets arrived and took up jobs in Sao Paolo (Moraes-Silva and Paixao, 2019; 216). In the 1929 Brazilian Congress of Eugenics, Anthropologist Edgard Roquete-Pinto predicted that Brazil's racial make up would be 80% white, 17% indigenous, 3% mixed and no black people by 2012 (Schwarcz, 1990). What Latin American elites sought was to secure white European immigrants who were to whiten and 'civilise' local populations. In this light, elites perceived Latin America as a deviation from a European civilising project (Sulmont and Callirgos 2019).

Between 1880 and 1930, some Latin American countries attracted significant numbers of European immigrants, most of whom moved to the southern cone. Argentina, for instance, was the main destination of Spanish, Irish, German, Austrian, French, English and Swiss (Chasteen 2001), but the largest group was that of around 3 million Italians (Castles et al. 2009). Brazil welcomed Italians, Portuguese, Spanish, German and Eastern European Jewish immigrants who, as stated above, moved to cities such as Sao Paulo (Chasteen 2001). By 1930, Brazil's foreign-born population was about 4,240,000 people (Rhenals Doria and Florez Bolivar 2013). Although in a smaller scale but through explicitly selective migration policies, Chile also intended to attract European immigrants. In 1882, Chile's General Immigration Agency was established in Europe and offered families Chilean land in uncultivated areas; between 1883 and 1895, more than 31,000 northern Europeans settled in the southern colonies of Llanquihue and Valdivia (Doña Reveco and Levinson 2012; Doña-Reveco 2022). By the beginning of the 20th century, Croatians settled in isolated regions in both the north and south of the country and, by 1920, Chile's foreign-born population amounted to 114,114 people, 51% of whom were Europeans (Doña Reveco 2022). Outside the southern cone, Cuba also became home to around 1.2 million foreigners, mostly Spanish immigrants who settled in Havana and other cities to work as store clerks and artisans (Gilbert 2004; Chasteen 2001).

Some other countries such as Peru, Mexico and Colombia also attempted to attract European immigrants, but they were less successful. For instance, about 30, 000 Spanish immigrants lived in Mexico by the 1920s (Salazar Anaya 1996) while 106,000 immigrants resided in Colombia in 1928 (Rhenals Doria and Florez Bolivar 2013). In this context, it is worth reminding ourselves that European immigration to Latin American is closely associated with ideas of pigmentocracy; a race-based view that still has an effect on the social structure of many Latin American countries where witheness is a desirable trait and a symbol of high status (Fitzgerald and Cook Martin 2015; Augustine-Adams 2015).

Global economic factors have also contributed to the reconfiguration of Latin American societies. For instance, the Great Depression of 1930 and World War II caused a "slump of agrarian produce" and a "disruption of international trade for industrial goods" (Munck, 2012: 44). These events derived into an inward-oriented economic development led by Latin American governments, which advocated an Import Substitution Industrialisation (ISI). This consisted of "establishing domestic production facilities to manufacture goods that were formerly imported" (Baer, 1972: 95) and laid the foundations of heavy industry in countries such as Argentina, Brazil and Mexico. Although industrialisation had begun in 1930 in Argentina, state-owned enterprises controlled sectors of the economy such as iron, steel and petroleum, energy generation, telecommunications, and transport in 1960 (della Paolera, et al. 2018). By the same decade, Brazil and Mexico could be characterised as semi-industrialised countries while Chile and Colombia were not lagging behind (Munck 2012). However, industrialisation was an uneven process across the región. Other countries such as Ecuador, Peru, Bolivia and Paraguay as well as those in Central America still relied on the primary-export model. For instance, Peru followed the primary export model to generate the trade surpluses that could pay for the machinery required in the industrialization process (Gómez-Galvarriato and Márquez-Colín 2017). In this context, it is worth taking on board that industrialisation as "an inward-oriented process was an attempt to address market conditions rather than change the economic bases of power" (Cardoso and Faletto 1979: 92).

The introduction of such policy as ISI also fostered rural-to-urban migration. This contributed to the accelerated urbanisation of Latin American societies, particularly in the largest cities between the 1930s and 1970s (see Brea 2003; Lattes et al. 2004). According to Herrick (1965), migration to cities was a two step-process in which people first moved from rural areas to small towns and then from small-towns to urban areas. It was not the poorest of the poor who constituted these migration flows but young people between 15 to 35 years of age who moved to urban centres in search of education, job opportunities and better service provision (Gilbert 2005; Elizaga 1972; Herrera 2013; ECLAC 2012). A major characteristic of these flows is the predominant presence of women. Although some women migrated as part of the family unit, a large number of them moved to the cities where they would take up informal jobs or find employment as cleaners, shop assistants and domestic workers for the affluent classes in urban spaces (Elizaga 1966; Hugo 1993; Elizaga and Macisco 1975; Rodriguez Vignoli and Rowe 2018).

Latin American societies were not only transformed by internal rural-urban-migration but also by intracontinental migration. An illustrative case is that of Argentina which became the destination of migrants from neighbouring countries such as Bolivia, Paraguay and Chile. Bolivian people, for instance, immigrated as seasonal, manual workers to the northwest of Argentina where the production of sugar mills and tobacco plantations expanded from the 1920s to 1938 (Villar 1984). According to Barlán (1988), this migration flow lasted for decades and was largely unregulated until the 1958 when a bilateral agreement was signed to protect Bolivian migrants. After the 1920s, Paraguayans constituted the main labour force required in the northeast of Argentina where industrial crops such as cotton, mate leaf and tea had expanded (Villar 1984). Similarly, Chileans would migrate to Patagonia (provinces in the south of the country) where, from the beginning of the XX century, timber yards and saw mills in the forest region as well as horticulture and fruit growing had become some of the important economic activities that required foreign labour (Villar 1984; Castles et al, 2009). However, migration from these three nations was not strictly rural-oriented. Eventually, many Bolivians, Paraguayans and Chileans concentrated in major urban centres in the northeast, northwest and south regions of Argentina where they would work in construction, domestic services, small shops and independent workmanship (Villar 1984; Jachimowicz 2006).

Venezuela is another country that received major flows from countries such as Colombia. Coffee crops have been a pull factor for Colombian seasonal workers whose increasing presence is also associated to oil-related economic growth and the reduction of European migration after 1958 (Castles et al. 2009). Furthermore, a 52-year armed conflict forced an estimated 1 million Colombians to migrate to Venezuela where they make the largest immigration group (Carvajal 2017). By 1995, 2 million persons were thought to have an irregular migration status in Venezuela, "most of them Colombian" (Kratochwil, 1995:33).

As scholars have stated, migration in the region was often spontaneous and unregulated. According to Lohrman, (1987), it was tolerated in the 1960s when unauthorised migrants could take up employment, which was not regarded as an illegal act. A decade later, state authorities' perceptions about migration changed and a number of measures were taken to regulate it. For instance, the Andean Pact on labour migration, ratified in 1975, regulated the movement of workers between member states to provide jobs and guarantee protection to migrants (Torrado 1979). The Andean Pact also entailed the creation of migration offices to supervise compliance of labour contracts, labour unions, social security benefits and the protection of migrants in repatriation cases (Torrado 1979). However, unregulated migration was still evident in 1980 when Venezuela legalized the migration status of some "280,000 to 350,000 out of estimates of 1.2 million to 3.5 million 'ilegal' residents" (Meissner, Papademetriou and North 1987:11). In this historical context, intraregional migration continues to shape Latin American societies in the early twenty-first century. For instance, Bolivians, Haitians and Venezuelans migrated to Brazil in 2003 when economic prosperity was anticipated (de Haas et al. 2020). Ecuadorian and a significant proportion of Peruvian women have moved to Chile where many of them find employment as domestic workers (Doña and Levinson 2007).

In addition to intraregional migration, people's mobility from Mexico to the United States is also an important migration phenomenon. As stated above, this is referred to as extraregional migration (Masferrer and Prieto 2021), which casts a wider light on the complex, historical transformation of Latin American societies. For instance, migration from Mexico began to become prominent in the 1920s when Mexico was reconstructing itself after the Mexican revolution. An estimate of 1,000,000 border-crossings were documented as a response to economic inequality that affected the popular sectors (Hernández 2015). In the following decade, the Great Depression would make migration from Mexico decrease but the Second World War would create a demand of Mexican labour. In 1942, the Bracero Programme, a Mexico-US bilateral agreement that allowed Mexican immigrants to work on short-term, agricultural labor contracts, was created. About 4.6 million contracts were signed and many *braceros* (farm labourers) were employed in Southwest and Northwest agroindustries (Hernández 2015). It is worth mentioning that the Bracero Programme was highly selective. Women and other Mexicans who lived in urban areas, owned land or were "too old" were not eligible for agricultural work in the US, which led many to migrate as undocumented workers (Cohen 2006). As some scholars have suggested, the Bracero Programme contributed to the reification of class and gender ideologies in that male Mexican workers were expected to learn from the American experience and were positioned as ideal actors of modernity upon their return to Mexico (Rosas 2006). The Bracero Programme was terminated in 1964 due to the exploitative conditions in which many Mexican migrants worked.

However, migration from Mexico and Latin American countries to the US did not stop as US policies and international politics developed. On the one hand, the passage of the 1965 Immigration and Nationality Act intended to replace the exclusionary national origins quotas of 1920 with a new migration system that allocated residence visas based on family reunification and labor force needs (Massey and Pren 2012). As foreign-born people were granted legal status through Green cards, their presence increased from 4.2 million in 1970–79 to 6.2 million in 1980–89 (de Haas et al. 2020). People of Mexican origin would make up most of the migrant population that would rely on irregular crossings and would work in lower skilled jobs (de Haas et al. 2020). On the other hand, the Cold War also contributed to migration from Central America, Andean and Caribbean countries to the US. El Salvador, Guatemala and Colombia were badly affected by US intervention in its fight against communism in Latin America (Massey and Pren 2012; de Haas et al. 2020). For instance, an estimate of 150,000 low and highly skilled Colombians migrated to the United States due to violence, inequality and political instability by the early 1970s (Carvajal 2017). In Cuba, emigration from the island would increase after 1959 when the US-supported Batista's regime was ousted by Fidel Castro. Most Cubans would be admitted after citing communist oppression and they would become lawful permanent residents after living in the US for one year as established by the Cuban Adjustment Act (CAA) that US congress passed in 1966 (Batalova and Zong 2017). By the 1970s, there were 439,000 Cubans (Batalova and Zong, 2017). In 1980, Castro's regime declared that people wishing to emigrate to the US were free to leave from the port of Mariel where approximately 125, 000 people boarded boats that reached Florida (Card 1990). As scholars suggest, Castro's government allowed them to leave as an escape valve for dissidence and excess labour (Batalova and Zong 2017) and as a test to US hospitality (de Haas et al. 2020). The US President Jimmy Carter negogiated with the Cuban counterpart to end this migration in November 1980 (Engstrom 1997).

The implementation of the North Atlantic Free Trade Agreement (NAFTA) in 1994 also brought about significant changes in migration flows from Mexico to the US. Although it was expected to encourage economic growth in Mexico and thus reduce migration flows, NAFTA created economic dislocations and unemployment that badly affected Mexican workers (Martin 1993; Martin and Taylor 1996). Mexican peasants, for instance, were unable to compete with US large corporations that exported subsidized corn and other agricultural products and, in many cases, were driven to debt, rent or sell their land or migrate (Nail 2015). In addition, maquiladora plants situated in border cities such as Mexicali triggered both internal and international migration. Labour was and still is predominantly constituted by women who often received low salaries and face human rights violations in unsafe labour conditions, which have also been migration-triggering factors that have made jobs more attractive across the border (Hernández-Suarez 2008). Since the implementation of NAFTA, migration from Mexico to the US increased from about 4 million people to 8.4 million people in 2000 (Passel and Cohn 2010; see also Gutierrez 2019).

Migration flows to the US have not only been regulated through economic policies. For instance, the 9/11 terror attacks increased the securitization of migration through the 2001 Patriot Act. This materialised in increased funding for surveillance and deportation of foreigners without due process and contributed to the reorientation of migration flows from Latin America into other parts of the world (Lacque 2011; de Haas et al. 2020). I will return to this in section 1.4. Nevertheless, the US would figure as a major immigration country for seasonal agricultural workers whose presence went from 28, 000 in 2000 to 196, 000 of whom 180, 000 were of Mexican origin in 2018 (de Haas et al. 2020: 159).

The complexity of people's mobility in the region is enhanced by migration flows from Central America through Mexico to the US. Economic insecurity and civil war forced people from Nicaragua, el Salvador and Guatemala to leave to Mexico or travel through the country to the US where they would apply for asylum in the 1970s and 1980s (see Gzesh 2006). Since the 1990s, gang violence has also been a major migration push factor (see París Pombo 2017). After the deportation policies of the US, the presence of gangs known as *Maras Salvatruchas* began to both increase and gain power over urban spaces in the Northern Triangle countries - Honduras, El Salvador and Guatemala- whose populations have had to deal with forced recruitment, extorsions, violence and a war tax that the gangs have imposed (Bailey 2014: 125). For instance, teenagers have had to emigrate as a strategy to escape forced recruitment while small bussiness owners have had to close and leave their bussinesses due to extorsions (París Pombo 2017). Natural disasters have also acted as major migration catalysts, mainly from Honduras. In 1998, Hurricane Mitch damaged crops, left thousands of people jobless and displaced 1.5 million people approximately (Reichman 2013). It is also after this event that Honduran emigration increased as suggested by the number of Hondurans being aprehended at the US southern border where the apprehensions rose from 10, 600 to 18, 800 between 1988 and 1999 (Reichman 2013). In subsequent years, migration from Honduras continued to grow and there were 283,000 in 2000 and close to 523,000 Hondurans in the US in 2010 (Reichman 2013).

As political and economic instablity worsened, migration flows from Central America through Mexico to the US diversified. In 2005, an estimate of 418, 000 Central American migrants crossed Mexico and, in 2014, the presence of unaccompanied minors caught scholars' attention when more than 50 000 unaccompanied minors made it to the Mexico-US border (Rodríguez, 2016: 9). In 2019, the US border patrol aprehended more than 850, 000 people (U. S. Customs and Border Protection [CBP], 2019), most of whom (64.5%) were family units made up by a female adult with a child or unaccompanied children (París Pombo et al 2021: 14). In this light, Mexico can be regarded as a major transit country for migrants from Honduras, El Salvador and Guatemala. Their journey is often a perilous one due to the presence of criminal organisations that force their recruitment or extorsions made by authorities (See París Pombo 2017).

Migration from the Caribbean, particularly from Haiti, is a phenomenon that also deserves attention. It has been multidirectional due to both economic factors and natural disasters to which some countries temporarily responded by making their migration policies flexible. After the 2010 earthquake, the US granted Temporary Protected Status to Haitians while Brazil offered them humanitarian visas and family reunification options (Duffard Evangelista, 2016; Méroné and Castillo, 2020). Haitians mainly moved to Brazil where the construction industry provided many Haitians with jobs as Brazil was to improve its infrastructure to host the 2014 World Cup and the 2016 Summer Olympics (Yates 2021). As to 2014, there were about 50,000 Haitians living in Brazil (Fernandes and Gomes De Cast, 2014). However, factors such as the 2016 economic downturn, racism and the fact that the newly elected Brazilian government did not allow Haitians to renew their five-year humanitarian visa, made many of them move to other countries such as Chile (Moreno-Mena 2018). Here, Haitians' presence numbered 103, 000 in 2017, but a year later the Chilean government began requiring visas to enter the country where they increasingly faced workplace discrimination and limited job opportunities. (Yates 2021). In 2020, an estimated 183, 000 Haitians lived in Chile (Doña Reveco 2022), but many began to head north to the US.

The North-bound journey involved passing through a number of countries that could take months or years. Haitians have had to traverse Peru, Ecuador, Colombia, Panamá, Costa Rica, Nicaragua, Honduras, Guatemala, México to reach the US or, in some cases, Canada (París Pombo 2018). As it has been documented, migrating by plane is a rare option and Haitians must hitch-hike, use taxis, boats and buses to cross most of those countries that often present them with life-risking dangers (Méroné and Castillo 2020). As they transit the region, the duration of their journey could depend on needs to find temporary work or the time they are detained in some countries (Yates 2021). In 2016, many Haitians reached Mexico's border towns such as Tijuana and Mexicali where they, however, were forced to wait due to recent changes in US migration policies. Except for pregnant women and those accompanying minors (París Pombo, 2018), the US began deportations of Haitian people in the same year arguing that conditions in Haiti were safe (Méroné and Castillo 2020). This policy change resulted in an estimate of 4000 Haitian people staying in Mexico's border cities where many men have found employment or have continued their studies after a nearly four-year wait (Yee Quintero 2017; Ramírez-Meda 2022).

In October 2018, Central American migrants drew on a collective strategy that could enable them to cross Mexico and reach the US. Although the origin of migrant caravans dates back to the migrant viacrusis in 2011 when a group of Central American mothers began to look for their dissappeared sons and daughthers in Mexico, migrants have drawn on them to protect themselves from the extorsions and kidnapping that many of them face in Mexico (see París Pombo et al. 2021). However, migrants' collective efforts to cross Mexico have been constrained by a number of local policies that respond to international economic interest. Although Mexico's federal government initially took on a humanitarian attitude to migrants by providing visas, former US president Donald Trump implemented a policy that made Mexico a *de facto* third safe country through the Migration Protection Protocols (MPP), a policy also known as Remain in Mexico. The MPP was enforced from January 2019 to January 2021 and it meant that Central American migrants applying for asylum to the US must wait for their asylum determination hearings in Mexico (OrtegaVelazquez. 2020).

Furthermore, in June 2019, the Trump administration blackmailed the Mexican government by threatening to increase tariffs on imports if migration flows were not stopped. As a response, the Mexican government is estimated to have deployed about 2400 National Guard members to stop migrant caravans in its south border (Observatorio de Legislación y Política Migratoria. 2019). It also mandated that coach companies ask customers to show an identity document such as a Passport or a voting ID that proves legal residence in the country to have the right to use their services (see Chisti and Bolter 2021). In this light, crossing Mexico illustrates the externalisation of borders that have influenced migrants' decisions to move to the US. That is, many Central American migrants have opted to apply for asylum in Mexico as it is evidenced by the increase of asylum applications that went from 1 296 in 2013 to 70 302 in 2019 (Comar 2020). Until 2015, most of the applicants were from Honduras, El Salvador and Guatemala (París Pombo et al. 2021). Although mexico has become an immigration option for many, it continues to be a major transit country for an estimated 300 000 and 500 000 people who cross it anually (Días-Prieto 2016).

Return migration from the US to Mexico has also foregrounded political arbitrariness and people's responses to it. During the Obama Administration (2009–2017), 2.2 million people of Mexican origin were deported in addition to the more than 1.56 million people deported in the Bush administration (2000–2008) (Masferrer 2021). However, two caveats are in order. On the one hand, our understanding of return migration should not overlook the social capital that people form since migrants may not cut their ties with kin, friends and other connections that may remain in a destination society. A case in point is that of migrant women returning to such a destination society as the US to reunite with their sons from whom they were separated after deportation (see Danielson 2013). In this context, return migration involves a circularity that makes it difficult to explain as something fixed and contained within national boundaries (Cassarino 2004; de Haas 2010). On the other hand, migrants may not be necessarily forced to return through deportation, but they may be compelled to migrate because they may face other abuses such as family separation (de Haas 2021), exclusion, racism and marginalisation experiences (see Cruz Manjarrez 2016).

Despite changing migration policies and the increased securitization of borders, the US has become a destination society for people from Latin American countries. According to the U.S. Census Bureau (2021), the "Hispanic" population reached 62.1 million in 2020 making it the nation's second largest racial/ethnic group. Hispanic is a term that deserves further attention and to which I will return below. The most numerous group is that of Mexican origin who were about 10.9 million people living in the United States in 2019 (Israel and Batalova 2020). In 2014, an estimated 1.2 million residents claiming Colombian heritage resided in the United States, making them the seventh-largest Hispanic group in the country (Carvajal 2017). The US has indeed become a major destination for other national groups. Venezuelans, Ecuadorians, Bolivians, Peruvians who have left their country of origin due to economic inequalities continue to reconfigure the spaces where they move (de Haas et al. 2020).

As noted above, the term Hispanic invites us to scrutinise it to avoid essentialist representations of heterogenous sociocultural groups. Indeed, Hispanic has become meaningful as it congregates people to observe Hispanic heritage month annually, for instance, and it is often used as synonymous with Latino in US official documents such as censuses. These, however, tend to lump together a very diverse group of people (Oboler 1998) that may identify with other terms and meanings. For instance, Fuller and Leeman (2020) report how a Dominican American teenager uses the term Spanish as a pan-ethnic label similar to Hispanic or Latinx. The latter has been more recently employed to challenge "traditional binary notions of gender" such as Latino/Latina (Salinas 2020: 153) and thus as a term that "recognizes the intersectionality of sexuality, language, immigration, ethnicity, culture, and phenotype" (Salinas 2020: 310). Identity self-ascription is more complex than what a census may intend to depict since other factors such as education attainment, discrimination experiences and immigration generation have also been reported to affect people's self-identification preferences for Hispanic, Latino/a, or LatinX (Thompson and Martínez 2022). In this vein, the apparent fixity of the term Hispanic is destabilised by people's contextual needs, identity-construction processes as well as social and migration trajectories that they have travelled. In other words, the meaning of these terms will hinge upon historically constructed contexts in which people situate themselves (see Fuller and Leeman 2020).

Migration from Latin America to Asia and Europe has also highlighted many Latin Americans' ancestry. For instance, Peruvian and Brazilian *Nikkeijin* (descendants of Japanese emigrants) have relocated their lives to Japan since the late 1980s (Takenaka et al. 2010). With no restriction to employment, both groups have satisfied labour demands in manufacturing (Kashiwazaki and Akaha 2006) that has led to their increasing presence over the years; while there is record of about 60,000 Peruvians living in Japan (Takenaka et al. 2010), an estimate of 286, 000 Brazilians has also been reported in the same Asian country (Tsuda 2000). People from Argentina have also moved to European countries such as Spain and Italy where applications for residence and citizenship are available to those with Spanish and Italian ancestry (Courtis 2011). However, Asian or European ancestry is not necessarily the predominant factor that may motivate people to leave Latin America. For those Latin Americans escaping economic instability, Italy has indeed become an immigration country. By 2009, there was an estimate of 77, 629 Peruvians and 80, 700 Ecuadorians in Italy where a large number of them are employed in domestic work and the health sector (Calvi 2011). In this light, people's mobility within, across and outside Latin America is intricately intertwined with economic, social and political factors along a historical continuum in which migrants' agency continues to transform the societies where their presence has become diasporic.

1.3 Diaspora

As we saw above, the history of Latin America involves not only sociopolitical, economic factors but mobility patterns that have shaped its social texture and have transcended intraregional geographic confines. In this sense, human mobility entails taking into account concepts that have historically informed it such as diaspora. This term derives from a religious text, the Septuagint that was the first

Greek translation of the Hebrew Bible in which diaspora refers to the threat of dispersion that the Jews would have to face if they did not abide by God's commandments (Dufoix 2017). The term carried a negative connotation implying a sense of loss and applied to the actual dispersion of the Jews; diaspora primarily referred to the Jewish experience (Brubaker 2015) and was generally associated with forcible displacement and the prospect of no return (Feist 2010).

However, as scholars have pointed out, the meaning of the term has not stayed put as there has been a '"diaspora" diaspora since the early 1980s in various academic disciplines (Sheffer 2003; Brubaker 2005). In Cultural Studies, diaspora began to be interpreted in relation to a recognised experience of heterogenous identities in migrant groups; that is, diaspora identities that (re)produce themselves through hybridity, transformation and difference (Hall 1993). The meaning has expanded to refer not only to overseas sociocultural groups such as the Armenians in exile or Palestinian refugees who have experienced displacement (Clifford 1994; Safran 1991), but categories such as victim, labour, imperial and cultural diasporas as well as trade (Cohen 1997). In addition, diaspora has also been understood as accidental diasporas in that the migration of borders have politically separated ethnonational communities such as Hungarians from their homelands (Brubaker 2000; 2005). The notion of the homeland has also been conceptualised to explain the emotional and social ties that labour migrants such as Mexican or Salvadoran in a destination society keep with their homeland (Sheffer 2003).

In the context of communication technologies, diaspora has also been developed. By observing "digital diasporas", there has been a focus on how migrants create "communities of belonging" to reaffirm connections with their homelands and establish new relations in both the host countries and across other ethnic diasporas (Ponzanesi, 2020; 989). Social media platforms such as Facebook, Twitter, Instagram and YouTube as well as apps such as WhatsApp, WeChat, FaceTime and Viber have been the sites in which researchers have also sought to understand how the experience of belonging is affectively conveyed through technological forms of immediacy and proximity (Ponzanesi, 2020). In this sense, the concept of diaspora has been (re)appropriated and reconfigured by a number of scholars to account for the "cultural, social, economic, and especially political struggles of those dispersed ethnic groups, permanently residing in host countries away from their homelands" (Scheffer, 2003: 7).

However, the evolution of the meaning of diaspora has been received with criticism that is worth considering. Tölölyan (1996) reminds us of possible assumptions that may treat populations as homogenous. Assuming them as monolithic may lead us to overlook the possibility that "populations may have possessed or may have enacted many different identities in their homeland" (Tölölyan,

1996: 8). Cohen (2008) also encourages us not to lose sight of the passage of time. As he states, not everyone may regard themselves as part of a diaspora, since:

> Many members of a particular ethnic group may intend to and be able to merge into the crowd, lose their prior identity and achieve individualized forms of social mobility. (The changing of ethnically identifiable names by new immigrants signals this intention.) Other groups may intermarry with locals, adopt or blend with their religions and other social practices (creolize) and thereby slowly disappear as a separable ethnic group. A strong or renewed tie to the past or a block to assimilation in the present and future must exist to permit a diasporic consciousness to emerge, while the active fraction of the incipient diasporic must have time to mobilize the group concerned (Cohen 2008: 16).

Additionally, Cohen also warns us of possible conceptual conservatism that may lead to empirical blindess. That is, we must consider what function diaspora is to serve "to the migrant groups that have adopted it since many social groups may want to be simultaneously ethnic and transnational, local and cosmopolitan, to have a comfort zone and a questing impulse" due to insecurities, tensions and adversities that people may encounter (Cohen 2008: 11). Indeed, scholars should be critical of both groupism as a general category into which migrant communities may be fitted and the sociopolitical conditions in which they may live. In the context of this study, Tölöylan's and Cohen's caveats pertinently remind us of the heterogeneous identities, divergent interests, motivations, social alignments and the historical time in which many Latin Americans have migrated.

Another important caveat to take on board is that diasporic movements are neither necessarily smooth nor are they undertaken by everyone. States still have the capacity to select, monitor and control people's movement through the creation of bureaucracies such as passports, visas, biometric devices (Torpey 2000; Brubaker 2015) and other forms of digital securitization that draw on systems of surveillance that aim to control the 'other' through databases such Frontex, Eurosur, Eurodac (Latonero and Kift 2018; Ponzanesi 2020). In this sense, these mechanisms that constrain mobility cannot be ignored in our understanding of diaspora since they are illustrative of regimes of mobility. As stated above, they could materialise in everyday bordering practices reflective of a hostile environment in the UK (Oliver 2014) or in bilateral agreements between the US and Mexico governments to stop the flow of Central American migrants (see París Pombo et al. 2021). Social class inequalities also matter as to who is able to move to another country since the poorest of the poor hardly ever have the resources to relocate their lives (de Haas et al. 2020).

Scholarly debate has also focused on the semantic overlap between diaspora and transnationalism. Faist (2010) has stated that diaspora conceptually intersects with transnationalism in that the experience of migration is neither limited to one single geographical space nor is it merely associated with traditional settlement and assimilation in host societies. He goes on to argue that both "diaspora and transnationalism deal with homeland ties" and "the incorporation of persons living 'abroad' into the regions of destination" (Faist 2010: 20). Indeed, transnationalism has been understood not as something new but as an epistemic move that explains "the processes by which immigrants forge and sustain multi-stranded social relations that link together their societies of origin and settlement" (Basch, Glick-Schiller and Blanck, 1994: 7). Therefore, clear-cut conceptual differences between diaspora and transnationalism are difficult to draw, and their theorisations will have to be contextually delimited in order not to contribute to an unreflective view of people's sociocultural practices and ways of organising themselves in space and time.

Bearing in mind the critical views of the semantic shift of the concept of diaspora, it can be argued that the term could be used to refer to national groups of people living outside their home countries due not only to religion or ethnic conflict but also to economic issues (Faist 2010). Diaspora can thus be understood as a "phenomenon that defines migrant groups that maintain a sense of belonging and culture over long distances" (Niewswand, 2011 in Marini, 2013: 134). Although long distances may be reduced and compressed by technological tools, these neither replace feelings of disjuncture that migrants may still experience nor eliminate a troubled relationship that they may have with the host society (Cohen 2008). In addition, the concept of diaspora often encompasses three features: dispersion, homeland orientation and boundary-maintenance. According to Brubaker (2005: 5), the first refers to "forced or traumatic dispersion or more generally as a type of dispersion in space that crosses national or state borders". The second refers to symbolic ties to the home country but more specifically to "the orientation to a real or imagined 'homeland' as a source of value, identity and loyalty" (Brubaker 2005:5). And finally the third involves the preservation of a distinctive identity vis-á-vis a receiving society; that is, cultural boundaries can be kept by an intentional resistance to assimilate to the host society (Brubaker 2005:6). As other studies have shown, this does not mean that migrants show reluctance to integrate, but it intends to stress the point that they cultivate sociocultural practices from their home country in their new society (see Brubaker 2005; Faist 2010). As described in the introduction to this book, this is exemplified by the various Latin American festivals in London in which I was able to participate and observe during fieldwork and that brought together migrants from Ecuador, Colombia, Peru, Mexico, Chile and other nationality groups to recreate meaningful cultural symbols such as dance, music, food, and clothing evocative of their homeland. In Italy, Latin Americans have demonstrated similar homeland orientation practices by the recreation of cultural symbols in restaurants and shops that they run and by engaging in homeland politics (see Calvi 2020). In this vein, the concept of diaspora entails observing people's practices that may acquire complex meanings that transcend national boundaries.

1.4 Latin American migration to the UK

Latin American migration to the UK is a South to North migration that draws attention to current global economic inequalities. As more people from developing countries are attracted to industrialised countries (see Martin 2013), their migration trajectories mainly reflect their disillusionment with sending societies in which a low income or the lack of both political instability and the rule of law usually acts as a major push migration factor (see McIlwaine, 2011; 2016). Their arrival, social and job insertion and lives in a receiving society such as the UK merit being observed and should therefore be contextualised within migration policies that, as it has been historically demonstrated, have an effect on routes to travel and the identities and living conditions of migrants (see Somerville 2018).

Latin American migration to the UK has increased significantly over the last three decades, but documenting their presence has not been an easy task. In his intent to capture the presence of 'Latinos' in London, Block (2006) refers to these challenges:

> in an interview with the Peruvian Consul General in November 2003, I was told that SSLs [Spanish-speaking Latinos] probably numbered between 200,000 and 300,000 in London, and that Colombians alone probably accounted for over 100,000 of this total. Elsewhere, in a newsletter published in Spanish for Spanish-speaking Catholics living in London, I read that 'Colombians alone numbered some 150,000 four years ago, and it is calculated that Latin Americans in general cannot be less than double this figure, that is 300,000'. Finally, in an interview with . . . [the] head of the Colombian Refugee Association (November 2004), I was told that the figure of 300,000, for the total number of SSLs in London, was certainly possible and that Colombians probably numbered at least 100,000 (Block 2006: 142).

Block's study draws our attention to some of the factors that could explain the lack of reliable information about the demographic size of Latin Americans. For instance, their invisibility due to irregular migration status as well as their geographical dispersion and dual nationality make it difficult to provide exact numbers about this sociocultural group (see Roman-Velázquez and Retis 2020). Since there are no official statistics on the size of this migrant group, recent studies drawing on the UK Labour Force Survey have also reported an estimate of 450,000 people of Latin American origin (Turcatti and Vargas-Silva, 2022). Despite these divergent figures, there seems to be a consensus about their presence. According to McIlwaine and Bunge (2016), approximately 250,000 people from Latin America live in the UK, of whom 145, 000 people live in London where they have been called the "Latin American community". Within these numbers, it is worth mentioning, there is also an estimate of 17, 100 irregular migrants and 17, 182 second generation Latin Americans (McIlwaine, 2015). Their nationality groups are made up by Brazilians (37%), Colombians (23%), Ecuadorians (8.6%), Peruvians (4%), Venezuelans (4.6), Mexicans (4.5%), Bolivians (3.2%), Chileans (3.5%), among other nationality groups (McIlwaine 2015).

The presence of Latin Americans in the UK is explained by political and economic instability in their countries of origin. In the 1970s, Chilean refugees escaping Pinochet's dictatorship, which was also backed up by neoliberal economic policies, began to arrive in the UK (McIlwaine, and Bunge 2015), and they were followed by people from Uruguay and Argentina who were also fleeing the same political unrest in their home countries respectively (Ramirez 2015; see Patiño-Santos and Marquez-Reiter 2018). Furthermore, Colombians also began to migrate to the UK through a work permit system whereby they worked in cleaning, domestic service and catering (McIlwaine 2008). By the 1980s, the work permit was withdrawn but Colombians kept migrating as both economic migrants and asylum seekers attempting to circumvent the armed conflict in their country (Bermudez Torres 2003), and Latin American migration continued to increase and diversified in the last decade of the last century (McIlwaine and Bunge 2016).

The 1990s is characterised by interrelated political and economic policies that acted as push factors such as the introduction of neoliberal economic reforms. It is reported that as Latin American countries renegotiated their foreign debts via privatisation and labour reforms, they had a negative effect on employment not only in Colombia (Moser and McIlwaine, 2004) but in many Latin American countries that deeply changed their socioeconomic structures and dismantled labour rights (Munck 2012). It is also argued that although the privatisation strategies enforced in many Latin American countries boosted their local economies initially, the recovery of their local economies was feeble and the structural disparities exacerbated as wages went down dramatically (Garcia Canclini 2002). In this light, the declining economy after successive trends of economic liberalisation, the weakening of the welfare state system as well as unemployment triggered emigration from Latin America to other continents (Castles and Miller 2009; Padilla and Peixoto 2007).

It must be added that the abovementioned phenomena did not happen in a vacuum. Some additional factors also motivated people to relocate their lives, particularly from Ecuador and Colombia. As to the former, an economic crisis worsened by natural disasters such as floods had a negative effect in export crops in the 1990s. These factors forced between 500,000 and 1 million people from Ecuador out of their country and sent them to the USA, Italy but mostly to Spain where Ecuadorians had previously lived (Jokisch 2014). As to the latter, the still palpable armed conflict along with the impact of the Asian economic crisis on Colombia forced nearly "1.9 million people to emigrate from their countries" (Reina and Zuluaga 2012: 5; see also Ribando, 2005). Although many went to Spain where bilateral labour agreements were made (Padilla and Peixoto 2007), it has been documented that after such phenomena the United Kingdom also became a receiving society for both nationality groups. McIlwaine (2008: 97) notes that "Colombians and Ecuadorians in particular applied for asylum during this period, many of whom were eventually granted permanent residence status through processes of regularization such as the family amnesty exercise in the UK in 2003". These two main nationalities have recently been joined by others such as Brazilians, Peruvians, Venezuelans and Bolivians who have also travelled alternative migration routes before arriving in the UK (McIlwaine and Bunge 2016).

Researchers have also noted that Latin Americans have moved firstly to Spain due to the economic and migration policy-associated advantages that the country has offered and that has been a gateway to the UK. The growing economy of European countries such as Spain's in 1995 as well as the increasing labour demand in sectors such as construction, tourism and domestic work acted as major pull migration factors for Latin Americans who could help fill such demands in both skilled and non-skilled jobs (Padilla and Peixoto 2007; McCabe et al. 2009; Mazza and Sohnen 2010; Vicente Torrado 2005). Furthermore, it is worth noting additional migration policies that favoured the entry of Latin American migrants into Spain before 2003. Latin American citizens did not require a visa but to be passport holders to enter and stay in Spain for up to three months, and after a two-year residence, they could apply for Spanish citizenship, which could guarantee mobility across European countries (see Zapata-Barrero and de Wite 2006). Such mobility to Europe must also be understood in a context in which former destination countries such as Argentina, mainly for Bolivians and Ecuadorians, and the USA ceased to be attractive immigration options. The former country was hit by an economic crisis in 1998 (Sveinsson 2007) while the latter, after the above-mentioned events of 11 September in 2001, introduced "tighter immigration controls such as the passage of the USA PATRIOT Act and the Enhanced Border Security and Visa Entry Reform Act (EBSVERA)" (Laque, 2011: 32). The above-mentioned factors help us understand and explain the reorientation of migration flows into Europe, particularly to Spain where in 2009 Latin American migrants totalled 2,365, 364 (Vicente Torrado. 2009).

Nevertheless, an important economic phenomenon has also contributed to the demographic growth of Latin Americans in the UK more recently. The economic crisis that hit Spain towards the end of 2008 resulted in high unemployment rates for low and middle-skilled workers and loss of work permits that had a major effect on the foreign-born population (Mazza and Sohnen 2010; Alba Monteserin et al. 2013). The latter that included Latin Americans was the object of return migration policies. According to Feline (2015) and Plewa (2009), and as I suggested above, the Spanish government created a voluntary return migration programme directed to documented migrants from Argentina, Brazil, Chile, Colombia, Ecuador, Paraguay, Peru, the Dominican Republic, Venezuela and Mexico.

Although many fell back upon such programme, a majority decided to stay due to kin or a dual nationality status that has allowed them to move to other European countries such as the UK (Feline, 2015; McIlwaine et al. 2011). In this context, a secondary migration from Bolivians, Peruvians, Colombians and Ecuadorians into the UK has been documented (McIlwaine and Bunge 2016).

Secondary migration to the UK has been termed onward migration. This is often unplanned and a reaction to unemployment that often undergirds precarious living conditions that Latin American migrants attempt to overcome (Ramos 2017; Mas Giralt 2017; McIlwaine and Bunge 2019; Patiño Santos 2021). Onward migration also points to the intersections between multiple precarities that migrants experience from origin to transition and final destination country over time (McIlwaine and Bunge 2019). As stated above, the 2008 economic crisis in Spain badly affected many Latin American migrants who moved to the UK to assuage the economic pressures they faced (see Mas Giralt 2017). However, onward migration is also key to our understanding of Latin American migrants' transnational identities and development of networks. I will return to the idea of transnational identities in chapter 2.2. Networks have been instrumental for their incorporation in London, and exhibit that the place of origin and people's common interests largely organise their mobility patterns and influence their migration choices. According to McIlwaine et al (2011), the most important reason why Latin Americans choose to move to London as a new receiving society is explained by the existence of connections, family and friends who already live in the city. Such connections, in turn, provide newly arrived immigrants with accommodation and many times, they help them secure a job with future employers, which over decades has contributed to the continued growth of the Latin American community (McIlwaine et al. 2011).

Another aspect to take into account is Latin Americans' academic profiles and their arrival in the UK as they exemplify vertical migration trajectories. Latin American migrants to the UK are mostly well educated with university degrees, technical institute education, which many of them obtained before leaving their country of origin (Wright 2011; James 2005; McIlwaine 2011). Nevertheless, as it has been observed not only in the UK but in other European countries (see Saenz and Salazar 2009), the job market available to Latin American migrants involves socioeconomic stratifying patterns such as declassing, reclassing and deskilling in a host society (Yepez del Castillo 2007; Block 2017). While declassing refers to changes in an individual's life conditions such as the loss of economic power and prestige and status that formerly were a person's class position", reclassing "is about the reconfiguration and realignment of class position" in a receiving society caused by changes in an individual's life conditions (Block 2017:140). These processes are experiences encountered in my participants' migration trajectories in which their movement to a new location has involved a socioeconomically downward trajectory and has involved realignment experiences that have impacted their quality of life and identities. For instance, Linda's case, which we will see in chapter 5, exhibits an experience of declassing, a downward class movement in the sense that she has a B.A in psychology from her country of origin, Mexico, but upon her arrival her credentials are erased as she first obtained a job as a hotel maid in London. Keeping in sight declassing and reclassing processes that migrants face is relevant given that it can allow us to be aware of and understand how they are inserted in structurally differentiated sending and receiving societies (see Levitt 2004).

Half of the 85% of Latin American migrants in employment in the UK work in the service sector such as cleaning and hospitality, and their low ability to speak English has presented them with obstacles to improve their life conditions (Block 2006; Marquez Reiter and Martin Rojo 2015; McIlwaine 2005; 2011; Turcatti and Vargas-Silva 2021). Their learning English is often frustrated due to their nature of their jobs, which are often underpaid and involve "fragmented schedules that require them to work early in the morning or late at night as well as limited opportunities to interact with English speakers" (Ramos, 2017: 6). Other obstacles are also found in the workplace and their everyday life as they try to incorporate to a host society since many of them do not receive their salary for the work they have done (McIlwaine 2011). That is, many Latin Americans face exploitation practices that very often those with an undocumented migration status, on which I will elaborate below, do not denounce due to their inability to speak English (McIlwaine and Bunge 2016).

Recently tighter immigration controls in the UK have resulted in a more varied nature of migration routes. Alternative migration channels from Spain to the UK have also been fallen back upon and their illegal nature that may involve people smugglers and fake passports are pointers to the complexity of migration; however, it is worth mentioning that these migration routes are rarely travelled (James 2005; McIlwaine 2015). More recently, the arrival of Latin American students and professionals in the UK adds to the heterogeneous composition of LA migrants. It is noteworthy that many LA migrants enter the UK with tourist visas; however, their overstaying them leads them to an irregular status (McIlwaine and Bunge 2016). Certain nationality groups such as Ecuadorians, Colombians, Bolivians and Brazilians find themselves in such status (see Wright 2011; James 2005; McIlwaine 2016).

The above phenomena must also be taken on board as they can help us explain why people congregate in specific physical spaces. That is, an irregular status as well as high rents can also encourage domestic segmentation (Castles 2002). Although Latin Americans are dispersed across London, certain boroughs that are often associated with poverty (Aldridge et al. 2013) such as Haringey and Southwark, for instance, have become the places with the largest concentration of Latin American migrants in London (Marquez Reiter and Martin Rojo 2015). This last statement should be interpreted cautiously since it does not mean that all Latin Americans are necessarily poor but they may live in such area due to their intent to save money that they could remit back home (see McIlwaine 2016). In addition, there is a significant and evident presence in other areas such as Lambeth where, as we saw in the introduction to this book, there are restaurants and other bussinesses run by Latin American migrants. The conditions in which many of them live in these boroughs are inappropriate and "often exemplify cases of overcrowding among different nationalities such as Ecuadorians, Paraguayans, Bolivians" (McIlwaine, 2016, p. 29), and it is also documented that "many of them live with people they do not know" (Ramos, 2017: 6). In contrast to these living conditions, people from other nationalities such as Argentinians and Mexicans are usually based in Chelsea Westminster, Camden and Kensington, often because of their higher socioeconomic status (McIlwaine 2016).

The presence of Latin Americans has also contributed to their politically recognition and the emergence of Latin American-oriented organisations. Latin Americans have received recognition as an ethnic group in the London boroughs of Southwark and Lambeth where they are concentrated as well as in the borough of Islington (CLAUK 2015). This means that they aim to underscore not only their presence but also their needs as they seek inclusion in terms of policy, services and political participation. In addition, organisations such as The Coalition of Latin Americans in the United Kingdom (CLAUK), Latin American House (LAH), the Indo American Refugee Organisation (IRMO), Latin American Women's Rights (LAWRS), Movimiento Ecuador en el Reino Unido (MERU) as well as el Teléfono de la Esperanza UK, etc., are some institutions that they have created and that attempt to address Latin Americans' needs. These range from offering workshops about labour rights among other services on which I will elaborate in chapters 3, 4 and 5 where we will learn of their role in context.

Latin American migration to the UK is an example of the complexities of present-day migration routes and channels, and a phenomenon that since 2000 has remained largely understudied (Block 2006; McIlwaine 2011). Natural disasters, internal as well as external political and economic factors have damaged the societies and stability of countries of origin for decades and have transformed the social texture and interaction in both sending and receiving countries. Migration policies in recipient countries have also interacted with political and socioeconomic conditions of sending societies and have contributed to the intensification and orientation of migration outflows and Latin American immigrants' status. It is in this context where the distinction between the local and the global dilutes as processes of economic globalisation and neoliberal policies have surpassed borders and have had a harmful effect on the economic and political stability of non-elite groups of people. Thus, the above-mentioned factors draw attention to Latin American migrants' current contexts as their places and conditions of origin still bear an imprint upon their arrival in a global society. Nevertheless, migration from Latin America and other European countries where they have resided should be viewed as a strategy to which people resort in order to both circumvent economic adversities, join family and friends as well as look for better job opportunities in remote areas to improve their living conditions.

1.5 Community formation

As noted in the previous section, Latin American migration to the UK is characterised by a complex interconnection of natural disasters as well as political and economic factors. These, encourage us to think of the varied motivations and resources with which they emigrated from their countries of origin and, in this context, their interests, aspirations as well as socioeconomic backgrounds contribute to the diversification of what has been called the Latin American community.

Community has been defined as a construct that metaphorically depicts people living together and it is suggestive of favourable conditions and social spaces in which people cohabitate. As Bauman (2001) put it:

> Words have meanings: some words, however, also have a 'feel'. The word 'community' is one of them. It feels good: whatever the word 'community' may mean, it is good 'to have a community', 'to be in a community'. If someone wandered off the right track, we would often explain his unwholesome conduct by saying that 'he has fallen into bad *company*.' If someone is miserable, suffers a lot and is consistently denied a dignified life, we promptly accuse society-the way it is organized, the way it works. Company or society can be bad; but not the *community*. Community, we feel, is always a good thing (Bauman 2001: 1, italics in original).

Bauman's view can be further explained by arguing that the word community contains an affective element to it; it carries feelings of belonging and membership and a shared emotional connection. Thus, community can be defined as "the commitment and belief that members have shared and will share history, common places, time together, and similar experiences" (McMillan and Chavis 1986: 9). That is, people in a community could be "bound together by a common set of beliefs, values, practices, language and artefacts" (Block, 2006: 25). Under this interpretation, the notion of community rests upon the presence of commonalities, which can act as an incentive on people's aspirations to come together for particular and shared interests. A case in point is the ethnic recognition that Latin Americans have achieved in the London boroughs that I mentioned above and which suggests that feelings of belonging and mutual needs could also be mobilised for political representation. Furthermore, the organisations that they have founded to help those in need provides further evidence of a sense of community.

However, processes that help us explain community formation in the context of Latin American migration need to be brought to the fore and put in a historical context. Community formation in receiving societies involve a range of factors. These encompass economic, political and social causes as well as migrants' motivations to be together in order to cater for their needs by the creation of businesses and different types of associations (see Castles and Miller 2009). The Latin American community and its gradual formation in London exhibit these traits. Roman Velázquez (1999) documents how individual Latin American entrepreneurs who settled in London started commercial initiatives that contributed to the visibility of Latin Americans in London. She states that Latin Americans by the creation of shops, small businesses and restaurants in areas around the boroughs of Lambeth and Southwark began to gain presence; however, there are two spaces that are fundamental in the formation of the Latin American community: The Latin American House and the Elephant and Castle shopping centre (see Figures 10, 11 and 12; Roman-Velázquez 1999).

Figure 10: Latin American House (LAH) housing a Brazilian restaurant (Photo taken by Daniel Morales).

The Latin American House, one of the first Latin American oriented places in London, emerges as a consequence of local policies that attempted to cater for minority groups in London in the mid 1980s. Roman Velázquez (1999) states that the labour-controlled Greater London Council (GLC) intended to address inequalities and injustices, which were due to class, race and ethnicity. At the same time, the GLC aimed to help the poor, women and ethnic groups by improving housing, creating jobs and providing transport for them (Roman Veláquez 1999). According to this author, it was in this historical moment in which the GLC provided funds to buy a building in Kilburn in which and NGO known as the Latin American House has been located and functioning since 1986 to solve some of the problems with which the presence of Latin Americans dealt. Nevertheless, the purchase of this building entailed political instability and economic pressures that to a great extent influenced its acquisition and explain its location. The money to buy the house, £ 200,000, was granted close to a date when the GLC was to be abolished, which not only resulted in the quick purchase of the house but generated disagreements about its suitable location (Roman Velázquez 1999). Indeed, although the Latin American house has attempted to address many Latin americans' diverse needs since its creation, its location may be problematic due to the geographical distance that it has with sites where they have a stronger presence. For example, as we will see in chapter 5, a Chilean mother who was unable to speak English was motivated to learn it to address communication needs and social interactions in such institutional sites as hospitals. Since she was looking after her son who had cystic fibrosis that required constant care, she could not attend English classes due to both the geographical location of Latin American House and the economic costs involved in commuting from her house to Kilburn.

Apart from the building acquired in Kilburn, there is another culturally and economically meaningful site that deserves attention. As stated at the introduction to this book, The Elephant and Castle shopping centre was identified as a place with a distinguishable Latin American presence that should also be contextualised in times of economic instability. The shopping centre was open in 1965 in Southwark, an area characterised with high unemployment and severely hit by the economic recession towards the end of 1980s (Hall 1992; Roman Velazquez 1999). The adverse economic situation at the time led to the closing of almost all the shops, but it was also an element that contributed to the presence of Latin Americans in it. Low rent in the shopping centre was a stimulus to move into it at the same time that by means of loans they started their businesses, usually in locations that had been closed or had not been used for years and which they repaired themselves to open their shops (Roman Velazquez 1999). The gradual growth of Latin Americans in the shopping centre started in 1992 with the opening of *La Fogata* restaurant followed by Inara Travels whose manager played a

Figure 11: Services and other activities offered by the Latin American House (Photo taken by Daniel Morales).

central role in encouraging other Latin Americans to start their businesses in the shopping centre, and by 1994 ten Latin American shops had opened (Roman Velazquez 1999). At the time of this study there were more than 90 shops within the shopping centre and around it (see also Marquez-Reiter and Martin Rojo 2015; Paffey 2019; McIlwaine 2016; Patiño-Santos and Marquez-Reiter 2019). The Elephant and Castle shopping centre and its surrounding areas have been iconic places where Latin Americans created and found employment and thus reignited part of the economy of the area. Furthermore, their presence and business activities also exhibit cultural practices that demonstrate how they have transformed, appropriated and resignified this space. As I noted above, many of them from different nationalities and backgrounds got together with their families and friends to eat and interact in Spanish in the shopping centre.

It must be noted, nevertheless, that the economic conditions in which a Latin American entrepreneurial spirit can be seen also sheds light on important distinctions that should not be obscured. Processes of globalisation have contributed both to "the disembeddedness of traditional forms of collectivities from their traditional foundations" and "have engendered new notions of community of membership" that are worthy of scrutiny (Sassen 2002: 218). In a globalising world where human mobility has intensified and economic inequality has increased, the term community may conceal important distinctions and particularities. Variables such as eth-

Figure 12: Colombian restaurant, La Bodeguita, in the Elephant and Castle shopping centre in Southwark (Photo taken by Daniel Morales). As stated in the introduction, demolition of the shopping centre occurred in 2021 and left 40 Latin American traders without a job or place to relocate their bussinesses.

nicity, socioeconomic class, education capital, language variation, gender, migration trajectories and statuses could be found within one single nationality group or even regional origin (Guarnizo et al. 2003). This multiplicity of variables should still be delved into since despite their apparent fixity they are constantly negotiated and are factors that throw light on our understanding of how people relate to one another in various domains of social life. In other words, the complexity of present-day societies forces us to observe social interaction within groups with common national ties that term themselves communities and that may exhibit hierarchical relations. For instance, McIlwaine (2008) notes that there is evidence of diverging loyalties in immigrants of Colombian origin in London. She reports mistrust among undocumented migrants who feared being reported to the Home Office after disagreements that had usually started in the country of origin and that were often linked to contrasting political views (McIlwaine 2008). Additionally, practices of exploitation, discrimination, feelings of envy, distinctions of migration status and jobs as well as neoliberal self-responsibilisation ideologies also appear to influence their social relations (McIlwaine, 2016; Patiño-Santos and Márquez-Reiter 2019). These instances suggest what could be the superdiverse and multi-layered composition of social groups (see Vertovec, 2007), which demand attention particularly in a larger conglomerate of experiences and nationalities that make up the population under study in a globalised economic system. As we will see in chapter 4, the migration raid of which many

Latin American cleaners were object illustrates the tensions and divergent interests of people from the same region.

In light of the above, it has become imperative to pay attention to a population whose heterogeneity is the norm and whose various worldviews, expectations, level of resources, and levels of social satisfaction and aspirations may influence a need for affiliation in a city such as London (see Kingston et al. 1999). The latter has been described as a multicultural city where a great diversity of nationalities and languages are encountered; but it has also been described as a complex site where there is a stratified class of professionals (see Sassen, 2002). In this stratified structure, many Latin American (non) professionals have also various levels of linguistic proficiency and exhibit a varied socioeconomic background, which have been determinant in their social and labour insertion and which adds to the complexity of stratification processes and interactions in such city and even with members of the same geographical origin. As it will be shown in chapters 3 and 4, there are practices of social distancing and tension among Latin Americans living in London, which suggests that their linguistic, educational, socioeconomic capital is also accompanied with values that could be grounds for either inclusion or exclusión. In this vein, the notion of community in a global city should also be interpreted as a construct that also produces context-based negotiations among its members as they may build their social relations in a way that they also reveal their social class backgrounds and interest.

1.6 Social class

Researchers seeking to find a definition of what class is in our contemporary societies have returned to Marx's work as the foundational explanation of it. This task has required a number of interpretations of what class may mean since it has been agreed that Marx throughout his work did not provide a clear definition of it (Giddens 1973; Calvert 1982; Block 2014; 2018). It is even argued that there is no consensus about how to define it (Wright, 2005). Nonetheless, a useful way of beginning to understand it is by referring to what social scientists call objective class markers. This means that class is interpreted in relation to people's income and wealth that explains their material standards of living and (lack of) property (Wright 2003). In objective terms, class indexes the economic conditions in which people live and in which gradational terms such as upper class, upper middle class, middle class etc. are commonly used for locating people in a social structure (Elbert and Perez, 2018). It must be added that such a notion of class is not without its critics who argue that it merely concentrates on monetary aspects of social life and that classifies people into discrete categories (see Eidlin 2014; Wright

2003). However, I argue that class, as a measure of wealth or lack of it, could still be an analytical tool that helps us explain people's living conditions and relations. This argument is intended neither to suggest a clear-cut dichotomy between the wealthy and the poor nor intimate a reductionist interpretation of the relationship between the haves and the have-nots since class divisions and relations are complex and dynamic. It is rather an intent to begin to explore inequality and social distancing, and this study partially and initially draws on such interpretation as in a context of migration, economic resources and (lack of) access to them significantly matter in Latin Americans' migration routes, their lived experiences and their relationships with co-ethnics in London.

Social class is a construct that should incorporate a pertinent multidimensional understanding of it (Snell 2020). In this vein, this study views class as:

> a social category which refers to lived relationships surrounding social arrangements of production, exchange, distribution and consumption. While these may narrowly be conceived as economic relationships, to do with money, wealth and property, . . . class should be seen as referring to a much broader web of social relationships, including, for example, lifestyle, educational experiences and patterns of residence. Class, therefore, affects many aspects of our material lives. (Bradley 1996: 19)

Bradley's interpretation of social class resonates with what Bourdieu (1986) called capital, habitus and field. As to the first concept, capital is initially understood as economic capital in terms of material property and wealth, but it can be complemented by other symbolic interpretations of it to explain class distinctions (Bourdieu, 1984). Capital can also present itself in two interrelated and additional forms such as cultural and social capitals. Cultural capital is symbolically articulated in the embodied state; the objectified state and in the institutionalised state. That is, it is embodied as it becomes manifest "in the form of long-lasting dispositions of the mind and body (Bourdieu 1986:17). This is what Bourdieu called habitus and on which I will elaborate below. Furthermore, it is objectified in the form of cultural goods such as books, dictionaries, ornaments, clothing, etc. These are possessions that indicate good or poor taste. Additionally, cultural capital is institutionalised in the sense that it becomes objectified through academic qualifications (Bourdieu, 1986). These stand for the skills, credentials, degrees that state institutions could sanction and that an individual and society recognise as legitimate knowledge. Nonetheless, as stated above, these states of cultural capital are not independent of economic capital since in order to achieve the accumulation of the former, a prolonged process of acquisition is necessary in which an investment of time is needed, i.e., "time free from economic necessity" as "the precondition for its initial accumulation" (Bourdieu 1986: 19).

Cultural capital also interrelates to social capital. This can be defined as the "aggregate of the actual or potential resources which are linked to possession of a durable network of more or less institutionalised relationships of mutual acquaintance and recognition" or "to membership in a group" (Bourdieu 1986: 21). That is, it stands for connections and belonging to various groups in society. Its acquisition is dependent upon the economic and cultural capital that an individual possesses or accumulates and that is recognised by others in different social domains (Bourdieu, 1986). For instance, a person being from an economically privileged background is usually more likely to make it further in education than a person from an economically deprived one, and thus may have developed the connections and network that could enable them to acquire good jobs and a higher social position. For my participants, as we will begin to see in chapter 3, social capital is also central for how they integrate themselves and how they face economic, language and even legal challenges in a new society. In this sense, different forms of capital intertwine and their interrelationship becomes more complex in a set of dispositions situated within particular domains.

As stated above, an interpretation of class from a Bourdieusian perspective also involves an analysis of both habitus and field. Habitus is defined as "both a system of schemes of production of practices and a system of perception and appreciation of practices. And, in both of these dimensions, its operation expresses the social position in which it was elaborated" (Bourdieu 1989: 19). This means that habitus is a "socialised subjectivity" in the sense that one's social trajectory or origins influence perceptual and behavioural dispositions (Edgerton and Roberts 2014: 198); "different conditions of existence produce a different habitus" (Bourdieu, 1984: 170). The latter argument does not mean that the concept of habitus does not recognise human agency or that individuals can be inserted into ready-made class identities. Bourdieu reminds us that habitus "is endlessly transformed, either in a direction that reinforces it, when embodied structures of expectation encounter structures of objective chances in harmony with these expectations, or in a direction that transforms it" (Bourdieu 1990a: 116). This means that habitus is interpreted as a set of dispositions that both generate and classify a range of social practices that are reflective of and situated in the material conditions of the existence of an individual. One of these generative and classifiable practices is associated with the embodied manifestation of habitus. That is, it may express itself through body language such as "a way of walking, a tilt of the head, facial expressions, ways of sitting and of using implements, always associated with a tone of voice, a style of speech" (Bourdieu, 1977a: 87). Such expressions may also involve matters of etiquette, dress, deportment, dialect, vocabulary (Goffman 1951), and may constitute symbols of class membership as they are charged with social meaning and recognition that are valued in a particular field.

The concept of field is also relevant for our understanding of habitus as context-based. Field may be conceived of as domains of social life such as the field of education, politics, the media, and art, which are interrelated to one another and to larger socioeconomic forces (Grenfell 2011). For instance, the field of education is associated with larger economic forces in the sense that school curricula and degree programmes are designed to meet economic interest. At the same time, a field is dynamic and interest-laden due to its agents' pursuit of positions of power and distinction, positions of the dominant or the dominated that are conditioned by mainly an agent's economic and cultural capital that is set against that of other agents within the same field (Bourdieu and Wacquant 1992). Within this logic, field is a "locus of competitive struggle" (Bourdieu, 1975: 19), a site in which individuals, as we will see in chapter 5 where two immigrant mothers enter state-sanctioned sites, may have the ability or inability to mobilise their capital due to the historical conditions in which it was acquired and that needs to be contextualised in the study of language and society as well as migration.

Class is, as stated above, a complex phenomenon whose interpretation hinges upon the society in which it is studied and upon the discipline that intends to account for it. Sociolinguistics, for instance, has paid attention to the relationship between language and class from different perspectives such as the variationist perspective (Labov 1966; Trudgill, 1974) and from an ethnographic approach in educational settings (Rampton 2006; 2010). Indeed, Rampton (2010:1) made a case for "the resuscitation of class" as the construct began to be obscured by a strong focus on ethnicity, gender and generation in sociolinguistics. In the context of migration, Block (2014; 2017; 2018), who to a great extent draws on Marxist and Bourdieusian interpretations of class to examine language and identity issues, proposes an integrationist approach that he calls a constellation of interrelated dimensions of class.

Block's (2014; 2017; 2018) integrationist approach is a model on which this study draws to connect the socioeconomic conditions from which the participants speak to other symbolic class markers that emerge in their discourses. Block refers to a first category that he calls material life conditions. This category includes a dimension of 'relations of individuals and collectives to the means of productions', that is, 'the circumstances of the provision of labour power to those who own and control the means of production' (2018: 92). This is a Marxist view of the exploitation-based relations of classes in the sense that there is a propertied class and a property class in which the former benefits from and appropriates the product of the latter's labour. A second category is entitled economic resources, which comprise the dimension of 'property' that could stand for 'land, housing, electronic goods and other material goods as well as income and accumulated wealth' (Block, 2018: 92).

As stated above, Block's model does not only concentrate on so called objective social class categories such as wealth and property. As a third category, he refers to sociocultural resources that comprise a dimension of 'occupation, education, technological knowhow, social contacts and networking' (2018: 92). Additionally, behaviour as a fourth category refers to a symbolic class dimension that pertains to 'how one moves one's body, the clothes one wears, the way one speaks' (2018:92). Finally, a fifth and sixth categories are socio-political life conditions and spatial conditions respectively. The former pertains to three interrelated dimensions such as political life, quality of life and a type of neighbourhood, each of which are understood in terms of one's relative position in hierarchies of power in society, physical comfort or psychological wellbeing as well as a 'type of neighbourhood', whether it is a working-class, middle-class neighbourhood or an area to be gentrified. The latter refers to a dimension of 'type of dwelling' such as 'trailer, house (detached/semidetached), flat (studio, small, large) etc.' (Block 2018: 93). Such dimensions are relevant to account for the participants' very different living conditions in London since many Latin Americans and some of my participants live in very different conditions; some may live in small rooms with four more people. For instance, Andres, an immigrant of Colombian origin that I will introduce in chapter 5, lived in a small room with two more families and has two jobs in order to pay for his rent in London.

Block's model of class is not free of criticism that accuses it of "compartmentalising class as though it is meant to *represent* it" (Block 2018: 91 emphasis in original). In response to this criticism, Block argues that the model is intended to be a heuristic and flexible one and thus not represent class as something fixed but as something that is constantly revised and that it can be reordered and reorganised as societies themselves change; it is, as he states, a model that helps him and could help us think about class (2018). I would also add that the dimensions described above allow us to reflect upon and take into account the various resources with which migrants relocate their lives, the migration routes they travel and how they have an impact on their quality of life.

In addition, Block's dimensions can also help us understand why immigrants live where they live, who they live and work with as well as the social relationships they form and how they make sense of these realities in these contexts. In other words, they allow us to connect the socioeconomic conditions about which and from which Latin American immigrants speak to other symbolic class markers that emerge in their discourses. These are value-laden ways of speaking indexical of how class in its different dimensions is invoked and mobilised directly and indirectly through the participants' self-presentations and categorisations of others and themselves. In chapter 3, for instance, we will see how one of the participants with an M.A from Brazil talks about her experience of migration. Her economic and sociocultural resources as well as her connections and living conditions influence how she self-presents and distances from the figure of the migrant. Her socioeconomic reality differs from that of a Peruvian participant that we will see in chapter 5. Although he holds a BA, he has been declassed and deskilled and lives in a flat with four more people working in the service sector. Both experiences illustrate how the material intersects with the symbolic at the same time that they evidence both horizontal and vertical trajectories. These may also influence the opportunities some of the participants in this study may have to learn and speak English and may intertwine with ideologies of neoliberalism.

1.7 Neoliberalism

Neoliberalism is a widespread historical phenomenon whose effect and influence have been felt by societies across the world economically, socially and politically. That is, neoliberalism is an economic doctrine and an ideology that, although it claims to seek to reduce state intervention, is still undergirded by the advocacy of the state. It is an economic doctrine in the sense that it holds that the free market will benefit all "if individual competition is given free reign" (Stiglitz, 2000: 74 in Piller 2015: 163). This means that the market is assumed to be self-regulating and should be free from state control and intervention, a *laisses-faire* rationale that prioritises continued economic growth for human progress (Smith 2007). As an ideology, neoliberalism is characterised by a system of ideas that "valorises autonomy as a state of being and as an ethics of self-interest and personal responsibility" (Wrenn and William Waller 2017: 499). In this context and as I have noted elsewhere (Morales Hernández 2021), two distinctive characterisations of neoliberalism arise, one of which is that of competition and another which is the notion of individual responsibility that, as some authors have argued (see Shin and Park, 2016; Bourdieu 1998) are penetrating and changing various domains of social life. This suggests that neoliberalism is not contained in an economic field but it transcends it and shapes individuals' social organisation and interaction by extrapolating a competition-minded logic that implies that there are winners and losers. In other words, neoliberalism as a doctrine and ideology fosters and praises individual merit and accomplishment while holding out an economic reward.

However, neoliberalism does not have a life of its own since it must be predicated by specific means. Harvey (2005:7) and Munck (2012: 70) respectively remind us that "economic models are politically determined" and that "states are not external but central to neoliberalism". Instances that support these arguments are found in Latin America (Munck, 2012; Roberts 2009), the UK and USA where governments have played a significant role in deregulation, restructuring and cuts in welfare provisions that have resulted in high levels of inequality (Sapiro 2010) and that are closely related to Latin American immigration to the UK.

Neoliberalism is palpable in social inequality and it is not a spontaneous economic model, but one that should be put in a historical context. The term neoliberalism dates back to the Colloque Walter Lippman in Paris in 1938 when a group of scholars such as Friedrick Hayek, Michael Polany and Whilelm Ropke met and used the term for the first time (Stedman-Jones 2012). According to Stedman-Jones (2012: 18), the purpose of such a meeting and the use of the term was respectively to "consider the implications of Walter Lippmann's book, The Good Society (1937) and address the concerns of the time; reclaim and defend freedom and individualism as notions that the Nazi party in Germany and Stalinism threatened" (see also Block 2018). However, the Second World War broke out and the meeting had to be postponed. It was not until 1947 when Friedrich Hayek summoned a group of intellectuals to Switzerland to discuss how liberalism could be defended from the above-mentioned threat and from New Deal liberalism, which involved programmes that supported the unemployed such as the Public Work Projects, as well as from British social democracy (Stedman-Jones 2012). The intellectuals included Ludwig von Moses, Milton Friedman, Karl Popper (Harvey, 2005), and academics from the London School of Economics, the University of Manchester, the University of Chicago as well as a group of Austrian exiles in the USA and a group of French intellectuals (Stedman-Jones 2012). They formed the Mont Pellerin Society (MPS) and it is after this meeting that important concepts with which neoliberalism is associated such as freedom, the individual, laissez faire economics began to emerge (Block, 2018). Furthermore, it is also after this, in a 1949 article that Hayek wrote, The Intellectuals and Socialism, when we begin to see the neoliberal intention that "individual liberty within the framework of free markets could only be protected by an elite-driven and elite-directed strategy of opinion formation" (Stedman-Jones 2012: 5).

As scholars have discussed, opinion formation was a phenomenon that took place neither overnight nor in a social vacuum. To disseminate the idea that free markets work for the benefit of all, it was important to harness and promote it through particular means of information although their impact was not felt equally in the societies that it penetrated. The popularisation of the idea that free markets were desirable was conducted by the media and politicians as well as business-sponsored think tanks such as the Institute of Economic Affairs in the 1950s, the American Enterprise Institute (AEI) in the 1960s (Harvey 2005; Carroll and Carson 2006), the Heritage Foundation in 1973 in the USA (Birch and Mykhnenko 2010). In the UK, The Foundation of the Centre for Policy Studies in 1974 and the Adam Smith Institute in 1976 were important idea centres (Birch and Mykhnenko 2010). Likewise, business schools in universities such as Princeton and Harvard as well as Chicago played a key role in the promotion of neoliberal ideas as they were training grounds for foreign economists that imported their ideas to their local governments such as the Chicago boys in the 1970s (Harvey, 2005). The 1970s was a crucial decade in which neoliberalism was not only spread by institutions but imposed by coercion, for example, after a coup d'état in Chile, which, on the one hand, helps us explain the first immigration of Chilean exiles to the UK and subsequent emigrations from Ecuador and Colombia that we have seen in chapter 1.3 (McIlwaine 2011). On the other hand, it is also probable that in this 1970s context neoliberalism began to be associated with its negative overtones (Boas and Gans-Morse 2009).

However, socioeconomic and political conditions at the time of the emergence of neoliberalism also enabled it to gain momentum. In the 1968 USA, for instance, there was discontent and resentment against the state for its restrictions on personal behaviours and for "its incompetence and failure to address issues such as civil, sexual and reproductive rights" (Harvey 2005:42). In addition to this, "the bureaucratic and rigid structures of unions as well as their lack of flexibility were significant factors that also made neoliberal ideas of flexi time arrangements and flexible specialisation influential and attractive for workers" (Harvey, 2005:53). In the UK, the population held a similar discontent against the government's management of welfare, which the media criticised and increasingly promoted individualism and freedom in contrast to the ineptitude of the state (Harvey 2005). However, within this complex combination of socioeconomic and political aspects, scholars in the history of neoliberalism agree that what characterises the US and UK cases are disputes over labour relations and a fight against inflation that led to the enforcement of neoliberal policies (Harvey 2005; Prassad 2006; Birch and Mykhnenko 2010). Their result was the reduction of welfare, privatisation of state enterprises, free trade, tax cuts and the undermining of labour unions in both the UK and the US during Thatcher's and Reagan's administrations (Steger 2010). For instance, Thatcher's consent to the introduction of foreign investment in the steel, shipbuilding and the automobile industry caused union power to disappear and allowed Japanese companies to settle in the UK and hire non-unionised workers (Harvey 2005). In this light, allowing foreign private capital to manage previous state-run enterprises also begins to point to globally evident business practices that characterise money-motivated policies.

An increasingly noticeable profit-led practice that illustrates a neoliberal logic and that is relevant for the context of the present study is that of outsourcing. This is "an agreement in which one company contracts-out a part of their existing internal activity to another company" (McCarthy and Anagnostou 2004: 63). An instance of this is the hiring of cleaning services by hotels, universities, hospitals through a third party, a scheme under which many Latin American immigrants and some of my participants working in the service sector in London are contracted (McIlwaine 2015; Woodcock 2014). The nature of this type of contract, however, carries negative implications for workers. That is, wage and benefit responsibilities are shifted to third parties (Castillo Fernández and Sotelo Valencia 2013), and jobs that were once stable have under this new scheme become temporary or part-time leading to a dismantling of labour rights and precarious lives (Celis Ospina 2012). It is also noteworthy that outsourcing is a widespread business and hiring scheme that has reached Latin America and, as we saw in section 1.4, has a strong connection with Latin American immigration to the UK in the 1990s. It has been reported that in Argentina, Brazil, Mexico and Uruguay 30–40 percent of the formal workforce is outsourced while in Colombia, Ecuador and Peru it constitutes nearly 40–50 percent (Castillo Fernandez and Sotelo Valencia 2013). These neoliberal tactics of hiring, apart from aiming to reduce labour costs, promote so-called job flexibility that works under a principle of efficiency as a way of responding to market-dictated needs; euphemisms that conceal the freedom to hire and fire combined with a type of vocabulary that influences individuals' ways of behaving.

An instance of such neoliberal vocabulary that is also explicitly and implicitly used by the participants of this study and that helps us understand their identities and relations better is that of 'the entrepreneur'. As one of the first thinkers to describe the entrepreneur, Jan Baptiste Say referred to such figure as "one who shifts economic resources out of an area of lower and into an area of higher productivity and greater yield" (Drucker 1985: 23). The entrepreneur is an economic agent who "must at least be solvent, and have the reputation of intelligence, prudence, probity, and regularity; and must be able, by the nature of his connexions, to procure the loan of capital he may happen himself not to possess" (Say 1971: 330). Capital and moral principles were, for Say, possessions that characterised the entrepreneur as a superior human being (Block 2018b).

The meaning of the entrepreneur as well as the values it promotes could also be located in later writings of those who support capitalism. Ludwig van Mises, a member of the MPS, for instance, wrote about the role of the entrepreneur and stated that:

> like every acting man, the entrepreneur is always a speculator. He deals with the uncertain conditions of the future. His success or failure depends on the correctness of his anticipation of uncertain events. If he fails in his understanding of things to come, he is doomed (von Mises [1949]; 2007: 290).

As we can gather from this quote, speculation and uncertainty are conditions in which the figure of the entrepreneur works and makes rational decisions; that is, it is associated with a knowing-risk taker and, interestingly, failure or success is an outcome for which the entrepreneur is held responsible. It must be said that Van Mises' argument is framed within the context of profit and loss in markets, but it is a logic with a strong focus on the individual that important political leaders have explicitly and implicitly promoted. As Holborow (2015:73) have noted, the current meaning that the figure of the entrepreneur carries "received its badge of respect in the early days of neoliberalism" when Thatcher and Reagan are respectively referred to as "the entrepreneurs' prime minister" and the president who regarded entrepreneurs as a "special breed". While Reagan in his inaugural speech in 1981 stated that "there are entrepreneurs with faith in themselves and faith in an idea who create new jobs, new wealth and opportunity" (Reagan 1981) Thatcher produced the often-cited phrase "there is no such thing as society (Ritzer and Dean 2014: 95). The social significance of these phrases lies in the fact that they were produced in a time of high unemployment and precariousness along with arguments and ideas such as "the government is the problem" or people misunderstand that "it's the government's job to cope with it". (Reagan 1981; Thatcher 1987). In other words, what they promoted was the ideological construction of an individual who is encouraged to take charge of him/herself and who should bear the economic burden on his/her shoulders. Within this logic, the responsibility to lift the country out of economic crisis seems to be shifted onto the individual who is thus interpellated to "being for himself his own capital, being for himself his own producer, being for himself the source of [his] earnings' (Foucault 2008: 226). A self-sustaining figure of the entrepreneur constructed on values of individuality that does not depend on the state and that has been extended into other contexts.

The concept of the entrepreneur is also found in the context of migration, for instance in Irish migration stories. Holborow (2015: 75) notes that the figure of the entrepreneur is contained in Irish culture in the form of the "rags to riches ideal". This is a notion that depicts the successful Irish emigrant to the US in pursuit of the American dream that holds the promise of wealth and fame away from rural poverty (Holborow 2015); that is, the individual as the architect of one's own destiny who is able to make it by his own efforts despite his adversities. Additionally, other studies document this idea of the entrepreneur in people's attitudes towards learning. Ullman (2012) explores how neoliberal discourses of individualism and entrepreneurism characterise the ways in which Mexican immigrants in Arizona talk about themselves as learners of English. Her participants, some of whom were undocumented immigrants, attempted to learn English on their own through a self-taught method called *Inglés Sin Barreras* (English without Barriers) and "in a context in which publicly funded adult language classes disappeared and English only had been passed as the official language of Arizona (Ullman 2012:461). She notes that her participants exhibited a will, a drive and a sense of personal responsibility to self-fund and educate themselves in English as well as to prepare for economic and political instability (Ullman 2012). Their failed attempt to learn English, however, resulted in discourses of personal disqualification or assumed lack of self-management and inability to use the learning materials properly; a type of blame culture that did not question external economic and political factors. In this light, the figure of the neoliberal entrepreneur carries interesting implications, one of which is the idea that "individuals succeed or fail by dint of their own self-discipline, hard work, personality, ambition, and effort (Bansel 298: 298). This idea will also be pursued and better illustrated by the language use of my participants that we will be able to see in more detail in chapter 5 where they describe the personal traits of the individuals with whom they relate as well as the attitudes they devalue. Another implication is that this individual-centred view takes into account neither the economic constraints that people may face nor the inequalities caused by other forces (Holborow 2015; Ullman 2012). Furthermore, what Ullman's study illustrates is another effect of a neoliberal ideology that not only promotes entrepreneurism and self-responsibilisation but language as a desired possession for social inclusion and market-oriented ends.

In light of the above, language has been commodified. Duchêne and Heller (2012) have drawn attention to the way in which ideas about language are framed in economic terms as a matter of added-value and not in national and political terms as a matter of rights and citizenship. That is, language has been constructed as a commodity and desired skill for socioeconomic mobility (Heller et al. 2014). It must be acknowledged that the notion of language as a commodity has not escaped criticisms due to the often lack of definition of what is meant by it (see Block 2019). The notion of language as a commodity has also been the object of ontological disagreements. Scholars have posed the question whether language really is a commodity, or whether it simply appears as a commodity (Simpson and O'Regan 2018). From a materialist, Marxist view, they contend that language cannot be the product of labour, rather language has acquired the form of a commodity; "it appears as commodity fetishism in the absence of any labour being expended upon it" (Simpson and O'Regan 2018: 161). Thus, the authors argue that scholars should pay more attention to the concrete labour that produces value in commodities to learn more precisely about the relation between language and capitalism (Simpson and O'Regan 2018).

Despite these criticisms, the notion of language being commodified still lends itself to explain that language has been metaphorically constructed as a tangible capital that the participants in this book also seek to obtain. It is also argued that language is treated as a part of a bundle of skills (see Urciouli 2008) in which people increasingly invest (Duchêne and Heller 2012); "an investment in cultural capital which can then be exchanged within the global labour market' (Rassool 2007:

148). In this vein, Song (2010) describes how Korean parents support their children's early English education. They are part of a trend of Asian families that draw on transnational migration to English-speaking countries so that their children obtain not only overseas educational credentials but "acquire English as economic capital in the global market" (Song, 2010: 23). Song's study reported that some parents in Korea teach their children English to make their investment "as profitable as possible" and that others view English as the "sine qua non skills" and thus equate English with a better job and education (Song 2010: 31).

However, the relationship between language, in this case English, and economic mobility is not straightforward and should be treated sceptically. There may be other factors that may come into play and that may affect a person's socioeconomic mobility. As Penycook has pertinently pointed out:

> English holds out promise of social and economic development to all those who learn it (rather than a language tied to very particular class positions and possibilities of development); and that English is a language of equal opportunity (rather than a language that creates barriers as much as it presents possibilities) (Pennycook 2007: 101).

His argument very well problematizes and captures the ideological dimension of English learning and as the language of socioeconomic mobility. It points to structural differences, inequalities and obstacles that, as we will see in chapter 5, both make a difference in how and under what circumstances people may want or need to learn the language to specific ends and that are usually erased in such process. In this light, issues of class arise but also migration trajectories and teaching practices that are consequential on people's identities and realities. For instance, Warriner (2007) documents the challenges of adult immigrants and refugees enrolled in an English as a Second Language (ESL) programme to prepare for entry-level employment in the USA and become self-sufficient in usually three to six months. Her participants, whose level of literacy and language background are heterogeneous, take grammar-focused classes that are repetitive and frequently take standardised tests whose scores are regarded to be "indicators of language proficiency and students are thus deemed ready to take up a job" (Warriner 2007: 315). She notes that although the tests seem to provide fair access to the workplace, their ESL classes do not enable adult learners to engage in real life meaningful communication that could be instrumental for them during job search or other needs such as "defending their rights with potential landlords or employees or communicate with their children's teachers" (Warriner, 2007: 319). Her study demonstrates that some of her participants, who also bought into the promise that English held, ended up with temporary part-time shift jobs in the service sector and although their jobs allowed them to get some income, they did not enable them to obtain the economic stability that they and their families needed (Warriner, 2007). Warriner's study contrasts with the case of the transnational Korean families described above. It exhibits that their socioeconomic background and resources reflect different migration trajectories and status, which are consequential in how their realities may be lived.

Nevertheless, Warriner's and Song's studies illustrate a converging theme: the belief that English will guarantee socioeconomic mobility. Within this logic, the attitudes reported in the studies above resonate with what Foucault (1988) and Althusser (1971) called "technology of self" and "interpellation" respectively. The former being a "means for fashioning a subjectivity compatible with dominant practices and beliefs" (Urciuoli and Ladousa 2013:177), and the latter being an "ideology that 'hails' individuals and that transform them into subjects with specific ideological and social positions" (Milani 2008: 181). That is, individuals are urged to acquire a language as a tool, a skill that will prepare them for life and for which they will be economically rewarded after hard work and self-discipline in an allegedly level field of competition to which they enter voluntarily. In chapters 4 and 5, we will see how these attitudes and ideologies come forward in the participants' accounts as they describe their realities and metalinguistic experiences as well as their relations with other Latin Americans.

Neoliberalism is a historical elite-driven economic doctrine and process that has materially transformed the social organisation of life. Privatisation and outsourcing are some of the clear practices and instances that show how people's lives are economically valued and humanely devalued, and governments and institutions such as think tanks and universities have played a significant role in the promotion of such an economic doctrine. Neoliberalism as an ideology has also reconfigured many aspects of the social conception of life and relations, which is evident in an orientation to individualism that inculcates an entrepreneurial spirit through which the individual seeks opportunities and embraces challenges in an environment of job precariousness and uncertainty. In such a context, as Bourdieu put it, a Darwinian world emerges – it is the struggle of all against all at all levels of the hierarchy, which finds support through everyone clinging to their job and organisation under conditions of insecurity, suffering, and stress (Bourdieu, 1998). In a competition-driven society, language is also reconceptualised as a skill and as a commodity, which can have an exchange value in market economy (Bourdieu 2003).

Chapter 2
Language, identity and society

2.1 Introduction

After having offered the reader a history of Latin America, intaregional migration patterns that have shaped the region as well as discussion of social class and neoliberalism, this section will now concentrate on the relationship between language and identity. It is important to note that here I will use the term language as in language use and not language as Spanish or English. The aim of this section is to describe how this study interprets identity as well as draws our attention to how we can understand the various language-mediated spatial contexts that the participants of this study cohabit and in which other identity markers are made relevant. In this sense, identity is understood from a social constructivist thinking; identity does not precede language, it is simultaneously multidimensional and a dialogical process. In a context of mobility, an interpretation of identity as transnational is instrumental to both capture the dual political loyalties that the participants enact since many of them are EU passport holders and engage in interactions with home countries. These interpretations of identity are closely related with the construct of intersectionality (Crenshaw 1989; 1991) that allows to point to other identity markers such as class, race, ethnicity and gender which will be discussed in detail due to their explanatory relevance in the participants' stories and sociolinguistic experiences.

Subsequently I offer a discussion of the concept of ideology. Its historical origin will be explored to understand the bad connotations it carries and with which it has been historically associated. In this sense, reference to Marx's ([1846] 1988) and Gramsci's (1971) interpretations of ideology and hegemony will also be made before I offer a definition of ideology for the purposes of this book. The definition offered will be linked to the field of Linguistic Anthropology to locate language ideologies outside a realm of ideas with which they are usually associated and emphasise their sociopolitical influence. A discussion of the language ideologies under study will follow before I move on to the relationship between language and society conceived and informed by a CDS perspective within which I include sociocognitive and dialogical-relational approaches as well as relevant units of analysis such as metaphors, topoi, and lexical units. As we will see in chapter 3, an analysis focused on these units of analysis allows for the examination of what speakers can socially accomplish in terms of their social relations, alignments and experiences in context. In addition, the concept of interdiscursivity is also central in the analysis and, in order to theoretically ground it, this will be preceded by a discussion of Bakhtin's heteroglossia, voice and dialogism (1981), which will be followed by Kristeva's intertextuality (1986). These concepts will allow us see how the participants (re)produce other ways of speaking of social reality, challenge or help sustain a social order by contesting, negotiating or accepting certain social identities.

2.2 Identity

Identity has historically generated various theorisations that have led to disciplinary interpretations of it. As Benwell and Stokoe (2006) have stated, identity was understood as something fixed and stable, a major trait that ignored individual agency until the Enlighment period where the use of reason and a focus on individuality began to be recognised and emphasised. In the early twenty century, explorations of the human mind were conducive to current influential exegesis of identity. Freud's interest in the human psyche allowed for explorations of subjectivity, which, conjoined with his interest in complex interaction processes within the family and its psychological impact on the individual, intimated social aspects relevant in the understanding of the self; that is, a socialised self (Chinoy 2012). Freud's work has been foundational for a number of academic disciplines such as literary theory, sociology and discourse analysis (see Hollway and Jefferson 2005; Elliot 2020) where the construct of identity continues to be reformulated.

Identity is an elusive and fleeting concept whose examination involves analytical complexities due to its plurality of definitions and manifestations. Outfit, music, sexual or professional identity (Blommaert 2005) illustrate some instances of complex identities. It may also refer to the political construct of national identities such as Colombian, Mexican, Ecuadorian, Bolivian or other nationalities, and it can even refer to a larger category such as Latinos. These are indeed important interpretations of identity as they are meaningful for the people who associate with these views of identity as they may "provide grounding for an individual's day to day experience" (May 2001: 39) and, as we saw in chapter 1.4, they can be important for political representation in the context of Latin American immigration to the UK. However, they are alluded to as all-encompassing, stable identities and important distinctions must be drawn in order to distinguish one individual from another (De Fina 2011). This is pertinent in order to avoid essentialist identity attributions that might engender stereotypical representations of an allegedly recognizable ethos as well as see how identity matters in Latin Americans' lives and relations. In this vein, how is identity to be explored and revealed?

Language is key to the exploration and understanding of identity since it acts as the vehicle through which the participants' identities emerge. As Bucholtz and

Hall (2005: 588) have stated in relation to this conceptualisation "identity is best viewed as the emergent product rather than the pre-existing source of linguistic and other semiotic practices and therefore as fundamentally a social and cultural phenomenon". This argument is better understood by considering that people employ language in their day-to-day experience in various social domains in which they use socially and culturally meaningful words and statements, which express values and describe ways of representing, being and acting in the world. This notion that identity does not precede language is also consistent with what other scholars have argued in terms of spoken language. Le Page and Tabouret-Keller (1985) consider utterances an act of identity; that is, through the use of language, all individuals perform an act of identity and reveal their sense of who they are. This view, as stated by Block (2006), is simultaneously multidimensional in the sense that different dimensions of identity such as ethnicity, nationality, gender, social class, etc., arise from people's utterances without a clear-cut separation. As we will see, one of the participants, Marcia from Brazil, says she is not an immigrant anymore and that she has integrated into her society. Her words index a way of (not) being in society but also point to other non-linguistic elements implied in the process of integration such as socioeconomic resources; notions of social class and its relationship with identity that I will explore in more depth later on.

It must be added that the complex emergence of identity through language is also related to a type of social action in situ. Language use is regarded as a social practice in context through which we reflect and construct our own individual experiences and social environment. In this light, the language and identity link is inseparable from the social domains in which we interact since the language choices we make are context-bound. Thus, the variability and diversity of context-based language use intimates that we cannot have one single identity rather context-dependent identities. In this sense we are a number of interpretations in language, we are manifold subjects (Barker and Galasinski 2001). Such a view is further supported by stressing that "identity is a discursive construct which continually shifts in the local contexts in which social actors enter" (Meinhoff and Galasinski, 2005: 7). The case of David in this study is illustrative of this contextual nature of the relationship between language and identity. In chapter 3 he talks about his experience as an illegal immigrant unaware of his rights and depicting different ways of acting while in chapter 4 he describes his work experiences as a diligent individual involved in labour rights movements. The words and utterances produced by a language user are evocative of important situational personae who are historically co-constructed in relation to specific social groups and events.

In light of the above, identities are never independent but always attain social significance in relation to and interaction with other available identity positions and other social agents (Bucholtz and Hall 2009). In other words, a great deal of what happens in identity construction is also a dialogical process and it "must be recognised by others in order for it to occur (Blommaert 2005: 205). Thus, identity construction is founded upon the multiplicity of our identities and roles we take on "in relation to who it is we are with, where we are" (Joseph 2004: 8) and who and what we allude to. In a similar vein, it can be stated that identities are not predictably aligned to one single identifiable entity, they are unstable and through the linguistic references to which people turn, we learn of the associative or dissociative constructions of the other to whom individuals might show adherence. In chapters 4 and 5, for instance, we will see how the participants use particular language choices through which they align themselves to a certain type of Latin American before they distance themselves from other Latin Americans who they regard as uneducated, dishonest or ignorant. Consequently, in Edwards' words (2009: 23) "the simultaneous possession of many different social roles and masks is uncontroversial, identities are certainly in flux, allegiances vary both diachronically and synchronically". That is, the variable ways in which we use language reveal our personal and social identities in situ as it is an undeniable fact that language is intertwined with various domains of our social, political, cultural contexts where we find ourselves (Cheshire, 2002). The situational and relational discursive construction of identity hinges on the socioculturally and temporally diverse realisation of a number of our everyday experiences.

Identity, as stated above, is understood as emergent in context-based language use and is relational and attributive. That is, the question about "who" we are hinges upon the relation to and interaction with other social actors (Joseph, 2004). Social class may also be conceived of as relational given that one's identity may become manifest through social actors' symbolic and material resources that others might recognise and thus sanction as belonging or not to a particular social group when entering a social space or interaction. Class involves a sense of place where we tend to both associate with "people like us" (Bottero, 2004: 995) and where there may be a "fellow feeling, a sharing of beliefs . . . ways of looking at society" that mirror and seem to be congruent with our worldview (Calvert 1982: 207). The latter notion, nonetheless, entails a distinction not merely of who we are but of who we are not; that is, class as relational also invokes us vs them social practices through which individuals "draw boundaries of differentiation from them" (Savage 2000: 102). Within this logic, understanding class as relational and part of one's identity will also help us shed light on the social distance that some of the participants of this study discursively draw to delineate the social groups with whom they (dis) associate within the Latin American community.

Migration trajectories, as stated in chapter 1.4, may also leave an imprint on people's transnational identities. These are what De Haas (2010: 248) calls "double national loyalties" that, in the context of this study, cast light onto many Ecuadorians, Colombians and Peruvians with EU passports after having lived in Spain and having escaped from the economic crisis. Furthermore, Brazilians also hold EU passports after having lived and worked in either Italy or Portugal (see McIlwaine 2011; Marquez Reiter and Martin Rojo 2015). 22% of the Latin Americans living in London hold an EU passport while 31% has British citizenship (McIlwaine and Bunge 2016). Their dual citizenship may also be explained by the European ancestry that, as noted in chapter 1, many of them have. In this sense, their double loyalties challenge notions of assimilation and assumptions of clear-cut national distinctions (Jordan and Düvel 2003). In this respect, a conception of identities as transnational also captures the development of and use of technology that allows many migrants to stay in touch with both sending and host societies; it allows for a reconceptualisation of the relationship between time and space, which have also reconfigured how the migration experience may be lived either physically or virtually (see Harvey 1989).

However, it must be acknowledged that not all migrants may embody a transnational identity. As some scholars have suggested, people who emigrate forever do not have access to the same resources or networks that allow them to engage in transnational behaviour (Castles and Miller: 2009). Their caveat is a reminder of important differences in migrant groups that other scholars have also observed. Samers (2010: 115), within the same logic, questions whether migrant practices reflect a sense of "transnationality" or social categories around gender, multiple ideas of nationhood and social class. Indeed, transnational identities and connections should not be reduced to a binary link between two local points but rather we should see how they integrate with other horizontal and vertical connections that may transcend borders (Levitt 2004).

In light of the above, an important construct that can further enable us to capture the complex relation between social class, transnationalism and identity is intersectionality. Its conceptual use originally emerged in critical feminist and anti-racist thought through the work of Creenshaw (1989; 1991). Her ideas mainly in Black feminism aimed to "denote the various ways in which race and gender interact to shape the multiple dimensions of Black women's employment experiences" (Creenshaw 1991:1244) and began to draw attention to and challenge what she called "the tendency to treat race and gender as mutually exclusive categories of experience and analysis" (Creenshaw 1989: 139). Such treatment is problematic since isolating and treating these categories separately, Creenshaw argued (1989:140), is both "failing to recognise the particular manner in which Black women are subordinated" and erasing them in the conceptualisation and remediation of race and sex discrimination by limiting the analysis to the experiences of privileged members of the group. That is, Black women's experiences cannot be subsumed into either "women's experience" or "the Black experience" and thus important distinctions must be drawn since they go through double-discrimination on the basis of race and on the basis of sex (Creenshaw 1989:149). Below, I will contextualise the relevance of this significant distinction. In this sense, Creenshaw's framework questions essentialist assumptions of the concept of woman that, as some authors have also stressed, was dominated by White Eurocentric knowledge in that "the experience of women was that of White women" and thus veiled Black women's identity and marginalised their voices and experiences in feminist struggles (Bhopal and Preston 2011:2), which also to some extent attempted to address relevant social class differences (hooks 1990; Corona and Block 2014).

Intersectionality, as class, identity and other concepts, is difficult to define due to the varied contexts in which it is employed to account for the phenomena on which it intends to shed light. Intersectionality, nevertheless, is here understood as a "framework to understand the ways in which multiple identity axes such as class, sexual orientation, race and gender intersect and influence the well-being of individuals" (Corus and Saatcioglu 2015: 415; see also McCall 2005). In other words, this understanding of intersectionality helps address essentialist interpretations of identity that may treat seemingly discrete identity categories such as the ones mentioned above as unrelated, and it therefore responds to the need to concentrate on the multiplicities of identity, their interactivity and thus acknowledge that social experience cannot be taken in isolation (Bhopal and Preston 2011). In the context of this study, the deconstruction of identity categories in relation to social class is significant to account for the social identities and migration experiences of the participants. As it will be noted in chapters 3 and 5, the participants' phenotypical characteristics, on which I will elaborate below, are influential on both the sociolinguistic experiences that they narrate and how they self-present. For instance, a participant in this study whose pseudonym is Karla and who is a White middle-class, M.A. educated immigrant woman from Latin America does not go through the same experiences as another participant, Sonia, who is a Black high-school educated female immigrant also from Latin America; while the former describes a story of a comfortable life style, the latter is the subject of discrimination practices. Their narratives exhibit how social positions intersect with race and stress the need to recognise important distinctions to look beyond "fixed" identity categories such as gender.

Gender has been traditionally associated with notions that concentrate on the female and male-female dichotomies in which physiological characteristics define who people are. Such a notion entails a biological determinism that has often been used as a justification for the assignation of gendered-work roles and social positions that have affected women, and a number of approaches to gender have attempted to shed light on this issue. For instance, Bucholtz (2014) refers to three approaches such as liberal feminism, cultural feminism and radical feminism. By eradicating barriers to women's full participation in all aspects of society, liberal feminism seeks to "establish equality between women and men", particularly through a focus on equal pay, abortion rights and domestic violence (Bucholtz, 2014: 26). Cultural feminism focuses on women's "ways of thinking, acting and speaking, practices attributed to a distinct women's culture" (Bucholts, 2014: 27). The third approach, radical feminism, views gender inequality as the main cause of social inequality. This is based on patriarchy understood as a "system of opresion from which every man benefits even without deliberately participating in it" (Bucholtz, 2014: 30).

However, these approaches have also been known as "difference" takes on gender; a type of criticism also associated with essentialism. As Bucholtz (2014) states, they do not treat women's experiences as unique but rather as universally shared and thus overlook important distinctions among women. For instance, liberal feminism benefitted middle class women more than other social groups to have access to traditionally male institutions of power such as politics and the law (Bucholtz, 2014). Their analytical purchase, nonetheless, is still valuable to examine issues of inequality in a number of social domains at different scales.

In this book, gender is understood in the sense that it applies to all human beings and it transcends the usual dichotomy mentioned above; in other words:

> Gender is a complexity whose totality is permanently deferred, never fully what it is at any given juncture in time. An open coalition then, will affirm identities that are alternately instituted and relinquished according to the purposes at hand; it will be an open assemblage that permits of multiple convergences and divergences without obedience to a normative telos of definitional closure (Butler 2002:22).

Butler's view of gender challenges essentialist views of it at the same time that it defies ideas such as having a stable identity by pointing to its opennes and fluidity that in turn rejects the notion of clear boundaries. In addition, Butler (1990) states that gender is performative in that it comes into being through repeated "discursive enactments of cultural norms" (Bucholtz 2014: 37). Performativity, a term borrowed from Austin (1962), refers to a performative speech act in the sense that language use creates a new social reality by carrying out the act it names (Bucholtz 2014). By drawing on it, Butler's argument both stresses that gender is an act rather than a permanent attribute and brings to centre stage its discursive element that has influenced other researchers.

An approach to gender that has been influenced by Butler's views is poststructuralist feminism. The latter views gender as socially constructed and thus asks questions such as "why gender differences are being constructed that way"? instead of asking "what are the gender differences?" (McElhiny 2003:24). What characterises this poststructuralist stance is that it offers a more dynamic approach to gender that avoids seeking already pre-determined gender categories at the same time that it holds that gender is something that one continually does; "gender as activity, gender as performance, gender as accomplishment" (McElhinny 2003: 27). It can thus be argued that gender is not binary but a combination of various characteristics that could be understood as depending on the context and relationships involved (Jule 2017).

In addition, gender is the result of social practices such as language use. This resonates with what I stated above, identity does not precede language but it emerges through language, and it is encoded in linguistic and symbolic representations, normative concepts and social identities (McElhinny and Mills 2007). For instance, Cameron (2014) notes how gender is discursively done and ascribed as well as it points to important differences within what is conceived of as a monolithic category. She gives the example of the fishwife, which is a term ascribed to women who did low-status work such as cleaning and selling fish and which currently people may use to label them as "uncouth, unrefined and coarse-mannered" (2014: 284). Through that label, she goes on to state that the social identity of women is not only constructed as vituperative but associated with a working-class group regarded as "unfeminine" due to the way their language is evaluated and contrasted with higher-social status attitudes of refinement and politeness; behaviours and attitudes of desirable femininity based on a norm that is Western, White and middle class (Cameron 2014:285). In this light, her analysis enables us to keep in sight identity categories that we have seen above and that intersect with gender; that is, people's social class, race, on which I will elaborate below, and ethnicity that may be made salient in the contexts and situations where they may find themselves (see Eckert and McConnell-Ginet 1992).

Discussions about race, as in gender, often touch upon biologically based interpretations that attempt to provide allegedly objective categories that fixedly define who and what people are. Such views that also carry essentialist notions of individuals' physical and cognitive attributes have been contested, rejected and proven to be innacurate by a number of specialists from various disciplines and agree that pure races do not exist (Marger 1997; Edles 2004). A view of race that this work advocates and on which many agree is that it is a social construct that has resulted from events and processes rooted in European colonisation, which also evidences the ideological character of it (Chinoy 1966; Gilroy 2000; MacMaster 2001; Wade 2010). Race is not a natural phenomenon but a notion and construct that people develop in pursuit of particular interests.

However, it must be noted that race as a social construct still deserves a great deal of attention and we should not dismiss it as being encapsulated in a terrain of ideas. The construct of race indeed, matters because:

> if people discriminate on the basis of their ideas of race, this is a social reality of paramount importance. Equally, people may lay claim to a racial identity that represents for them central aspects of their person – indeed in the US, racial identity is so politicised that no one is really complete without one (Wade 2010:13).

Wade's statement reminds us of two important aspects in debates about race that also relate to identity. It points to the idea that race is attributive and relational in the sense that racial categories are both externally constructed and form relationships based on arbitrary distinctions. But what are they based on? Various scholars have argued that common distinctions of race are drawn in terms of physical appearance or, as Bonilla Silva (1999:903) has stated, they are social categorisations that rest on "the language of the phenotype". Phenotypical features are used to differentiate groups of people from another and they often revolve around ideas of being black, white or coloured at the same time that they evoke questions such as what are you? (Edles 2004). Nevertheless, this argument should be treated cautiously as I do not intend to present it as a biological or an objective basis for racial recognition but rather to refer to how phenotypes may also be socially mobilised to either exclude or include and that they are part of the social perception and experience of race.

Also, another term interrelated to class, gender and race is that of ethnicity. This, it is worth mentioning, also entails complexities in definitions and interpretations and is often conflated with and treated as synonymous with race. As Pilkington (2003:27) puts it, ethnicity and race "may empirically overlap with people defined as race becoming over time an ethnic group". Indeed, clear-cut distinctions are difficult to draw.

Nevertheless, two interpretations of ethnicity on which there seems to be general consensus is that, as in the case of race above, it is also a social construct (see May 2008; Wade 2010), and rests on perceptions and experience of cultural differences. By cultural differences I mean dress, customs, dance, language. In this logic, as Puri (2004:174) states, ethnicity "is a form of collective identity based on shared cultural beliefs and practices, such as language, history, descent, and religion", and, he goes on to argue, "even though ethnicities often allude to enduring kin-based and blood ties, it is widely recognised that they are cultural, not biological, ties". This interpretation, on the one hand, allows us to shed light on the intricacies and multiple dimensions of ethnic identity at the same time that it invites us to avoid a primordialist view that may treat it as either biologically determined or fixed. On the other hand, it is not unproblematic in terms of the language element given that not all Latin Americans in this study, who also identify as an ethnic group, speak only Spanish but also Portuguese and English. Thus, we should not rush to conclude that ethnicity is a bundle of cultural traits that can be studied and listed to establish differences between other ethnic groups (Barth 1969; May 2008). Instead, we should bear in mind that ethnicity also involves a two-way process between an individual's subjectivity and external agents; that is, "it is the result of a dialectical process involving the individual's self-identification and outsiders' ethnic designations – i.e., what *you* think your ethnicity is versus what *they* think your ethnicity is (Nagel 1994:154 italics in original).

In addition to the above, ethnicity is also viewed as instrumental. Although this approach to ethnicity is often associated with negative overtones such as Nazi Germany (see May 2008), this means that ethnicity can also be used by people as a social and political resource in the quest of political ends, that is, "a group organices along ethnic lines in pursuit of collective political ends" (Stack 1986:5). The fact that Latin Americans in London have achieved status as an ethnic group in London demonstrates how powerful symbolic ties are and how they could be employed for their benefit as a collective in political and civic participation in a host society. This should not be interpreted as a view that holds that ethnic groups are internally homogenous since they are indeed heterogenous, rather it should be interpreted as a way of understanding how "a chosen ethnic identity is determined by the individual's perception of its meaning to different audiences, its salience in different social contexts and its utility in different settings" (Nagel 1994:155).

The notion of identity and its portrayal by an individual viewed from an essentialist standpoint is an argument difficult to sustain. The language and identity nexus is part of a social practice that must be conceived of as dynamic rather than stable; that is, identity is "always open to change; multifaceted in complex, contradictory ways; tied to social practice and interaction as a flexible and contextually contingent resource" (Miller 2000:70). The various social domains that act dialogically with people's language use unveil the multi-layered, multidimensional phenomenon of identity given that individuals turn to various discourses in a socially conditioned situation (Pietikainen and Dufva 2006).

2.3 Ideology

The word ideology was introduced by the French philosopher Destutt de Tracy in his 1796 *Memoire sur la faculté de penser*. In it, ideology was proposed as a branch of zoölogy that could explain the content of our human minds (Woolard 1998). That is, an analytical science that would dissect ideas into component parts to scrutinise the perceptions on which they were founded (Rehmann 2014). Ideology was meant to allow us to understand the "causes of incertitude and logical error" in order to improve the human condition by developing our mental faculties (Silverstein 1998: 124). For Tracy, ideology was the only science that could provide the foundations of all other sciences; "the knowledge of all knowledge" (Foucault 1994).

However, the origin of the word ideology is situated in a time of historical and political tensions. Ideology emerged in the post-Jacobin period of the French revolution as a research project of the so called *ideologistes*. They and Tracy were a group of scholars who held leading positions in the education system under the regime of the Directory whose Thermidor, a counter revolutionary stage, was influenced by their ideas (Rhemann 2014). Tracy and his circle wanted to use ideology to transform and stabilise post-revolutionary France (Kennedy 1979). They were involved in the foundation of the *Institut de France, the École Normale Supérierure* and *the Institut National*. The latter was a state-institution where Tracy introduced the concept of ideology to a number of republican intellectuals who gathered to debate the reorganisation of the education system (Kennedy 1979). In this context, ideology was meant to preserve the achievements of the republic while ridding of 'plebeian' demands (Deneys 1994) and was to become the foundation of grammar, education, morality and "finally the greatest of arts"; the regulation of society (Kennedy 1979: 355). Ideology was then designed "to regulate society in a way that man gets the most possible aid and the least possible harm fom his peers" (de Tracy 1992: 39). In this light, ideology was not apolitical since it was meant to influence people's perceptions and opinions through "a centralised education system" (Rhemann 2014: 17).

In addition, ideology sought to promote individual liberties and the integrity of representative assemblies, and one of its defining characteristics was its anti-religious stance, which contributed to its semantic shift with negative overtones. Ideology intended to foster a secular education in the *Écoles Centrales* and eliminate religious components in public education. This aim, nevertheless, was criticised since, on the one hand, the children of the propertied classes were to receive education in the *écoles centrales* while an abridged education was to be provided to children of the popular classes (Kennedy 1979). On the other hand, a secular education differed from one with religious components that Napoleon sought to inculcate as part of an alliance with the Catholic Church (Rehmann 2014). Since secularization did not align with Napoleon's agenda, ideology was reduced to metaphysical revery (Kennedy 1979). The *ideologiste* began to be called *ideologues*; the "class of windbags and ideologues who have always fought the authority", "dangerous dreamers who deprived the people of religion and salutary illusions" and who always distrusted authority "even when it was in their hands" (Kennedy 1979: 358). A vilification campaign went on as they, the *ideologues*, were even made responsible for Napoleon's military defeats by Russia. In 1812, Napoleon claimed: "we must lay the blame for the ills that our fair France has suffered on ideology" (Kennedy 1979: 360). As some scholars have concluded, the concept was mobilised by an Emperor to silence his opponents (Thompson 1984) and gradually shifted to signify a sphere of disconnected ideas (Eagleton 1990).

The meaning of ideology transcended national confines and developed into a number of conceptualisations and interpretations. Marx and Engels employed it in a number of contexts and in complex different ways, one of which is that of distortion. In *The German Ideology* they draw on the idea of *camera obscura* to describe ideology as an upside-down, distorted view of the world held by ideologists who "regard their ideology both as the creative force and as the aim of all social relations (Marx and Engels 1845: 420). Marx and Engel's use of ideology was a criticism directed to the young Hegelians who held that people's ideas would allegedly transform men's consciousness and thus reality. Such view exhibited a 'false consciousness' since 'it is not consciousness that determines life but life that determines consciousness' (Marx and Engels 1845: 36). In this sense, ideology is critically used to demistify mistaken ideas about indivduals' material living conditions and a social existence.

In addition, ideology is also associated with power within a social class system. As Marx and Engels stated:

> The ideas of the ruling class are in every epoch the ruling ideas; the class which is the ruling material force of society, is at the same time, the ruling intellectual force. The class which has the means of material production at its disposal, has control at the same time over the means of mental production, so that thereby, generally speaking, the ideas of those who lack the means of mental production are subject to it (Marx and Engels 1988: 67).

As we can gather from this passage, power could be exercised at interrelated intellectual and material levels. That is, ideology reflects the perspective and serves the interests of the ruling class by upholding an unequal system of power since it could be understood as system of thought intended to justify existing modes of production and exploitative social relationships that emerge from them (Kennedy 1979). In this sense, ideology may not only offer a distorted view of the world but obfuscates oppressive mechanisms from the lower classes (see Heywood 2003). Although Marx and Engel's statement is not free of criticism that claims that it ignores 'internal fractioning of the ideological universe of the dominant classes' (see Hall 1988), their formulations of ideology have lent themselves to questioning historical systems of oppresion and regulation that may be presented with a universal hegemonic character.

In light of the above, Antonio Gramsci made significant contributions to theorisations of ideology by linking it to the notion of hegemony. This was indeed a Leninist conception that originally sought the leadership of the proletariat over the peasantry; "political leadership conceived of as class alliance" (Mouffe 1979: 179). Although Gramsci did not offer a definition of hegemony, other scholars have set out to offer insightful interpretations of it:

> Hegemony emphasizes the ways in which power operates to form our everyday understanding of social relations, and to orchestrate the ways in which we consent to (and reproduce) those tacit and covert relations of power. Power is not stable or static, but is remade at various junctures within everyday life; it constitutes our tenuous sense of common sense, and is ensconced as the prevailing epistemes of a culture. (Butler 2000: 14)

Butler's take on hegemony allows us to advance our understanding of it by foregrounding power that may be articulated by either coercitive or consensual means. Indeed, it brings us closer to two major tenets of hegemony discussed by Gramsci: 'supremacy of a social group manifests itself in two ways: '*domination*' and '*intellectual and moral leadership*" (1971: 57 emphases added). The former refers to physical force that could involve the military, the police or the prison system. The latter stands for the winning over of potentially antagonistic groups (Block 2022) through 'civil society' institutions such as schools, the press, family or the Church. These are regarded as "hegemonic apparatusses" (Gramsci 1971: 228), which play a role in manufacturing indivuals' consent to subscribe to the values and norms of a dominant social group; as he put it "the normal exercise of hegemony is characterised by a combination of force and consent which balance each other so that force does not overwhelm consent but rather appears to be backed by the consent of the majority, expressed by the so-called organs of public opinion (Gramsci 1992: 156). Hegemony manifests itself as 'common sense'; a view of the world that shapes our daily experience and that implies government by the consent of the governed.

The idea that common sense shapes our daily, mundane practices does not intend to suggests that hegemony does not encounter resistance nor does it attempt to make the claim that the ideas of a dominant class determine social values. Indeed, Gramsci recognised individuals' agency and ability to change social order; "man is to be conceived as an historical bloc of purely individual and subjective elements and of mass and objective or material elements with which the individual is in an *active* relationship" (Gramsci 1971: 413 emphasis added). Rather, Gramsci's interpretation of hegemony draws our attention to the various social levels and domains interspersed by ideology. In the context of religion, for instance, he referred to Catholicism as "a multiplicity of distinct and often contradictory religions; there is one Catholicism for the peasantry, one for the petit bourgeoisie and the town workers" (Gramsci 1971: 420). The Italian thinker, in this sense, does not offer a reductionist perspective of civil institutions, but points to their various structures in which hegemony may be historically embedded and thus encourages us to challenge common sense views that could be rearticulated into new realities.

In light of the above, ideology has a long history of theorisations that attempt to account for the intricate social phenomena that we set out to explore in different disciplines (see Althusser 2014; Luckács 1971). In this book, as a way of clariying how ideology is to be treated it is important to state what ideology is not. As van Dijk, states "ideologies in our perspective are not merely systems of ideas, let alone properties of the individual minds of persons. Neither are they vaguely defined as forms of consciousness, let alone 'false consciousness' (van Dijk 1995: 21). Ideology is thus understood as a "worldview that constitutes social cognition; complexes of representations and attitudes with regard to certain aspects of the social world" (van Dijk 1998; Wodak and Reisigl 2016). Ideology stands for "specific basic frameworks of social cognition, with specific internal structures, and specific cognitive and social functions" (van Dijk 1995: 21). Within these interpretations of ideology, we should not ignore individuals' social positions that may influence views of the world and that we can also observe in relation to language.

2.4 Language ideologies

Research about language ideologies has been growing over the past decades, particularly from scholars working within Linguistic Anthropology. The work of Woolard (1998), Kroskrity (2004), Gal (1989) and Silverstein (1979; 1992) paved the way to critical observations about ideas, beliefs or attitudes about language and language use in various contexts. Their examination has also led researchers to explore and understand how individuals build their inclusion or exclusion in social groups in situations of language contact (Barat et al. 2013), and in a context of high mobility as well as for the purpose of this study, their study becomes highly relevant as people along with their linguistic, economic and education capital move into and interact in new societies. The latter are conceived of as spaces where people may find other intersecting notions such as class or ideologies of neoliberalism, both of which I will address below, and interests that may be either contextually divergent or convergent. Language ideologies in the context of globalisation and migration are multifarious and dynamic since they permeate the social experience of the individual. However, what are they?

The definitions and interpretations of language ideologies are diverse, which responds to the complex and context-based events in which they occur. However, two interrelated definitions lend themselves for the analytical purposes of this study. Woolard (1998:3) states that "representations, whether explicit or implicit, that construe the intersection of language and human beings in a social world are what we mean by language ideology". In this line of thought, she later on states that language ideologies are "socially, politically and morally loaded cultural assumptions about the way language works in social life and about the role of particular linguistic forms in a given society (Woolard 2016: 7). These interpretations interrelate in that they point to the social and political roots and basis of language ideologies and are thus instrumental in that they enable us to come away from what at first glance seems a cognitive domain as their main origin and terrain. This is an important caveat in our initial understanding of language ideologies that also adds clarity to it since, as other researchers have noted, although ideologies pertain to mental phenomena, beliefs or ideas, they cannot be merely located within a realm of ideas about language or be reduced to individual responses to language (Woolard 1998; Milani and Johnson 2010; Paffey 2012).

The above still requires that we delve into what factors influence the production of language ideologies and that we consider a wider sociocultural spatial frame in which they may emerge. Various researchers have observed and have agreed that language ideologies, as suggested above, have a social origin and that they respond to the experience of a particular social position (see Woolard et al 1998; Errington 1998; Gal 1998; Irvine 1998; Silverstein 1998). Kroskity has pertinently underscored this by arguing, "language ideologies are profitably conceived as multiple because of the multiplicity of meaningful social divisions" (2000: 12). His argument draws attention to the complexity of social structures in which education, gender, ethnicity, social class, generation, religion, etc., should not be ignored as factors that have an effect on how reality is viewed and experienced as they may evidence a situated and partial character of conceptions and uses of language (Errington 2001). In this light, it can be argued that language ideologies apply to everyone and are grounded in the speaker's sociocultural experiences from which therefore attitudes and beliefs about the value, the purity or superiority of a language originate (Kroskrity 2004; Silverstein 1992). In addition, our analyses and debates to understand language ideologies should not be reduced to language users' textual representations of their experiences. Indeed, ideology is discovered in linguistic practice, in metalinguistic discourse, in explicit talk about language (Woolard et al. 1998) but language ideological debates, Blommaert states:

> They develop against a wider socio-political and historical horizon of relationships of power, forms of discrimination, social engineering, nation building and so forth. Their outcome always has connections with these issues as well: the outcome of a debate directly or indirectly involves forms of conflict and inequality among groups of speakers: restrictions on the use of certain languages/varieties, the loss of social opportunities when these restric-

tions are not observed by speakers, the negative stigmatization of certain languages/varieties, associative labels attached to languages/varieties. Language ideological debates are part of more general socio-political processes (Blommaert 1999: 2).

His statement leads us to both remember and think of fundamental and interrelated aspects in the examination of language ideologies. By referring to conflict and inequality, it reminds us that their study is not merely about language but it concomitantly involves the scrutiny of historically situated events in which the exercise of power is sought (Woolard 1998). In addition to this, by pointing to nation building processes, Blommaert's argument indexes political phenomena and institutions on which societies have been founded and which have played a major role in the promotion and dissemination of particular interests and ideas about the world, society and also language. In this vein, language ideologies are multiple, varied and may be encountered in various social domains and scales that constitute our social space and interaction and, thus, they must be identified in the social context in which they are reproduced.

One of these ideologies is that of the one-nation-one-language ideology that has both a political and linguistic dimension at interrelated levels. Such ideology holds that one single language is the glue that holds a nation together and an identity marker that fosters national unity (Piller and Cho 2015). However, instances that evidence the political and partial interest of particular groups intending to mobilise one language and marginalising others for the sake of the nation can be found by looking at history and the mechanisms used by those in power. For instance, in the context of the French revolution, Billig (1995) and Blommaert and Verschueren (1998) note how the French language was spoken by a minority and used as an administrative vehicle of what later on will be the State. They go on to argue that the declaration of the Rights of Man and the Citizen benefited neither Bretons nor Occitans due to the imposition of French as the language of instruction in the schools of France, which resulted in the reduction of linguistic diversity in the arbitrary and ideological process of nation-building (Blommaert and Verschueren, 1998). Similar instances are encountered in the UK where Welsh was officially banned in schools and their speakers punished for using their native language (see Sallaband 2011). Also, more recently, the English only movement in the US also provides instances of the one nation-one language ideology. Its advocates argue that "English is a common bond" that has allowed Americans from various backgrounds to overcome differences and that language diversity leads to language conflict and political separatism (Crawford 2000:6; see also Baran, 2017). At the core of these historical and political events we find what Blommaert (1999: 427) has termed "the dogma of homogeinism", which promotes the idea that "monolingualism is the norm or the desired ideal for society" and that, nonetheless, contradicts the factual presence of multilingualism in the overwhelming majority of societies including the UK, USA, etc.

It must also be added that the one nation-one-language ideology is also associated with ideologies of linguistic assimilation. This promotes the idea that linguistic diversity is a danger for social cohesion or an obstacle for individuals to integrate in a host society (Martin Rojo 2002), that bilingualism hinders academic progress by creating confusion (see Heller, 2018) or that multilingualism creates a babel-like social environment that is not conducive to communication. This is problematic given that, as we will see in the participants' accounts in chapter 6, this ideology suggests exclusion and inequalities in various social domains and it also carries overtones of moral judgement. In other words, those who speak a language other than that of the state-sanctioned institutions may be regarded as people who deviate from the norms and do not do the right thing, and at times face antagonistic attitudes that are nationalistic (Billig 1995). This ideological representation of a monolingual nation is inconsistent with their current linguistic constitution and it may become manifest at institutional level or individual level, which reminds us that ideologies of language could apply to everyone and it draws attention to an ideology that is also closely related to identity.

Accent is the way of pronouncing words as well as individuals' property that indexes their identity (Anderson and Trudgill 1992). Nonetheless, we often hear statements such as "I have no accent", "my accent is neutral", or, as we will see in chapter 6, "people have a hard accent" that imply a social evaluation of ways of speaking that are often categorised as proper or improper and ideologically constructed for particular interests. Lippi Green (2012), for instance, has referred to the standard language ideology, which is the belief that there is one single correct form of accent and that promotes a variant of the white-upper middle class in the USA. In a similar vein in the UK, researchers such as Carter (1999) and Milroy and Milroy (1998) refer to Received Pronunciation also described as RP, Oxford English, the Queen's English or BBC English, which is also an ideological construct of the upper classes since it has been found that only 3% of the population speak in this way (Milroy 2001). In other words, what is regarded as the standard accent is based on a class interest that uses the linguistic as proxy in the pursuit of social prestige and power, and that often delegitimises other variants. In this vein, Bourdieu mentions that a nonstandard accent, either class-based, regional, or foreign, "might be perceived as a particularistic trait that disqualifies the speaker in public deliberations" (Woolard 2016: 29). His statement is also pertinent in a context of mobility in which both speakers of a variant of a particular language or second language speakers' accents may be ideologically labelled as inadequate or equated with deficient cognitive abilities or sounding inauthentic (see Gal 2006).

Ideologies of authenticity are also present in society and they are often found in perceptions of a speech variety and language teaching. In terms of a speech variety, Woolard describes authenticity as something that "must be perceived as deeply rooted in a social and geographical territory in order to have value. To be considered authentic in this ideological frame, a speech variety must be very much "from somewhere" in speakers' consciousness, and thus its meaning is constituted as profoundly local" (Woolard 2016: 22). This means that, as we will see in this book in chapter 4 and 5 respectively, to speak English one must sound like being from the UK or to speak Spanish with a Spanish accent one must be from Spain. Within this frame, having the authentic accent or speech variety provides its speaker with value and credibility and may create social conditions in which "to profit from linguistic authenticity, one must sound like that kind of person who is valued as natural and authentic" (Woolard 2016:23). Linked to this idea of authenticity is the ideology of the native speaker in language teaching. This is the belief that native speaker teachers are the authentic linguistic model whose speaking is to be emulated or are "the models of correctness" (Kubota 2009 in Creese et al. 2014: 938). It is also related to a territory-based idea of authenticity in the sense that it is often associated with notions of citizenship and belonging to a nation state as well as ideas of language as a fixed system with a homogenous speech community (Doer 2009 in Creese et al. 2014). These beliefs, however, should be carefully and contextually examined as they may either promote or instantiate discourses of deficit, illegitimacy, exclusion and dominance (Piller 2001; Jenkins 2009). It has been documented that when applying for either teaching or non-teaching jobs native English speakers have been given preference over non-native speakers, which have material and discriminatory effects on people's social realities (see Holliday 2013; Doan 2016).

People's realities are also located within a context of globalisation in which economic conditions of competition have been created and have influenced perceptions about language usefulness. English, for instance, has been, on the one hand, constructed as the language for socioeconomic mobility and progress (Penycook 2007). On the other hand, it is often perceived as a language intrinsically superior to others and better equipped for the technological demands of our times (Milroy and Milroy 2005). As to socioeconomic mobility, it reflects an ideology of marketization in which English is constructed as a desirable skill for employment, academic and economic success, and its learning is often presented as a rational decision that the individual must make (Duchene et al. 2013; Miller 2014). Its ideological nature, nevertheless, emerges in the power asymmetries and inequalities evident in present-day mobile societies in which other resources such as economic, cultural, social capital, having the "right" accent as well as other forms of cultural dispositions may have a stratifying effect (Garrido and

Codó 2017: 33). In addition to this, the alleged rational decision to learn it exhibits a common-sense view that interacts with a neoliberal discourse of entrepreneurship in the sense that, as we saw in chapter 1.6, the individual is held responsible for their own success or failure in either global market or receiving society (Miller 2012; Holborow 2015).

As to the alleged intrinsic superiority of English over other languages, it could be described as exhibiting what has been called "social Darwinism" (Mocek 1999 in Moreno Cabrera 2008: 19). This biological metaphor is often used to explain that languages are born, develop and die in order to justify a belief that some languages are more naturally fit to survive, progress and thus triumph over others as a natural, unquestionable result and not as a consequence of economic or political factors or inequality (Moreno Cabrera 2008). In chapter 5, we will see how this ideological representation of language is produced by one of the participants who characterises English as a naturally better equipped language than Spanish and suggests that English is superior to other languages in domains such as education and technology. Her view will also enable us to gain insight into how such ideology may influence the selection of social relations and how they are constructed as investments in a globalised city.

The study of language ideologies does not merely involve the study of beliefs about language or metalinguistic descriptions. This idea should not be interpreted as an underestimation of their study but rather as reminder of their complexity given that their examination, as stated above, also entails the scrutiny of power relations in which individuals interact with other social actors across different domains and scales in social life. These, due to the different processes of globalisation and migration, are increasingly complex and unequal and can be conceived of as sites where social actors associate with or dissociate from others whose (non) linguistic resources, expectations and aspirations may or may not coincide with or reflect the interest they pursue.

2.5 Critical Discourse Studies (CDS) and society

Given that this book aims to analyse Latin American immigrants' discourse, it is necessary to state what I mean by this. This section, thus, will concentrate on the relation between language and society viewed from a Critical Discourse Studies lens (CDS) and it aims to provide a description of how this study approaches such a relationship that will help us understand the social spaces and events of which the participants talk.

Critical Discourse Studies (CDS) is an interdisciplinary field of inquiry that integrates different approaches to the study of language and society issues. It is mainly formed by a discourse historical approach (DHA), a dialectical-relational approach, a sociocognitive approach (Wodak 2016; Fairclough 2016; van Dijk 2016), on which this study will draw and I will elaborate later on, among other approaches. Although the methods that constitute CDS vary in how they approach and examine language and society issues, studies in CDS are generally characterised by common research interests. These include the deconstruction of ideologies and power through the systematic "examination of semiotic data" such as written, visual or spoken data, "the critical investigation of social inequalityas it is expressed, constituted and legitimized by language use (Wodak and Meyer 2016:4–12), "the understanding and resistance of social inequality" (van Dijk 2001: 352). By 'critical', what is meant is not taking things for granted and it thus involves challenging reductionism in order to make unclear structures of power and ideologies manifest (Reisigl and Wodak 2001); that is, being critical implies being sceptical about and taking on a dissenting attitude towards common sense views (van Dijk 2013). Taking on a critical stance towards, for instance, the widespread use of the adjective and noun 'illegal' in the context of both immigration and this study enables me to challenge commonly accepted views of immigration and bring to the fore relevant sociopolitically distinctions that matter for and affect the realities of Latin American immigrants as we will see in the next chapter.

As noted above, language use for the aims of this study is viewed from a CDS perspective. This decision rests upon the notion that language use "involves an interest in the ways social members categorise others and themselves" (Van Dijk 1997a in Ainsworth and Hardy 2004: 236) as well as "exploring patterns in and across the statements and identifying the social consequences of different discursive representations of reality" (Jorgensen and Phillips 2002:21). Furthermore, it must be added that categorisation is not unidirectional; as Ainsworth and Hardy (2004: 238) have noted "practical categorisations are brought into being with practical effects for those targeted by such discourses as well as those involved in their construction". Within this interpretation, categorisation also involves the dialectic construction of social identities in the sense that language users by stating or categorising who the other is, are also suggesting who they are not. Such an understanding of discourse becomes instrumental for this study since, as we will see in chapters 3 and 4, it will help us inform the analysis of the participants' contextualised language use in order to understand how they self-present and categorise other Latin Americans and (dis)associate themselves from other members that constitute the Latin American community.

Language use also involves different ways of speaking. These ways of speaking in this study are treated as synonymous with discourses in that the latter, as Fairclough (1993:138) has noted, refer to a particular discourse such as a "feminist discourse, a Marxist discourse, an environmentalist discourse, a neoliberal discourse" (cited in Jorgensen and Phillips 2002: 67). What characterises each of these discourses and distinguishes one from the other is the particular, partial social interest they pursue as well as the values they seek to promote; that is, while a Marxist discourse is often associated with collectivism and egalitarianism, a neoliberal discourse seeks to promote contrasting values such as that of individualism (see Heywood 2003). This interpretation of discourse is central in exploring the participants' ways of speaking given that it can enable us to gain insight into their different views and interests that constitute the Latin American community, particularly the neoliberal discourse that some of them use to make sense of their relations and that carries values that I will address in subsequent chapters.

Discourse in this study is also seen as a social practice that is not merely a reflection of social life. Fairclough and Wodak (1997:258) have drawn our attention to the two-way relationship between discourse and social life within this frame of interpretation by stating that "describing discourse as social practice implies a dialectical relationship between a particular discursive event and the situation(s), institution(s) and social structure(s), which frame it: the discursive event is shaped by them but it also shapes them". This means that discourse is socially constitutive and socially conditioned and that it has the capacity to transform or sustain social life within particular social domains. Furthermore, discourse as social practice also transcends the local situation in which it is produced. Fairclough (2013:30), for instance, refers to the interconnectedness of social activity by pointing to "the networking together of different social practices across different domains or fields of social life (the economy, education, family life) and across different scales of social life (global, regional, national, local)". This interpretation is best captured in the discursive construction of migration in which its representation from a political domain through various channels such as the media has been badly depicted and which has generated social attitudes of antagonism and distancing not only in a political terrain but in the everyday life of social actors that are part of this study. In this light, discourse can be interpreted as a multidimensional social practice that permeates social experience.

It is also important to note that the production of discourse for the purposes of this book is to be regarded as deliberate and non-neutral. In other words, discourse is "mostly intentional, controlled, a purposeful human activity" (van Dijk 1997: 8), a form of action. Indeed, it is mostly intentional since there are certain parts of discourse, to which I will return later, which are under "a speaker's control" and that must be examined in relation to the social context of its production as well as its functions (van Dijk 2001:99). Within this logic, once those parts of discourse under analysis have been identified, discourse is not neutral given that it is selective and has a consequential effect on how we relate to one another and our social environment. Fairclough and Wodak (1997: 258) have pointed to the effects of discursive practices, which can be ideological in that "they can help produce and reproduce unequal power relations between (for instance) social classes, women and men, and ethnic and cultural majorities and minorities through the ways in which they represent things and position people" (cited in Wodak and Meyer 2016: 6). In other words, discourse may be associated with processes of inclusion and exclusion that language users can accomplish throur particular discourse units.

However, the consequentiality of discourse also hinges upon other non-linguistic factors. Bourdieu (1997: 2003) has noted that the power of language is not strictly an inherent characteristic of it but it is associated with "the social position or status of the speaker" as well as the situation or, as stated above, context in which the communicative event occurs. This will be clearly seen in chapter 5 where two of the participants' experiences depict discursive processes of exclusion and discrimination in state-sanctioned spaces. Therefore, the social conditions under which discourse is produced are fundamental for our exegesis of the research participants' statements. They forefront the social events in which the research participants partake as members of a community embedded in a larger socioeconomic, political and cultural context. In other words, by looking at language use through a CDS lens and its relationship with different social structures we can establish links between "the micro-social" and "the macro-social frames of analysis of any sociolinguistic phenomenon" (Silverstein 2013: 193). Language use is neither divorced from the social environment nor separated from the historical and political conditions in which it is produced; as stated above, they are in a dialogical relation. In this manner, a CDS informed view of language as a deliberate social practice that forms society also helps us contextualise the research participants' accounts in the present migratory movements to a cosmopolitan city such as London and thus examine the identities that their discursive moves disclose.

The particular use of language of the Latin American immigrants in this study lends itself to a critical analysis of their personal experiences. They are social situations that exhibit power relations that lead to the polarisation and fragmentation of social relations, exclusion and discrimination, and their occurrence as many other social phenomena are subject to critical investigation through a CDS approach (Wodak and Meyer 2016; van Dijk 2001). In this light, my motivations, on the one hand, to select an approach of CDS as method of investigation lie in its problem-oriented nature that probes critically into social inequality that is expressed explicitly and implicitly in language use (Wodak 2001; van Dijk 2016). On the other hand, by looking at Latin American immigrants' metalinguistic discourse and the way they self-present, interpret events and categorise people via language use, we gain valuable insights into their identities, ideologies and social relationships with themselves and other groups of people since language use is socially constitutive (see Wodak 2013; van Dijk 2013; Wodak and Mayer 2016). Furthermore, as I mentioned above, the tools CDS offers allow me to take on a critical attitude to problematise assumptions, commonsensical ideas and views in discourse since they can become reified in the ways we regulate and organise our social interactions (van Dijk 2001; Machin and Mayr 2012).

A CDS-informed view of language, nevertheless, should acknowledge its criticisms. CDS has been accused of being selective of texts known to be contentious, as putting a high price on textual analysis or as either too ambitious for social change or invalid as a discipline (see Blommaert 2005; Simpson and Mayr 2010; Hammersley 1996; Jones 2007). It is also criticised for putting a strong emphasis on textual analysis disregarding context (Blommaert 2001; 2005). In this vein, Breeze also notes that sometimes critical discourse analysts have not paid enough attention to aspects and characteristics of the immediate context where discourse is produced, "which has led to interpretations which are pragmatically inappropriate or remote from the concerns of the participants" (2011:520). This means that context within CDS studies is often interpreted as the macro-context into which analysts make huge jumps leaving the day-to-day experience and the situation in which social actors produce discourse ignored. Such criticisms should neither discourage analysts from pursuing what they are after nor should demotivate them to abandon discourse analysis as a method of analysis. Rather, such observations should be taken on board, as I will attempt to do so in this book, in order to both capture the participants' discourses in situ and incorporate the social encounters and interactions with them so I offer a richer description and critical analysis of their narrated realities. Furthermore, by considering context we can attempt to gain better insight into the participants' various and intricate social practices and relations that could be explored by the particular version of CDS to be employed in this study.

For the analyses in chapters 3, 4 and 5, I will initially draw on van Dijk's sociocognitive approach. This approach is one in which the interpretation of the relationship between discourse and society is mediated by mental models (van Dijk 2001; 2016). These are subjective representations of individual personal experiences categorised as situation models and context models (van Dijk 2016). I will say more about these two below. According to van Dijk (2016: 66), "mental models are multimodal and embodied", and define and control human beings' perception and social interaction as well as the production and comprehension of discourse. They are multimodal in the sense that they may "feature information of social experiences" that encompass the visual, the emotional, the auditory, and the evaluative (van Dijk 2016: 66). In other words, mental models are "the interface" between sociocultural experience and discourse that represents or constructs social events from the perspective of an individual (van Dijk 2016). In addition to this, mental models also feature social cognition. This is a more general, abstract knowledge about the world shared with other individuals with whom we may also share attitudes about, for instance, immigration (van Dijk 2016). In this vein, mental models do not only construe or interpret personal experiences in a seemingly isolated cognitive domain but on the basis of a partial social cognition (see van Dijk 2016).

As noted above, mental models are categorised as situation and context models. Situation models, also called semantic models, "represent the situation a discourse is about" (van Dijk 2016: 67). Such models, which are also subjective representations of events, people or actions, account for implications and presuppositions that can be derived from the explicit information a discourse contains or that a communicative exchange conveys (van Dijk 2014). That is, language users draw inferences about a topic or a situation given that situation models define the gist of text and talk (van Dijk 2014). For instance, producing a phrase such as "we've got a situation" makes us think of, infer an event or action laden with a particular connotation. In this light, semantic models also define the meaningfulness and coherence of a situation. That is, a language user may want to talk about a personal experience or a topic by producing sequences of sentences that express temporal or causal relations between events or that have functional meaning relations (van Dijk 2014).

In addition to the situation models discussed above, discourse production in a sociocognitive approach also involves paying attention to context models. These are also called pragmatic models and they account for the appropriateness of the communicative event, how a personal experience should be described in a specific context. For instance, the way we relate an accident to a friend will differ from the way we tell it to a physician since these mental models organise the selection and production of information by keeping track of our intentions in discourse as well as the setting and the participants of the situation language users describe (see van Dijk 1998; 2014; 2016). In this manner at the micro level of discourse production we frame how Latin American immigrants verbalise their personal social experiences using particular ways of speaking such as positive or negative (self) presentation, categorisation, etc. that exhibit how they understand and construe them in particular and contextually relevant social environments. Nevertheless, their individual experiences must be located in wider spatiotemporal frames with other social actors with which they interact.

Latin American immigrants are members of larger social groups with whom they may or may not share ideologies. The latter, as stated in chapter 2.3, are a system of ideas with a social formation, "worldviews that constitute social cognition; complexes of representations and attitudes with regard to certain aspects of the social world" (van Dijk 1993: 258 in Wodak 2016: 9) and they are the basis of knowledge and attitudes of certain groups such as "neoliberals, feminists" and

2.5 Critical Discourse Studies (CDS) and society — 95

other groups (van Dijk 2001: 115). In a sociocognitive approach of CDS, ideologies influence language users' mental models since they affect how people plan, understand and interpret their social practices as well as they influence the representation of basic characteristics of social groups such as their identity, values and norms (van Dijk 2016). In this vein, Latin American immigrants' discursive representations of their personal experiences do not occur in a vacuum since they contain traces of ideologies that contribute to the definition of the communicative event (see van Dijk 1998). Thus, by recognising such traces we learn of the various social identities and practices that influence Latin American immigrants' relations amongst themselves and with other social actors, phenomena that can be criticised through particular features of their discourses.

It must be said that a full, detailed analysis of Latin American immigrants' discourse is not an ambition of this study since such aspiration exceeds its aims and it is not a plausible result of CDS approaches (see van Dijk 1985; 2001). Consequently, I will carry out the subsequent analyses by focusing on the global and local meanings of the participants' discourse. Global meanings stand for what the participants' discourse is about; that is, the topics that are intuitively derived from the participants' word choices and that characterise the meaning of a discourse as speakers choose to foreground or background information that resonates with their interests (van Dijk 2000; 2001; 2016). Local meanings account for lexical meanings, pronouns, word repetition, metaphors, and rhetorical strategies such as topoi, disclaimers, hedging, implicitness, presuppositions, implicatures and other argumentative moves that help us scrutinise the participants' self-presentation and group description such as other-descriptions as well as language ideologies. It must be added that both global and local meanings will be under analysis depending on the contextuall relevance of some other discourse units.

Furthermore, I will also concentrate on two important rhetorical strategies, one of which is metaphor. By metaphor I mean the use of language to "refer to something other than what it was originally applied to or what it literally means, in order to suggest some resemblance or make a connection between the two things" (Knowles and Moon 2006:3). In other words "the essence of metaphor is understanding and experiencing one kind of thing in terms of another" (Lakoff and Johnson 2002: 5). It must be noted that the use of metaphor is pervasive in everyday language and it carries social significance. Lakoff and Johnson (2002) have studied and have demonstrated how a metaphor can transcend its rhetorical purpose in that it regulates our habitual functioning and structures social relations given that the way people choose to talk about social phenomena contributes to a certain kind of understanding of what society is (Antaki 1994). In a context associated with this study such as migration, van Dijk (2006:738) has underscored the social relevance of metaphors and has referred to how "abstract, complex, unfamiliar, new or emotional meanings may thus be made more familiar and more concrete". Common metaphors to represent migration, for instance, are the use of "military metaphors" which are used for representing immigrants and refugees as threats and as an invasion by big numbers of dangerous "aliens" or "parasites" (van Dijk, 2006: 738). I argue that the study of the use of metaphor in this research study is socially relevant not only as a discursive strategy but as a way of understanding what speakers can socially accomplish in terms of their social relations, alignments and experiences in context in which other discursive strategies are concomitantly employed.

The second important unit of analysis in the participants' discourses is the use of topoi. They are here understood as "central parts of argumentation that belong to the premises. They justify the transition from the argument(s) to the conclusion. Topoi are not always expressed explicitly but can be made explicit as conditional of causal paraphrases such as 'if x, then y' or 'y because x'" (Reisigl 2014:75). In other words, topoi are "the common-sense reasoning typical for specific issues" as well as "the most typical elements of the argumentative and persuasive nature of debates on immigration, integration and the multicultural society" (van Dijk 2000:97–98 in Blackledge 2005:68). Having this definition in mind, both the implicit and explicit production of topoi for the analytical purposes of this study should also be identified and captured within three main types: topoi of culture, topoi of history and topoi of burden.

Topoi of culture refer to essentialising characteristics attributed to a group of people as in "problems arise because a group's culture is as it is" (Blackledge 2005:70). An instance of this was given by Mexico's former president, Enrique Peña Nieto, who stated that corruption in Mexico was a cultural problem and not one associated with the particular interests of political parties or specific actors in positions of power (Proceso 2014). Topoi of history are here interpreted as an argumentation strategy intended to show that a present situation can be relevantly compared to earlier events (positive or negative) in history and that therefore history teaches us a lesson; that is, people's attitudes, present-day events are explained and reduced to an alleged law of history (van Dijk 2003). The direct or indirect numerical representation of immigrants is typically related to the topoi of burden. This may also be articulated by a view that depicts immigrants as either passive or negatively agentive in the sense that too many of them will undermine or abuse the resources or benefits that a host society provides. We will see instances of these in chapter 3.

In addition to the units of analysis mentioned above, an approach on which this study also draws is the dialogical relational approach in which discourse is treated as semiosis. This suggests that discourse analysis is concerned with the various semiotic analysis of which "language is only one" and "views semiosis as an element of the social processes which is dialectically related to other processes" (Fairclough 2010: 230). In this vein, a key construct that enables us to capture the multidimensionality of discourse is interdiscursivity (Fairclough 1993). This concept, on which I will elaborate below, derived from Bakthin's heteroglossia and subsequently was developed by Kristeva's intertextuality. As to heteroglossia, Bakhtin (1981) writes:

> The living utterance, having taken shape at a particular historical moment in a socially specific environment, cannot fail to brush up against thousands of living dialogic threads, woven by socio-ideological consciousness around the given object of an utterance, it cannot fail to become an active participant in social dialogue (Bakhtin 1981:276).

His interpretation of language, or more specifically of the utterance as being interwoven and in interaction with other dialogic threads enables us to think of, understand and view discourse as a verbal practice that is also associated with reference to another source, "full of transmissions and interpretations of other people's words (see Bakhtin 1981:338). In this sense, interrelated constructs such as voice and dialogism gain conceptual prominence to account for language use in a social milieu. Voice refers to the fact that words are not directly our own since they are spoken by someone else (Bakhtin 1981). That is, words are not produced ex nihilo; they are socially charged in that they bear traces of contexts in which they have been used. This does not mean that speakers merely reproduce meanings. Indeed, Bakhtin argued that the word is half someone else's but it can become one's own only when the speaker provides it with their "own accent" and adapts it to "their semantic and expressive intention" in context (1981: 293). Thus, Bakhtin recognised a dynamic social interaction between the word, the speaker and meanings.

In addition to voice, dialogism lends itself to a closer examination and conceptualisation of the word. Bakhtin (1981: 279) developed the term "dialogism" to criticise linguistics and the philosophy of discourse for treating the word as preconditioned, "excised from dialogue and taken for the norm" since such a view ignored "the internal dialogism of the word". That is:

> it is precisely this internal dialogism of the word, which does not assume any external compositional forms of dialogue, that cannot be isolated as an independent act, separate from the word's ability to form a concept of its object [. . .], this internal dialogism that has such enormous power to shape style. The internal dialogism of the word finds expression in a series of peculiar features in semantics, syntax and stylistics that have remained up to the present time completely unstudied by linguistics and stylistics (Bakhtin 1981: 279).

Dialogism sheds a wider light on the multilayered meanings of the word since it frees a conception of it from a structuralist view, and puts it in a much broader social realm in which it acquires socially contingent meanings. These are relationally and mutually constructed in the sense that dialogism consists in the fact that one's own word alludes always to the word of the other (Petrilli 2016). A word's meanings are in a constant interaction with others and they have "the potential of conditioning others. Which will affect the other, how it will do so and in what degree is what is actually settled at the moment of utterance" (Morris 1997:426).

Bakhtin's theoretical contributions have also been enriched by what Kristeva termed intertextuality. She used it to refer to "the insertion of history into a text and of this text into history" (Kristeva 1986: 39). Intertextuality is, in other words, "reference to the same events as the other texts or the reappearance of a text's main argument in another text" (Wodak 2009:319). Such a concept functions as an optic through which we locate and recognise discourse in a historical frame in which there has been an interaction of interrelated social voices.

These ideas, as stated above, have also derived in what Fairclough calls interdiscursivity. Fairclough defines it as "the property texts have of being full of snatches of other texts, which may be explicitly demarcated or merged in, and which the text may assimilate, contradict, ironically echo, and so forth" (1993:84). The relevance and analytical instrumentality of such concepts in the context of this study lies in that they help us become aware and identify that the discourses that the participants (re)produce voice other ways of speaking of social reality and intertwine with other discourses that, as stated above, are not necessarily our own but come from other sectors of society which we cohabit. In this vein, interdiscursivity in this study can also allow us to see how some of the participants' discourse challenges or helps sustain a social order by contesting, negotiating or accepting certain social identities. For instance, as we will see in chapter 3, the participants' depiction of immigration voice and reproduce discourses that are also found and come from other sources such as the media in which the figure of the immigrant is negatively constructed and is associated with danger and illegality.

The discursive representations of social events that the participants depict through specific verbal choices are worthy of scrutiny. They allow us to shed light on how they construct their identities, their social relations and how they make sense of their experiences in context. The latter is complex and dynamic, and, as stated above, should not be disregarded in the analysis of their discourse since it is not neutral and constitutes people's day-to-day lived reality that we intend to understand.

Chapter 3
Latin American immigrants' voices of immigration

3.1 Introduction

In this chapter, I firstly introduce three Latin American immigrants. Their introduction is preceded by how I met them in order to contextualise and locate their lives in London before I move on to the micro analysis of their experiences. They are included since they enable us to gain insight into how the length of stay, education, social and economic capital influences the self-presentations of the participants and thus construct identities that diverge from others here included. For instance, a participants' language use exhibits interdiscursive elements that voice negative representations of immigration found and originated in other sectors of society as well as other immigration countries, and her self-presentation as a successful individual in adapting to her new society suggests that she distances from features that allegedly defines who an immigrant is. Furthermore, another participant's discourses also show elements of interdiscursivity since they contain rhetorical strategies that exhibit a discourse of concern about immigration. In contrast, another participants' self-presentation as vulnerable is illustrative of his experience of migration as an event of misfortune that is concomitant with a social dispossession and downward mobility explained by economic circumstances. In the analyses, I take into account the construct of racial phenotype that intersects with social and cultural capitals that also help us understand the participants' self-presentation and thus the social position from which they speak and that in turn illustrates inequality in the Latin American community. Also, their discourses suggest an ideology of neoliberalism as the type of conventional knowledge that explains self-responsibilisation attitudes and that justifies people's presence in a host society where the migrant is presented as either a passive object or an agent whose social practices are negatively evaluated and from which they distance themselves.

The remaining discourses draw our attention to the social consequentiality of language use when other two participants self-present as illegals. Such self presentations underscore the implication contained in their discourses in the sense that they suggest a precondition of criminality as a normalised way of designating a presence that reproduces the topos of suspicion embodied by the social behaviour their discourses describe. However, we see that such a lexical choice as illegal blurs transcendental distinctions such as deportation and removal that could determine the conditions in which they can stay and re-enter the country. The discourses gathered in this chapter reflect a negative social meaning attributed to the figure of the migrant as well as reveal stratified social identities and relations; that is, by looking at how members of the Latin American community use language to talk about immigration and self-present, we will begin to see divergent social alignments and identities that both constitute their social relations and exhibit assymetrical realities. Thus, the subsequent analysis will also shed light on the different and stratified social structures in which Latin American immigrants live in a destination society.

3.2 Who is an immigrant? Social class and immigration

Marcia: 'This generation now has the idea that the migrant is a bad thing'

As a result of my observations, participations in workshops and conversations in cultural events with Latin Americans in various London boroughs, I gradually began to interact with people, one of whom was Marcia. After a number of emails, text messages and re-scheduled meetings due to her availability, we were able to meet near her workplace in Beckenham, London. Since the moment Marcia and I met, she showed an animated and open personality and immediately started speaking in Spanish to me, an interaction that developed spontaneously before, during and after the interview.

Marcia is a mixed-background woman who was born in Brazil to an Italian father and a Brazilian mother. At the age of ten, she and her parents lived in Paraguay where she attended school for six years and consequently, she learnt Spanish in addition to the languages she grew up speaking with her parents, Italian and Portuguese. Subsequently they moved back to Brazil and after she finished her university studies there, she moved to London to study a Master's Degree in Arts that she said she supported through her cleaning and waiting jobs in fast food restaurants. Later on, she obtained a second MA in Education. In such jobs, she met other Latin Americans with whom she shared a flat and interacted in Spanish and who she described as a strong support in times of adversity and made the work environment more relaxed and at times festive. At the time of the interview, she worked as a language teacher of Portuguese, Italian and Spanish in a school in London and was married to an English man with whom she had three daughters. She has been in England for twenty-three years.

In the interview, Marcia touched upon a number of topics, one of which was that she decided not to take British citizenship since she said that it was a way to avoid social pressure and be herself. However, she said that she had British values and ways of behaving that she described as a body language that is not as lively or expressive as that of Latin Americans. She also narrated the way she felt in a receiving society where a referendum to leave the European Union was to take place. I then asked her about her perceptions of immigration in this context since, as stated in the introduction to this book, her life story is not impervious from larger socio-political processes.

Excerpt 1: 'when I came here, the immigrant was necessary'

> esta generación ahora viene con la idea de que el migrante es una cosa mala es una basura que te están tirando en tu puerta y en la época en que yo vine aquí el inmigrante era necesario para la economía ellos estaban desesperados había mucho trabajo y poca gente para trabajar . . .

Translation

> This generation now has the idea that the migrant is a bad thing that it's rubbish being dumped at your door when I came here the immigrant was necessary for their economy, they were desperate there was a lot of work and very few people to work.

In excerpt 1 above, Marcia reports what she perceives are the prevailing attitudes towards immigration; that is, attitudes that echo wider discourses of immigration such as the ones disseminated by the media that remind us of the interdiscursivity of different social voices that I mentioned in chapter 2.5 and that exhibit an ideological representation of it. As to the interdiscursive element, Marcia's depiction of who an immigrant is echoes and brushes against other texts that are not strictly hers (Bakhtin 1981; Fairclough 1993); that is, immigration is portrayed through the typical lens of the tabloid press as the main source that she voices. Furthermore, in her depiction, the prominence of a particular topic accompanied with a frequently used rhetorical trope in media texts deserves attention. For instance, the organising topic of Marcia's depiction is that of the immigrant as a passive object, a representation that is reinforced by the phrase *the migrant is a bad thing that it's rubbish*. These in turn foreground the metaphor the immigrant is a pollutant, which objectifies the presence of immigrants and presents them as unwanted outside one's doorstep. The use of the generic *you* in the above phrase is also noteworthy but I will discuss it in more depth in the last excerpt where it is used repetitively. As to the metaphor, *it's rubbish*, its relevance lies in the fact that, as stated in chapter 2.5, it transcends its rhetorical purpose in the sense that it regulates our habitual functioning and structures social relations (see Lakoff and Johnson 2003; Cisneros 2008; Knowles and Moon 2006) since "the way people talk about social phenomena contributes to a certain kind of understanding of what society is" (Antaki 1994:102).

Furthermore, it is interesting to see that Marcia's description provides us with the setting of the attitudes to which she points; that is, temporal frames, *now, when I came here*, where she locates perceptions about immigration and herself respectively. The latter adverb introduces phrases such as *the immigrant was necessary for their economy, there was a lot of work* and *very few people to work*, which foreground the topos of money as the main ideology that informs her account above and that is used to explain why the presence of immigrants was justified then. It must be noted that Marcia reports a description of immigration that is not only found in the UK and it thus deserves to be connected to ideological discursive representations promoted in other immigration countries.

Santa Anna (2002), for instance, has studied the metaphorical representation of Latinos in media discourse in the USA and has highlighted how it shaped public perceptions and polarised social relations. In that context Santa Anna (2002) points to racist and debasing depictions of immigrants given that the dehumanising discourse resulted in what and not who immigrants are. Returning to the case of the UK, other studies have reported that media representation of migration has concentrated on a discourse of concern about high levels of immigration (see Allen 2016). Nonetheless, the role of the media in shaping public opinion does not seem to be determinant in such a context but it still demands attention since it is both argued that most of the information that we get comes from them (see van Dijk 2016; Allen 2016) and will continue to appear further below in Marcia's and Karla's perceptions of immigration. As Marcia's description progressed in the interview, she acknowledged that politics in immigration countries is not human-oriented but dominated by a money-centred view. Interestingly she said that if it was in her power to change it she would do it, but there seems to be ambivalence between her desire to change such a view and what she subsequently said.

Excerpt 2: "they cannot pay for their homes"

> yo tuve la suerte de ser de una generación de que que aquí ellos necesitaban de los inmigrantes y hoy no necesitan porque no pueden pagarles la casa del gobierno el sistema de salud está empezando a no funcionar o sea las cosas que eran buenas hoy ya no son buenas . . .

Translation

> I was lucky to belong to a generation that that here they needed immigrants and today they don't need (them) because they cannot pay for their homes the health service is not functioning, I mean the things that once were good now aren't good . . .

In excerpt 2 Marcia self-presents as a lucky person who felt welcomed in the UK and, as we have seen above, her description contains temporal frames. In them, she not only differentiates what her receiving society needed and what it no longer needs but apart from constructing a polarised discourse, it presents such situation as an assertion, *they don't need them*. In addition to this, her account of immigrants both resonates with that of the first excerpt and reinforces a description of their presence as passivized and undesirable. For instance, her use of such phrases as *they cannot pay their homes* and *the health service is not functioning*, seems to be informed by the topos of the immigrant as a numerous, heavy burden for the state since the former phrase implies that immigrants are recipients of social housing provided by the government, and the latter that they are the social agents that threat to undermine public institutions. Moreover, it is also worth noting Marcia's implicit depiction of the role of the state. It is painted as the bona fide provider of help that despite itself cannot offer assistance to what is suggested as excessive numbers of newcomers, which reproduces a disclaimer as in "we would like to welcome you but there are too many of you".

Marcia's above description, nevertheless, begs to be examined in a broader historical and social frame. According to some studies documenting immigration to the UK, negative perceptions and attitudes about immigration are not new. Blinder and Allen (2016), for instance, report that since 1964 the majority of people in Britain have believed that there are too many immigrants, and that they and their descendants have faced hostile attitudes for decades (Panayi 2010). In 2015, immigration figured as the most salient public concern in the UK (Arnorsson and Zoega 2018; Blinder and Richards 2020). Additionally, the passivized depiction of the immigrant that Marcia reproduces is also contestable given that it has been reported that immigrants are economically active and that they pay more in taxes than they receive in welfare (The Royal Geographic Society 2008; Dustmann and Frattini 2013; Wadsworth 2017). In this context, Marcia's description intimates two relevant intertwined discursive and social elements. On the one hand, her word choices, as stated above, index the interdiscursivity of texts since it points to another source of information and thus connote interpretations of immigration and events that are not strictly hers and which are not limited to our current times given that they echo those found in other texts historically reproduced. On the other hand, even though she voices a version of immigration that the media characterise, her depiction also suggests a class-based view of it that we can peruse below. When asked about how she felt in this context, she responded as follows.

Excerpt 3: "The name of immigrant does not apply to me anymore"

> A mí, yo siento que personalmente el, el ¿cómo te voy a decir? El nombre de inmigrante no me sirve más porque creo que ya pasé de este periodo de adaptación. Y como que *I made it* ¿no? Vamos a ponerlo así ¿no? Yo soy parte de esto, pero además que soy yo tan diferente y que ya, ya me incorporé en la sociedad. Yo creo que una vez para un inmigrante tener suceso es integrarse en su sociedad, en la sociedad que lo recibe. Yo creo que ese es el suceso . . .

Translation

> Me, I feel that personally the, the how can I put it? The name of immigrant does not apply to me anymore because I think I got past this, this adaptation period and like I made it, right? Let's put it that way, shall we? I am part of this, but apart from the fact that I am so different and that I already, I have already incorporated in society. I think that once for an immigrant to have success is to integrate in their society, in their host society. I think that is their success . . .

Marcia, in excerpt 3, openly rejects the name of the immigrant and her description conjures up a story of success that involved going through what she calls a stage of adaptation and incorporation into her local society. Interestingly the process to which she refers is presented as a concluded action that is accompanied by values that underscore her own agency. In other words, instances of phrases such as *I made it* and *I have incorporated* in the perfect tense are not only illustrative of a finite process but of a social behaviour indicative of her own social and cultural accomplishment. As she discursively moves on to make an assumption, *I think*, as to what being a successful migrant means, she reinforces that sense of an individual's agency, *to have succees is to integrate*. This last phrase seems to echo an ideology of immigration that points to beliefs about properties of immigrants who should be responsible for their own integration to a host society (van Dijk 2016; Ager and Strang 2008).

What does integration mean? Marcia did not specify what integration signifies, and to some authors there does not seem to be an agreement about what constitutes it in a world of mobility and flows of people (Grzymala-Kazlowska and Phillimore 2017). However, her biographic information can help us draw a conjecture of what it may mean to her. As stated above, Marcia holds two MAs and has a job that generates an income for her and her family and has access to an English-speaking social circle of friends with whom she reports to interact frequently and that she was able to develop through her husband with whom she lives in a house of their own. In this context, integration for Marcia seems to be synonymous with a particular lifestyle in which she has an income, a property and a social life that is oriented towards the host society. Interestingly the accumulation of cultural, social and economic capital may explain why she openly does not self-present as an immigrant, and it points to differentiated access to resources that construct a class-based figure of the immigrant. As the interview went on, she then continued to describe perceived attitudes towards immigration.

Excerpt 4: "the immigrant is a thing that you don't want in your garden"

> hoy el inmigrante es una cosa que no quieres en tu jardín, que no quieres que llegue y te tome más dinero de tu país porque está usando tus escuelas y tu hospital. Y yo creo que en aquella época, nosotros nos sentíamos que teníamos el poder financiero como se dice . . .

Translation

> Today the immigrant is a thing that you don't want in your garden, that you don't want to come and take money from your country because they are using your schools, your hospitals. And I think that back then, we felt we had the economic power so to speak . . .

We have seen in the previous excerpts how Marcia reproduces a media discourse that paints immigrants disparagingly, which, as stated above, exhibits interdiscursive feautures and is not limited to our current times; it is "the reappearance of a text's main argument in another text" (Wodak 2009:319). In excerpt 4, such discourse again becomes evident in a conspicuous metaphor evoked in *the immigrant is a thing that you don't want in your garden*. It conjures up the nation as home metaphor (Billig 1995) in the sense that the nation is discursively constructed as a property that must be protected from a foreign body; an unwanted weed that is to decimate what is cultivated in our territory. As Marcia continues to describe what current attitudes towards immigration are through a discourse feature such as *your* employed as a generic possessive pronoun and repetitively used in *your country, your schools, your hospital,* she also seems to achieve an interesting implicature that allows her to keep face. The generalised conception of the immigrant in the above excerpt functions as a disclaimer that enables Marcia to distance herself from the attitudes that she depicts given than she appears to be reporting what public opinion is and not hers. In this light, she self-presents neither as an anti-immigrant individual nor as an immigrant.

However, by temporally locating her discourse, we gain a valuable insight into how she negotiates her identity and with whom she associates, and we can do this by looking at phrases such as *back then we felt we had the economic power*. The former provides the setting and a clearly demarcated historical period in which Marcia produces a we discourse informed by a capitalist-oriented view with which she aligns herself. In this context, Marcia's descriptions and views must be located in a historical time where the presence of immigrants as well as social roles are interpreted through an economic ideology that generates a social distance that her self-presentation suggests. Her account thus suggests that education, social and economic capital play a significant role in and influence not only how immigration may be lived but narrated. In other words, the acquisition of such capital enables her to position herself within mainstream society. All of the above encourages us to probe into the various identities and alignments towards which the participants orient themselves in the different London boroughs where they live, work and socialise.

Miguel: "there are rooms where a Spanish and a Bolivian live together"

As I mentioned in chapter 1.3, the presence of the Latin American community is increasingly evident in various boroughs of London. One of these is Lambeth where restaurants as well as other shops run by Latin Americans are situated and where I met Miguel. As stated in the introduction to this book, he worked in a Mexican restaurant where we would have our frequent conversations before and after he shared his life story. Miguel is a high-school educated, white Venezuelan immigrant whose first experience abroad was in 2001 when he left for New York to accomplish his dream to visit it. However, he found this experience very gruelling and a month later, he decided to go back to Venezuela. A year later, he left his home country again and this time he stayed in New York for four years and worked as a kitchen assistant. He then went back to Venezuela and after a short time, he immigrated to Spain where he would live for 7 years. Miguel's ancestry enabled him to have Spanish citizenship as his father was born in Galicia. Without any connections in England and with his wife and daughter in Venezuela, he emigrated from Spain to escape unemployment. At the time of the interview, Miguel had been in England for three and a half years while his family still lived in Venezuela.

Miguel's life story implies negative attitudes towards the event of migration at the same time that it reflects his own situation as one of misfortune and contempt. As we will see, his account contrasts with that of Marcia, and in order to understand his discourse in his current social context, it is important to see how he refers to his experience living in Spain as a way to construct his identity and compare it with that in England.

Excerpt 5: "they still have that thinking of slavery"

> cuando estamos en España, nos damos cuenta que ese pensamiento de esclavismo, de esclavitud todavía ellos lo tienen de dominación sobre los latinoamericanos todavía. Y tratan al lati, al inmigrante en general, lo tratan con mucho desprecio . . .

Translation

> when we are in Spain, we realise that they still have that thinking of slavery, of domination over the Latin American and, generally they treat Lati the immigrant derisively . . .

The brief description that Miguel gives and that he attempts to extend to a generalised attitude towards immigration depicts his experience in Spain in an interesting light. It seems to be illustrative of a discourse of polarisation. For instance, for Miguel, the historical memory of colonisation that becomes evident in the negatively connoted nouns, *slavery, domination*, is what explains a hierarchical social treatment of Spanish people against Latin American immigrants, and the former are thus attributed cognitive characteristics of cultural superiority that defines them. In this light, the immigrant is presented as a victim and, as we will see below, as a vulnerable person. As to the above description, however generalised it may be, it is still worthy of attention given that it echoes accounts recorded in previous studies on Latin Americans in London who talked of leaving Spain due to the high levels of racism that they perceived (see McIlwaine 2011). As his narrative continues, Miguel depicts the experience of migration from Spain to England with negative overtones.

Excerpt 6: "They are both immigrants in a different country"

> actualmente estamos en Londres y el mundo da muchas vueltas. Actualmente hay habitaciones en Londres donde vive un español y un boliviano. En la misma habitación. Entonces, ya no puede ser despectivo, ya no puede ser denigrado denigrante, el español porque está viviendo en las mismas condiciones que el otro, que la otra persona. Son inmigrantes los dos, exactamente igual en un país distinto . . .

Translation

> currently we are in London and you never know where life will take you. Currently there are rooms where a Spanish and a Bolivian live together. In the same room. So, they cannot be derogatory, the Spanish cannot be denigrated denigrating because they are living in the same conditions as the other, as the other person. They are both immigrants in a different country . . .

Miguel's account is reminiscent of a larger economic and social event that affected the lives of many people in Spain that should not be omitted to understand his narration. As stated in chapter 1.3, in 2008 Spain was hit by an economic recession that left people unemployed and triggered emigration to various European countries (see McIlwaine 2011; Izquierdo et al. 2016). His description underscores adverse socioeconomic conditions that not only forced him, as we saw in his brief biography, but also Spanish people to relocate their lives outside their country to spaces that they cohabit with other migrants, *rooms where a Spanish and a Bolivian live together*. Miguel in this light narrates an event that denotes a downward social repositioning that places Spaniards in the same socioeconomic circumstances as other immigrants, *he is living in the same conditions as the other*. The description that Miguel provides is also indexical of people's economic resources when moving to another country as it attempts to reflect the living conditions of many immigrants in London that will also help us gain insight into his discourse.

As I stated in chapter 1.3, many Latin Americans either rent an apartment with two or more people or live in small, overcrowded spaces, and in some cases entire families live in a room where they also eat (McIlwaine 2011; 2015; Mas Giralt 2017). Other immigrants rely on this type of living as a tactic to save money that they can remit back home (Wills et al. 2009). Miguel himself rented a flat with two more people from European countries. In this context, these depictions along with Miguel's situate the lives of immigrants in a limited socioeconomic condition. That is, Miguel seems to portray and rationalise the experience of migration both as a form of social dispossession in which economic resources are lacking and as an event of misfortune with which immigrants have to come to terms. In the following excerpt, Miguel refers to the way he perceives his being an immigrant in English society.

Excerpt 7: "The immigrant is a vulnerable person"

> aquí el inglés es muy distinto es muy, en ese particular, es muy amable con el inmigrante. Es muy amable. No he tenido ningún tipo de queja con ningún inglés porque lo tratan a uno de una forma muy amable. Que eso, el inmigrante es una persona vulnerable y lo que necesita es que lo traten bien. Y aquí es un muy buen país para inmigrar porque los que son de aquí, tratan bien al inmigrante . . .

Translation

> Here the English are different in that respect, they are very kind with the immigrant. They are very kind. I can't complain about any English because one is treated kindly. The immigrant is a vulnerable person and what the immigrant needs is to be treated well and this is a very good country to immigrate because the locals treat the immigrant well . . .

As his narrative progresses, Miguel becomes reflective of his previous migration experiences as he implicitly evaluates them in relation to his current context, *here the English are different*. His word choices provide a picture where the English are positively presented, *they are very kind,* and that resonates with what he describes as a social environment of affability, *the locals treat the immigrant well*. Moreover, the adjective he uses to define immigrants generically, *a vulnerable person*, produces a discourse of empathy that, on the one hand, humanises them but, on the other hand, projects them as socially disempowered. In this sense, the immigrant is presented as a person in need of special care and protection. However, what may vulnerability mean in Miguel's context that could influence his self-presentation?

As I mentioned above, Miguel moved to England with no connections to escape unemployment. Additionally, he had two jobs, one of which is at the restaurant and another in a storehouse where he worked from Monday to Saturday due to his need to remit money back to his wife and daughter in Venezuela. These jobs largely influence his daily life given that he had a limited circle of friends mostly from Latin America who also had two jobs or did odd jobs to make their ends meet. I came to meet and interact with three of them. They were working-class Latin Americans from Colombia and Venezuela who had also left either Spain or Portugal in search of a better job and who were working in the service sector, namely cleaning. In this light, Miguel's discourse of vulnerability indexes two interrelated aspects of his social life that may influence his description of the migration experience as well as his social alignments: his pressing economic needs that forced him to a secondary migration as well as the absence of a stronger social capital.

Miguel's limited capital clearly contrasts with that of Marcia, and their descriptions and self-presentations are contextualised as stories speaking from two different social spaces. While Miguel speaks from a marginal social position as he associates with and self-presents as a vulnerable immigrant, Marcia self-presents as a successful person who speaks of being part of her receiving society and thus does not define herself as an immigrant. Moreover, Marcia's discourse about immigration is located within an abstraction of the perceptions of immigration while Miguel's focuses on the experiential. Thus, Marcia's and Miguel's discourses signal not only a socioeconomic condition in which they emigrated, but also education and social capital as valuable resources with which they travel to and arrive in a new society. In addition, two factors that impact and contribute to the differentiated quality of the lives of both Marcia and Miguel are their length of stay and their age when they arrived in the UK. This is a socially significant distinction that should not be dismissed given that it sheds light on both the processes of integration into a new society and the development of social networks that they both describe in their accounts. Marcia, after having lived in the UK for more than twenty-three years and, without ignoring her social and economic capital, arrived in the UK when she was twenty-two years old and had the opportunity to work and study as well as interact with people from varied backgrounds with no need to remit money back to her family. Her life in a receiving society thus suggests a contrasting and different reality compared to that of Miguel who is high school-educated and arrived in the UK at the age of forty-one and whose experience has not been conducive to socioeconomic mobility but rather reflects the economic constraints that he attempts to overcome with his two jobs.

The resources and circumstances mentioned above become crucial to understand how Latin Americans may form their social relations, how they live and with whom they may align. The way their experiences are narrated may suggest value-laden discourses that may shed light on the complex multi-layered composition and social class-based interrelations of the Latin American community.

Karla: *"he helps me with the language"*

The places that I visited and where I began to talk and interact with people from Latin America were Non-Governmental Organisations. NGOs are based in central, south and north London and provide Latin Americans with services and information through workshops, talks about labour rights or access to the health system, etc. After attending one of the many workshops offered in north London, I met Karla who held a secretarial job in a London-based NGO. Karla is a white woman from Chile and she holds a B.A in Journalism and an M.A in Anthropology from her country and moved to England in 2012. Originally, she arrived in London to take English-language courses and then she would move to France where she had been ten years ago and where she intended to study French. However, her plan changed as she met a Scottish man in the school where she was studying and eventually, they became engaged. At the time of the interview, she held a spouse visa. Language has been an issue for her profesional development as she described her job interview training as daunting and nerve-wracking due to limited language skills, which gradually she was able to hone through her English-speaking fiancé.

Excerpt 8: "when I am with him, it's different. They even crack jokes"

> es mucho más fácil para mí por por esa vía, a veces por el idioma también porque él me ayuda con el idioma, me corrige porque ahora todavía la policía te hace preguntas en el aeropuerto "a ver esta visa". Como que a veces ni siquiera leen bien "su visa se vence", pero cuando voy con él, es distinto. Hasta hacen bromas "¿de dónde vienen? ¿Están de vacaciones?" Entonces, todo bien, pero cuando voy sola, hay un poquito más de preguntas, pero cuando estoy con él, estamos de vacaciones, ¿me entiende? . . .

Translation

> It's a lot easier for me because of the language because he helps me with the language. He corrects me because the police still ask you questions at the airport "show me your visa". Like sometimes they don't check it properly "your visa is about to expire", but when I am with him, it's different. They even crack jokes "where did you come from? Are you on holiday?" So, everything is fine, but when I am alone, there may be a few more questions, but when I am with him, we are on holiday, you know what I mean? . . .

Karla's account provides us with a glimpse of the relevant role of social capital that could function as a mechanism of linguistic support when language capital may become devalued in a different country. At the same time, the symbolic value of Karla's social capital that she describes seems to materialise in such a regimented space as an airport given that it seemingly generates a type of social membership. The immigration officers' ambivalent attitudes that she reports are illustrative of this experience, *when I am with him it's different, they even crack jokes*, that nonetheless she mitigates through her phrase *there may be a few more questions*. The latter points to a discursive strategy that helps her negotiate the presentation of such attitudes, which are, in either the presence or absence of her fiancé, presupposed as given and unquestionable through her use of a rhetorical question, *you know what I mean?* In other words, being the fiancé of a local citizen enables her to be perceived as a member of an ingroup, which allows her to broker access to a new society less enquiringly. Moreover, there is an additional relevant aspect about Karla's social position that we could follow up below and that could help us gain insight into how she continues to self-present.

Karla, in the interview, stated that her friends are usually women who are in the same situation as she is; they are either married to or fiancées of English people. She and her fiancé sometimes get together with these couples for dinner or go out with her fiancé's co-workers with whom she also practices English. Before she joined the NGO, she said that she would go to museums or would spend her time visiting tourist sites. These activities draw our attention to a particular lifestyle with a relative comfort that are, nonetheless, clearly opposite to that of Miguel whose two jobs and a limited circle of friends of working-class Latin Americans constitute his lifestyle. They point to social class dimensions that I will describe in a more detailed manner below. As the interview progressed, I then asked her about her social situation and position as a Chilean in London in current times.

Excerpt 9: "My situation has been, let's say, easy to obtain a regular migration status"

> Yo he tenido una situación digamos fácil de obtener un estatus migratorio regular. es que, no, no podría ser tan radical en decir en el fondo aquí no le dan oportunidades a la gente, pero es que mi situación particular es. Hay, a ver, entiendo, entiendo también en el fondo que tampoco es mi situación, pero podría entender por qué la gente quiere venir para acá, que tienen el derecho, quizás, de poder quizá elegir . . .

Translation

> My situation has been, let's say, easy to obtain a regular migration status. It is because, I couldn't be so radical and say here they don't give people opportunities here, but that's because my particular case is. Let's see, deep down, I understand that it is not my situation either, but I could understand why people want to come here that they have the right, maybe, to be able to choose maybe . . .

In excerpt 9, Karla describes her own situation as unproblematic due to her regular migration status, and it allows her to position herself as different from a group of people implied as undocumented. Her self-presentation nonetheless discloses two particular features, one of which is the recurrent hesitation in Karla's discourse that evidences a face-keeping effort as she attempts to negotiate her ambivalent attitude towards immigration. That is, the vagueness contained in the modality of the phrase *I couldn't be so radical*, since it implies both possibility and ability, seems to suggest that she aligns to a non-migrant group in an effort to not ill-speak of her receiving society. Subsequently, through the phrase *let's see*" and the repetitive use of a verb of cognition such as *understand*, she attempts to step back from her own social position in order to give her opinion objectively and produces a discourse of empathy respectively. She recognises people's rights to mobility. However, her hedging epitomised in her use of *maybe* dilutes her alignment with immigration into the UK at the same time that it serves as a discursive strategy through which she distances herself from her statement.

Her discourse, in light of the above, illustrates non-linguistic features that allow us to understand her self-presentation. Karla is a white woman, and her racial phenotype is worth considering since it is not limited to a physical appearance but to a social representation and position of who is a migrant. As a number of studies have demonstrated, depictions of immigration often exploit the figure of the migrant as non-white and poor, and it is conflated with issues of illegality and with assumed attitudes towards disintegration (see Castles 2010; Lundström 2014). In addition to this, like Marcia, Karla is a well-educated woman whose capital matters and has not been lost after relocating her life. Before moving to the UK, she had a well-paid job in the Chilean government, and it was the means that allowed her to save money before her planned trip to England and then to France where she would take a three-month language course for which she had already paid. Apart from the linguistic support from her fiancé who also speaks Spanish, Karla stated that she also received economic support from him, which took her mind off any monetary issues. Additionally, before her secretarial job at the NGO, she did volunteer work for two years in the same site, which brings to the fore her situation of economic stability.

In this context, her discourse suggests two intersecting factors. On the one hand, it points to a social reality of a gendered outcome of her migration experience in the sense that she to some extent is economically dependent on her fiancé and resonates with what Weiss (2005) calls a "quality of space". This is a social space to which she had access, a new society to which she moved and that does not illustrate a downward or declassing process with which, as we will see below, many migrants deal but that she did not experience. In other words, she speaks from a privileged social position that she implicitly acknowledges. On the other hand, it suggests that the construct of race may also play a role in the constitution of relations in which it intersects with economic, social and cultural capitals that come to be organised and valued leading to a social location of structural advantage (see Skeggs 1997; Frankerberg 1993). These characteristics and those described above help us understand her self-presentation as different from the identity of the immigrant to whom she implicitly referred above; that is, an undocumented immigrant. At the same time her self-presentation to a large extent resonates with Marcia's and is different to Miguel's in the sense that, as stated above, it indexes social class as the main construct from which they speak. That is, the differentiated access to the sociocultural resources that the participants possess becomes manifest in the discursive depiction of who an immigrant is.

Excerpt 10: "about the real capacity to be able to sustain them all"

> Pero, a veces digo, sí, claro. Si todo el mundo quisiere quisiese emigrar, venir de la capacidad real de poder sostenerlos a todos. No lo sé. A lo mejor yo me sentiría a chile están llegando muchos extranjeros, quizás también yo allá desde esa lógica que están ocupando, pero no sé. Es compli, es complicado . . .

Translation

> But sometimes I say yes, of course. If everybody wanted to emigrate, to come, about the real capacity to be able to sustain them all. I don't know. Maybe I would feel like many foreigners are arriving in Chile. Perhaps, also me being back there, from that logic that they are occupying, but I don't know. It's compli, it's complicated . . .

Karla's attitude in the above depiction strikes a chord with that of Marcia. That is, the topic of immigration as a threat organises her discursive choices that, at the same time, exhibit the interdiscursivity of the description of immigration mentioned above by echoing dominant representations of it in the media (see van Dijk 2014; 2016; Wodak 2009). The occurrence of hyperbolic language such as *everybody* and the unspecified but culturally differentiated numerical representation of immigrants, *many foreigners*, foreground the generalised representation of immigration as big numbers of people coming into the country. Furthermore, her use of *sustain them all*, contributes to the characterisation of immigration as a heavy burden for a receiving society, which in turn, as we have seen in Marcia's discourse, produces the topos of money that implies that immigration is thought about in economic terms and not in human terms. Such lexical choices border on the discourse of concern (van Dijk 2016); that is, although she struggles to remain neutral, she presents immigration as a problem that threatens to take possession of a territory as suggested in the metaphorical process of the verb *occupy*. Consequently, Karla's self-presentation and attitude towards immigration oscillates between her avoidance to speak negatively about local authorities and society and her intent to understand people's rights to relocate their lives.

The dominant and organising topics of the three cases thus far presented along with the events foregrounded therein seem to confirm that language use plays a crucial role in the constitution of social identities and space if we regard language as "the architecture of social behaviour and relations" (Blommaert and Dong 2010b:7). It must be added that the words that the participants have chosen exemplify that there are no neutral terms to describe social experience given that they index a particular social position and status also suggestive of the construct of race and reflective of their education, social and economic capital. Block (2014) reminds us of the importance of economic resources as they intersect with social class differentiations that will continue to appear crucial in shaping the lifestyles and migration trajectories that David and Irma relate as they tell their stories.

3.3 Being "illegal"; deportation or removal?

David *'She wanted to have me legalised'*

The three different cases and contexts to which I have referred above have allowed us to catch a glimpse of their migration trajectory, and they have helped us to locate a Latin American presence in London that illustrates different socioeconomic realities, identities and alignments. The case that I now present is that of David who I met in a so-called Latin American festival that I atended in Newham. As I stated in the introduction to this book, upon my arrival to the site of the festival, the theme was predominantly dominated by political activism and there were information desks from which David shared out leaflets describing labour rights for cleaners. We talked at length and after telling him I intended to learn more about Latin Americans' experiences, he invited me to go to his workplace where we continued our conversations and shared his life story.

David is an Ecuadorian immigrant who has been working in the service sector for more than 10 years in a London-based university. His story exhibits an experience of declassing, which, as I stated in chapter 1.3, refers to changes in an individual's life conditions; that is, "the loss of economic power and prestige and status that formerly were a person's class position" (Block 2017:140) and with which many Latin Americans deal. David decided to leave Ecuador in 1999 due to a combination of factors. At the age of sixteen, he became a professional football player, a career that he was able to do in conjunction with a degree in Physical Education until the age of 21. At this age, his football career ended due to constant muscle problems from which he was unable to recover and the lack of job opportunities were increasingly pressing, as he needed to provide for his wife who was expecting their first child. In 1996, his sister came to England to study a Master's Degree in a medicine-related field and had no intention of going back to Ecuador. It was through her that David learnt of the existing and promising job opportunities abroad as she represented the social capital that helped him leave Ecuador.

David brought his wife to the UK in 2000 as they planned to work and save more money to go back to Ecuador as soon as they could since they had to leave their child with his mother in his country. Unfortunately, they went through a rough patch and were unable to save enough money and stayed in the UK longer than planned. Such a situation led them to live without their child for nearly four years before they were able to bring him to the UK. However, even though they were together, they faced other challenges. David and his wife worked without a work visa for all this time but his wife was able to have her migration status legalised eventually. However, the legalisation of her migration status was not necessarily conducive to his family's wellbeing and as his account suggests it could result in family separation.

Excerpt 11: 'They call it remove'

> mi esposa pudo lograr los documentos acá en un momento legalizarse ella.pero ella quiso legalizar a mí pero no pudo. y hasta que un día pues por medio de la aplicación que ella metió me fueron a ver a la casa y me dijeron usted no puede estar en el país.. incluso mi esposa ya estaba embarazada del segundo niño ella estaba embarazada y a ellos no les importó nada "usted está de ilegal y ella es la única que está legal y se puede quedar entonces y usted se va" me..bueno ellos dicen remove me removieron del país . . .

Translation

> my wife managed to get her documents here to become legal but she wanted to have me legalised but she was unable to until one day through the application she did they came to my house and told me "you can't be in this country" my wife was pregnant with the second child she was pregnant and they did not care at all "you are here illegally and she is the only one that is legal and she can stay so you have to go" . . . well they call it remove I was removed from the country . . .

Many authors and policy makers have argued against the use of the term "illegal" due to its overtones with criminal conduct (Sciortino 2004; Pinkerton et al. 2004; Dauvergne 2009) and have argued that the adjective undocumented or irregular has increasingly replaced the label illegal (Triandafyllidou 2012). This is, nonetheless, contradicted by the language use that David voices, and as we will see below that of Irma. As we have seen in the analysis of Marcia's discourse, the representation of immigration that her discourse exhibits contains interdiscursive characteristics that also appear in David's account. The use of the word *illegal*, which he reports immigration officers used to address and inform him that he was not allowed to stay in the UK, brushes against widespread and unquestioned depictions of undocumented migration. In other words, he is voicing wider discourses of migration that are not only found in the UK but are full of transmissions and interpretations of other people's words that make reference to another source and that are laden with the social intention to exclude (see Bakhtin 1981). In this context, David describes his migration status as illegal, and the seemingly normalised use of the verb *legalise* in conjunction with its object as well as the adjective that describes an immoral behaviour in his account carries heavy implications about his social identities. His evaluative self-presentation and that of his wife as the objects of the legalisation process implies a social precondition of illegality that is interpreted as a prohibition that becomes manifest in David's use of modality as in *you can't be in this country*. Such phrase both casts light on the process of differentiation between citizens and non-citizens and on the attributes and rights that demarcate them from us as David's use of a relational verb and modality confirms, *she is the only one that is legal and she can stay so you have to go*. However, it is important to point out that David's word choice in terms of legality blurs relevant distinctions, which we will see below, since his irregular migration status became reified in the top-down practice of removal. This exhibits the specificity and consequential effects of language.

Excerpt 12: "my frustration was that I was going to be deported"

> y claro pues yo no sabía que. pues la desesperación mía que me iban a deportar a mi país y yo he escuchado que si me deportan yo no puedo volver en cinco seis años entonces era la desesperación yo ya en Ecuador yo no tenía nada, como se dice tenía mi vida acá mis cosas mi trabajo ya mis hijos acá también entonces fue desesperante . . .

Translation

> I did not know that since my frustration was that I was going to be deported to my country and I have heard that if I get deported I can't come back in five years so that was my frustration in Ecuador I had nothing, I had my life here my belongings my work my kids here as well so it was frustrating . . .

Experts in migration law draw a relevant distinction between removal and deportation. The former is regarded as administrative detention that does not imply a criminal offence while the latter does or is enforced when it is "conducive to the public good" (Blinder 2016: 3). It must also be noted that, although David worked without a work permit, such violation is treated as an executive fault (see Blinder 2016), an administrative removal that determined the conditions and terms in which he was made to leave and later on did not prohibit him from re-entering the country. Nevertheless, his self-presentation as the object of the material process of removal conjures up knowledge of migration laws as the organising topic of his discourse, which in turn implies that such knowledge or the lack of it establishes the rules of social behaviour. Through verbs of cognition and perception, *I did not know*, *I have heard*, we gain insight into both David's mental processes and his non-agentive social position, which subsequently can be seen through negatively connoted lexemes such as, *frustration* and *frustrating*. These describe David's reactions, not actions, to his feared prohibition to return to the UK illustrated by modality, *I can't come back*.

David recounted that he was eventually removed to Ecuador after having been in a detention centre for one month, and his experience reflects the social and economic inequalities that largely affected his migrations status. Unlike Karla, David despite having a B.A did not have a job back in his country that could allow him to secure an income but rather the lack of it was an incentive to leave and attempt to provide for his family. Therefore, he could not save money that allowed him to have relative comfort upon his arrival to the UK with a passport. These structural differences in their home countries may explain why David got inserted into what has been called survival employment in other contexts such as Canada. That is, immigrants with tertiary education take on any jobs irrespective of how unrelated to any previous training or how low paid they are as long as they meet their immediate economic needs (iCreese and Wiebe 2012). At the same time, his story reflects that of many immigrants whose status becomes irregular. According to some studies, it is thought that most irregular migration to the UK is because people overstay their visa and that the vast majority of Latin Americans in such status face this situation (Wills et al. 2009; McIlwaine 2015). In this context, David's story exhibits a process of cultural dispossession such as his loss of education and another of social expulsion such as his removal from the UK. Subsequently, he described how he got back to his wife and kids in the UK.

Excerpt 13: "I had a spouse a spouse visa to be here with my wife and I could become legal"

> mi hermana en ese tiempo tenía un novio que era manager de pizza hut. y entonces, justo tuvo una vacante y me pudo conseguir un contrato en pizza hut. Todo legal ¿no? Contrato pedido y todo y ahí ya, a los cuatro meses pude venir. Ya tuve un spouse, un spouse visa para estar acá con mi esposa y ahí pude legalizarme y estuve con mis hijos y bueno. Por un lado, fue duro, pero por otra ya tuve tranquilidad de que tú dices ya estás con todos los documentos legales. Ya no tienes esa tensión de que tú sales mañana, alguien te denuncie que esto, que veía la policía me daba un miedo, me escondía. Entonces, fue como se dice, fue un mal, pero al final del día estuvo bien. Tuve ya, pude tener legalizados los documentos . . .

Translation

> my sister had a boyfriend back then and he was a manager at pizza hut. So he had a vacancy and was able to get me a contract in pizza hut legally, right? With a contract and everything and after four months I could come back. I had a spouse, a spouse visa to be here with my wife and I could become legal and I was able to be with my kids and well. On the

one hand, it was tough, but on the other hand, I felt relieved because you already are with all your legal documents. You don't have the tension that someone will denounce you if you go out the next day because I would see the police and I would be so frightened that I would hide. So, it was like bad, but at the end of the day, it was all good. I already had, I was able to have my documents legalised . . .

Through the topic of legality, David self-presents as both an agent and object of his own legalisation. On the one hand, his emphatic use of legal-related terms, *legally, right? With a contract and everything*, presents David as a rule-abiding individual that turned to authorised vehicles to his return. His use of legal-related terms also functions as an argumentation strategy to justify his own social reinsertion, a process of which he self-presents as the agent through the use of modality, *I could come, I could become legal*. On the other hand, behavioural processes contained in such verbs as *denounce* and *hide* present David as an illegitimate object that implies distrust and surveillance by society itself due to the social values attached to them. Thus, David's description of legalisation, removal and return produces the topos of suspicion that reveals processes of consensual differentiation in which the human is conflated with the inhuman as evidenced in the interchangeable object of legalisation, *I could become legal* and *have my documents legalized*. Illegality can thus be interpreted as "a space of forced invisibility, exclusion, subjugation" (Coutin 2000: 30), a discursive construction of self-regulation that can produce mechanisms of social disentitlement that we can further examine in Irma's account.

Irma: *"I was still illegal because my application was denied"*

Irma is an Ecuadorian woman who left her country more than twenty years ago, and I met her through another NGO that cater for Latin American women who have suffered domestic violence or who are economically disadvantaged. As stated in the introduction to this book, in one of my visits to this organisation and conversations with the General Operations Manager, I was told that the cases to which they provide assistance are very delicate such as domestic violence and that I would be very lucky if someone volunteered to tell me their life story after leaving my contact details. Nevertheless, Irma contacted me and we met after two failed attempts in central London.

In her life story, she described that as she was studying towards a university degree that she did not finish in her home country, she got word about job and better life prospects in Brussels from former classmates. She decided to join them in a flat in which she and nine more people were living. She recounted that she obtained a job as a live-in maid through her housemates who were also working as undocumented domestic workers. Two years later, she went to London to see her boyfriend from Ecuador for five days but in the end, she stayed longer and became pregnant. With no knowledge of English, no visa and in need of medical attention, she got help from a Latin American woman who submitted Irma's visa application. After two weeks, she got a letter from the immigration office that granted her temporary stay in the UK and she got the medical attention that she had been seeking for six months and gave birth to a girl. However, she narrated that her migration status changed from regular to irregular once again.

Excerpt 14: "because I was so unexperienced, I didn't speak English, I knew very few people, I bought it all"

> yo seguía de ilegal porque me negaron el caso con el tiempo y claro, todo mundo en ese tiempo había de que de pronto la gente te decía "mira las leyes están muy malas y si viene la policía te deportan enseguida". Te hacían asustar, te hacían tener miedo. Yo, como era muy nueva, sin hablar inglés, sin conocer casi a nadie, me creí todo. Me negaron mi caso y lo primero que hice el mismo día en que me llegó la carta, con el padre de mi hija, salimos de ahí. Corrimos de ahí solamente con el coche de mi hija. Pusimos lo que más pudimos . . .

Translation

> I was still illegal because my application was denied eventually and of course, everybody back then was like people would tell me "The law is harsh and if the police come, they deport you right away". They would scare you, they made you feel afraid and because I was so unexperienced, I didn't speak English, I knew very few people, I bought it all. My application was denied and, when I got the letter, the first thing I did, along with my daughter's father, was to leave. We ran out of there (house) we just took my daughter's pushchair. We put all we could in it . . .

In excerpt 14, Irma narrates how the absence of contacts and the inability to speak English seem to exacerbate her experience as an undocumented immigrant that in this sense is interpreted as a space of asymmetrical relationships. Irma's use of the word *illegal* to describe her migration status reflects the interdiscursivity also seen in David's account and thus reproduces a social voice of exclusion. In addition, it also shows how her social identity is vertically positioned since verbs such as *deport* and *deny* are indicative of top-down material processes of social expulsion. However, the subtle and significant difference between deportation and removal (Blinder 2016), as we have seen in David's case, is not a distinction of which Irma is aware. Such distinction becomes relevant to help us explain and gain insight into a behavioural process such as *run* that presents Irma's decisions as reactions rather than actions that place her in a peripheral social space. Therefore, this last process must also be understood as a consequence of a type of social knowledge to which Irma had access, *people would tell me the law is harsh, they made you feel afraid,* which sheds light on the complex social structures where discourses of immigration laws seem to circulate. In this context, the lack of linguistic and social capital that Irma describes particularly contrasts with that of Marcia and Karla whose regular migration status, social and economic capital draw our attention to issues of inequality.

Like Miguel and David, Irma left her country due to economic motivations rather than academic ones, and her boyfriend who was her main contact and motivation to come to England was undocumented and worked as a cleaner. As she and her boyfriend lived in hiding, she worked as a cleaner or as a domestic worker part time since she also needed to look after her daughter. In this light, Irma's migration trajectory and experience resonate with that of many Latin Americans whose lives and work are located at the lower levels of the socioeconomic ladder in a vulnerable position. In larger studies, and as I mentioned in Chapter 1.3, McIlwaine (2014) has documented that nearly half of all Latin Americans have moved to the UK for economic reasons and work in the service sector. Additionally, it has also been reported that those in an irregular migration status face a stratified sense of belonging that labels them as deportable (McIlwaine 2014). Thus, the combination of a low income with an irregular status places Irma's life in a precarious situation that she continues to relate.

Excerpt 15: "we were literally illegal"

> del miedo que supuestamente venía inmigración, no volvimos a esa casa. Nos quedamos prácticamente de ilegales mi hija y yo porque el padre de mi hija, ecuatoriano, era ilegal. O sea, no teníamos alternativa de nada . . .

Translation

> because we were afraid that supposedly migration [officers] would come, we did not go back to that house. We were literally illegal my daughter and I because my daughter's father, who is Ecuadorian, was illegal. I mean, we had no choice . . .

What Irma describes in this short account provides us with a depiction of how she perceived the presence and function of authorities, fear fuelled with an element of uncertainty, *supposedly*. Also, the potential presence of immigration authorities evident in the phrase *migration [officers] would come*, at the same time resonates with what De Genova (2002: 438) has described as "the palpable sense of deportability" in the sense that "what defines illegality is not deportation" but its possibility. Such dread, also evident in David's account, is what seems to regulate Irma's behaviour, *we did not go back to that house*. The latter description is also illustrative of a social identity whose free mobility is inhibited and consequently arrested to a social space of marginalisation. In this light she self presents as an individual who recognises that her undocumented status contravenes the rules that dictate the organisation of the society in which she finds herself and thus rationalises the prerogatives to which she was not entitled, *we had no choice*.

The spatial restriction that Irma narrates and that coincides with David's is explained by an irregular migration status, but the behaviour she depicts also suggests a social uncertainty that could lead to other consequences. As documented in other migrant populations inside and outside the UK, being in an undocumented or irregular status forces people into practices of invisibility that could result not only in limited social relations in order to avoid detection by authorities, but also in ill health such as depression, anxiety disorders or posttraumatic stress (McIlwaine 2015; Teunissen et al. 2016). Irma's story in this context also sheds light on processes of seclusion and alienation, which, as we will see below, restricts access to information and may lead to family separation. Later on in her life story, she related that her boyfriend made the decision to go back to Ecuador and take their daughter with him since, due to their undocumented status, their future was not promising; a decision with which she agreed. She also recounted that three years later she received a telephone call from the Home Office that a friend of hers helped her interpret, and who told her that they had indeed been looking for her for the same time to inform her that she had been granted indefinite leave to remain in the UK since then. Her account is the following and the label of being "illegal" again comes up.

Excerpt 16: "three years I was supposedly illegal in this country"

> a los pocos meses de que yo me salí de esa casa, mandó migración una carta con mi residencia para mi hija y para mi. Residencia indefinida. Tres años yo supuestamente de ilegal en este país . . .

Translation

> a few months after I left that house, migration [the home office] sent a letter with my residence for my daughter and for me. Indefinite leave to remain. Three years I was supposedly illegal in this country . . .

In excerpts 14, 15 and 16 we find a common organising topic that both informs Irma's account and reflects the social circumstances from which she speaks; the topic of fear that restricts mobility that is nonetheless not only constructed symbolically but as a physical barrier since it determined the places to which she could and could not move, *we did not go back to that house, I left that house*. Her reaction to leave the house for her presumed illegality to be unidentified at the same time implies that she moved to a place where she did not have true knowledge of her migration status as it becomes evident in the lexically present assumption, *supposedly*. Additionally, this physical barrier is also reinforced through the use of a negatively connoted adjective, *illegal*, given that, as we have seen in David's case, it produces the topos of suspicion that attributes criminalising characteristics to her social identity. That is, such an adjective is highly descriptive and constitutive of the identities of individuals since, in the context of migration, it indexes assumed expectations about behaviour. Thus, Irma's word choice functionalises her social role and relations as surreptitious and illicit. In this vein, the underlying assumption of her discourse implies that the dichotomy of legality and illegality renders "social identities as acceptable or unacceptable" (Flores Farfan and Holzscheiter 2011:142) and that access to particular sources of information and social capital shapes social relations.

As the interview went on, Irma explained that she had been informed that her indefinite leave to remain was granted through an amnesty in 2000. She then began to work in restaurants and saved money to bring her daughter back to England but her intent was unsuccessful and she stayed with her father in Ecuador. At the time of the interview, she ran her own event management business mainly directed to Latin Americans who also made up her main social network. Her life plan was to become a successful business woman and thus become a role model for what she called her community so they know there are more jobs and not only cleaning.

Summary

In this chapter, we have seen how five Latin American immigrants self-presented. Their self-presentations suggest, on the one hand, how they distanced themselves from the figure of the immigrant either openly or implicitly. On the other hand, they self-presented as vulnerable or "illegal" through a number of ways of speaking that nonetheless blur socially significant distinctions. Additionally, their discursive choices appeared to be influenced by another non-linguistic feature. The accumulation of education, social and economic capital in the lives of the participants seemed to have lent itself for the construction of a social space and a class-based view of who an immigrant is. This has provided us with pointers to a diversity of identities and practices that may influence social relations and alignments of Latin Americans in various social domains in which they have come to interact.

Chapter 4
Work and social interactions of Latin American immigrants in a neoliberal context

4.1 Introduction

In this chapter, I concentrate on the interactions of Latin Americans by looking at how they categorise other Latin Americans and themselves as they describe their work and social experiences in certain social domains. One of these domains is the service sector where a large proportion of Latin American immigrants working in London are concentrated (McIlwaine 2015). I will firstly focus on the experiences of Sharon from Colombia, David and Diego from Ecuador and Alfonso from Venezuela. Their accounts of working with other Latin Americans depict practices of exploitation and manipulation. I thus focus on negative 'other' representations, metaphors, topoi of culture and history as well as presuppositions and common ground knowledge that emerge in the participants' ways of speaking. Such units of analysis enable us to gain insight into how the participants justify attitudes of distrust, dishonesty and subjugation due to the assumed expected social roles that Latin Americans are to take on. The experiences of the Latin Americans here involved intimate social values and asymmetrical power relations that seem to disarticulate their social interactions. These interactions, nevertheless, are contextualised in a larger socioeconomic reality, such as a neoliberal economic model, that also affects other migrant groups and whose experiences in the same domain interestingly echo those of the participants in this book.

As I move away, from the examination of the participants' discourses in the context of the service sector, I will continue the analysis of their interactions by looking at the case of Linda from Mexico whose work experiences are told in the context of domestic work and Spanish language teaching. Linda's experiences introduce us into an exploration of Latin Americans' social relations in other social domains such as volunteer work, network marketing and cultural events that I will subsequently present as I include the descriptions of Mayra from Ecuador and return to Sharon before introducing Jazmin from Colombia. Their accounts foreground ideologies of neoliberalism that depict success or failure as the responsibility of the individual and that also intertwine with notions of social class that vertically demarcate in-groups from outgroups. These are attributed social behaviours and cognitive properties that categorise them as immoral, insecure, unpleasant or poorly educated individuals who, according to one of the participants, do not make a good impression of what being Latin American is supposed to mean, or do not know how to live in a receiving society. Additionally, we will see that their social relations and interactions also appear to be divergent and at times conflictual due to their language experiences, interests and views. These are influenced by the social and education capital that the participants possess and that surfaces as a distinctive trait that is mobilised by the participants to distance themselves from other Latin Americans.

The analyses and discussion in this section will benefit from reminding ourselves of and answering the following question: what insights into the social interactions of Latin Americans in London can we gain by looking at the social values and ideologies emergent in their discourses? As I said in chapter 1.4, Latin American immigrants are lumped together under the term community, which may conceal important distinctions and divergent interests due to their heterogeneous composition and, as we were able to gather from chapter 3, social class differentiations that constitute both their identities and social relations. In this context, an answer to this question through the intended analysis aims to enable us to explore and understand what might affect their relations in the social spaces in which they have interacted and how they make sense of the experiences that they describe. The discourses presented and examined here are both preceded by how I came to meet the participants and their biographies that will help us contextualise their experiences in London.

4.2 Assumptions and ideologies of Latin Americans in the service sector

Sharon: *"I frequently saw how a Latino manager from different nationalities treats his employees"*

I previously noted that my observations and interactions with Latin American immigrants were accompanied with serendipitous conversations and meetings in events and sites where they usually congregate and work. Some of these sites were shopping centres, cafes, cultural events as well as universities and markets. I met Sharon in the Elephant and Castle shopping centre after having been put in touch with her through one of the study participants from Ecuador to whom I will return in the next chapter.

Sharon is from Colombia and has lived in the UK for twenty years. The decision to move to the UK was not her own but her parents' as they faced pressing economic problems in their country. She was thrown into the service sector by the family's economic needs and found herself in a swim or sink situation. She started out as a cleaner, then she got promoted to supervisor and subsequently to manager in a cleaning company where she then was taken under the wing of another person and began to work in the accounting department. In this context, Sharon recounted that her work enabled her to understand Latin American workers' basic needs inside and outside the workplace as well as witness work interactions among them.

Excerpt 17: "I had been in their shoes, it was painful, you know what I mean?"

> veía mucho cómo un manager latino de diferentes nacionalidades trata a sus empleados y como yo empecé allí haciéndolo, estar en la otra posición, pues sí dolía ¿sí me entiendes? Entonces, se trataba de ayudarles de cooperarles con el mismo manager y con el mismo empleado. Es como ser una fuente allí ¿si me entiende? . . .

Translation

> I frequently saw how a Latino manager from different nationalities treats his employees and as I had been in their shoes, it was painful, you know what I mean? So, I tried to help them, to be the go-in between with the manager and the employee. It's like being a source there, you know what I mean? . . .

In excerpt 17, Sharon points to the different roles and positions of Latin American employees as well as her experience that helped her relate to them who she suggestively presents as being subject to asymmetrical interactions. In this context we see the emergence of a topic; the Latino manager, who Sharon represents as a figure that embodies practices that deteriorate Latinos' work relationships. The latter can be inferred by looking at her use of lexical items such as the verb *treat* and the adjective *painful*. The former begs the question, how does a Latino manager treat his employees as Sharon presents him as the agent of such treatment? The latter helps us draw conjectures of this type of work relationship by analysing its connotative use, which is indicative of adverse work interactions. However, Sharon negotiates her description of what she witnessed. For instance, she does not seem to want to expose such interactions by referring neither to a particular nationality nor to a particular tense event and she appears to suggest that she did not intend to side with a particular party but rather act as a negotiator. The latter role emerges as she uses the verb such as *help* and the phrase *the go-in between*, which not only exhibit Sharon's discourse of empathy but also imply conflicting work relations between the manager and the employee.

The description of this work interaction still merits further scrutiny as it may have been influenced by the public space in which Sharon was sharing her life story. Sharon and I met in a Latin American-run cafe and were surrounded by more people from Latin America. Such a setting needs to be borne in mind in order to understand the word choices and discursive strategies that the participants employ as they recount their work experience. I pursue this in David's following explicit account that helps us understand their interactions in the same context better.

David: *"Apart from robbing the company, they were robbing us too"*

As we saw in the previous chapter, David is an Ecuadorian immigrant who has been working in the service sector as a cleaner for more than 10 years in a London-based university despite the fact that he holds a B.A in Physical education obtained in Ecuador. His migration trajectory reflects that of more than 50% of Latin Americans who work in the service sector, many of whom deal with a downward social repositioning (McIlwaine 2015). He invited me to go to his workplace to tell me about his life story during his lunch break in which he not only touched upon his experience as an undocumented immigrant but as a cleaner who had faced exploitation. In the following excerpt, he relates his experiences with Latin American managers in the cleaning job that, at the time of the interview, he did through an outsourcing company at this site. As his life story unfolds, he recounts that he and his co-workers did not have many problems until Latin American managers took over management.

Excerpt 18: "Latinos to make matters worse as a manager"

> teníamos un manager inglés. por ahí sacarían cosas, pero no, nunca tuvimos queja. Nosotros trabajábamos, hacíamos horas extra, pero llegaron estos, Latinos encima de manager. Se complicó todo. Aparte de robar a la compañía, ellos nos robaban a nosotros también . . .

Translation

> we had an English manager they might have done certain things, but we never had complaints. We worked, we worked extra hours, but these people came along, Latinos to make matters worse as a manager. All got complicated. Apart from robbing the company, they were robbing us too . . .

This account contrasts with that of Sharon given that, in David's, the representation of the Latino manager is an example of a negative discursive categorisation that explicitly refers to their dishonest practices. By resorting to an argumentation strategy through which he mitigates the implied negative practices of the English manager, he foregrounds and emphasises polarised work interactions between Latinos. Illustrative of this interaction is his use of such a demonstrative adjective in Spanish as *those*, which carries a derogatory meaning about them and exhibits a strategy of distancing. Additionally, his discourse produces a topos of culture, a generalisation through which he intends to explain how Latinos exercise and abuse their position of power, *Latinos, to make matters worse*. This categorisation of Latinos is reinforced by the repetitive use of a negatively connoted verb, *rob*, which both presents the Latino manager as the agent of such practice and points to fragmentation between Latin Americans in clearly delineated in-groups vs outgroups. However, why does David speak so openly about exploitation and manipulation among Latin Americans?

As I noted in the introduction to this book, David and I met in a festival where he was handing out leaflets with information about labour rights for cleaners who were outsourced. Later on, I learnt that David had taken courses about labour rights and that he had acquired British citizenship. These practices and status contrast with his experience that we saw in the previous chapter as an undocumented immigrant who had to hide and go unnoticed. In addition to this, there are two important factors that will help us gain insight into David's discourse. One of these is his participation in demonstrations held outside his workplace that I was able to observe during fieldwork in which he would denounce exploitation practices and demand that he as well as his co-workers were directly hired and not outsourced by the university at which he worked. Another factor was the place of the interview. It was an unoccupied, quiet room on the third floor to which only he had a key in the building where he worked. Nevertheless, it must be added that as he narrated his experiences, David constantly looked out the window in order to make sure, as he later stated in the interview and our conversations, that his boss did not catch him giving an interview. In this context, his political activism, his access to information about labour rights and his British citizenship conjoined with a private room as the setting of our conversation generate the social conditions in which he, unlike Sharon, openly categorises Latino managers as unscrupulous. After hearing the above in the interview, I asked David whether he thought that the Latin American manager was presented with a challenge when working with more Latin Americans. My question, it must be acknowledged, was motivated by my assumption that there was comradeship between Latin Americans.

Excerpt 19: "they know how to manipulate the worker"

> No más bien encontró un tesoro. porque él conoce las debilidades de nosotros él sabe las políticas de la compañía ellos saben muy bien. tienen que representar la compañía y vinieron aquí y ¡bingo! porque saben cómo manipular al trabajador "te doy tanto" y mucha gente somos muy agradecidos el manager te dio cuatro horas pero te está sacando veinte sin darte cuenta tienes que tú sabes cómo somos los latinos . . .

Translation

> No, he rather found a gold mine because he knows our weaknesses, he knows the company's politics. They know it very well that they have to represent the company and they came here and bingo! Because they know how to manipulate the worker "I give you these hours" and a lot of us are very grateful the manager hired you four hours of work but in reality he hires you for twenty without your realising you have to you know what we Latinos are like . . .

David's answer depicts a picture of manipulation and exploitation in which assumed cultural characteristics seem to define the nature and the direction of the cleaners and managers' work relations. These are in turn characterised by a metaphorical representation that, as we saw in Marcia's account in the previous chapter, could help us explain how social interactions could be conceived of and structured (see Lakoff and Johnson 2003; Santa Anna 2002; Cisneros 2008; Knowles and Moon 2006). That is, David's word choices such as *gold mine* and *bingo* produces the metaphor the Latino manager's behaviour is mercenary given that it points to a conduct motivated by a personal economic gain at the expense of others. Furthermore, his negative categorisation of the Latino manager becomes emphasised since through the verbs, *manipulate* and *know*, he interpellates them as unscrupulous individuals who schemingly exploit workers.

In addition to the above, it is noteworthy how David seems to rationalise the behaviours he narrates and that my presence co-constructs. David's concluding remark, *you know what we Latinos are like*, again seems to be informed by a topos of culture as it presupposes that such deviant and dishonest practices are a defining characteristic of Latinos as in 'it is normal and expected that we Latinos carry ourselves this way'. In this sense, my position as a Latin American researcher who is supposedly to have inside knowledge of what Latin Americans are like is interpellated and am invited to agree with this common-sense view of what defines not them but all of us. Consequently, his representation of these events essentialises Latinos' interactions and behaviour which is to be explained and justified by a sociocultural shared knowledge that is not to be questioned.

Nevertheless, there is a lexical item that is worth attention. David's mention of *the company* is indexical of a business practice such as outsourcing through which many Latin Americans like David find a job in the service sector where they are either underpaid or hired for few hours of work (see McIlwaine 2016; Linneker and Wills 2016). Their job insertion, as stated in chapter 3 and as we will continue to see in the following case of Diego, is through contacts and other Latin Americans employed as cleaners. In this context, the role of outsourcing companies deserves further scrutiny. As we saw in chapter 1.6 and according to a report by the Equality and Human Rights Commission (2014: 69) outsourcing firms in an attempt to deliver a high-quality service at the lowest cost possible "can try to reduce their costs and improve their profit margins by reducing pay rates, increasing work intensity, reorganising work or creating a more flexible workforce", all of which has been proven to affect work conditions in the service sector negatively. David through his demands of fair labour rights for cleaners, as stated above, exhibits awareness of this business practice, but interestingly his description rather concentrates on traits that allegedly define Latinos and that explain the nature of their work interactions. In the next excerpt through which we will be able to pursue the above description, David continues to describe his work interactions and explains why managers exploit him and his co-workers.

Excerpt 20: "We are also very submissive"

> también somos muy sumisos ¿me entiendes? porque nosotros somos muy agradecidos "ah mira este trabaja" y "tengo que pagártelo" entonces abusan también ¿me entiendes? hasta que nosotros reaccionamos ¿me entiendes? . . .

Translation

> We are also very submissive you know what I mean? Because we are grateful "this one is hard-working" and "I am in your debt" so they take unfair advantage of that as well you know what I mean? Until we got tired of that you know what I mean? . . .

In this account, David points to characteristics embodied by cleaners and for which they are treated unfairly by the managers. According to David, the latter identify cleaners' industriousness and attitudes of gratefulness and indebtedness as exploitable qualities for their ends, attitudes which are presented by David's use of quotes through which he additionally intends not only to re-enact those events discursively but also present them objectively. Consequently the categorisation of the Latino manager as abusive by David foregrounds conflicting and contrasting values that in his narration appear to disarticulate and polarise Latinos' work relations.

However, the latter argument should not be treated as a definition of cultural essentialism or fixed work relations among Latin Americans in London since it reflects work interactions in a larger scale. Other studies have focused on Chinese migrant workers relations and employment practices with their co-ethnics outside and inside the UK. In the context of Australia, Li (2017) documents exploitation and low pay of Chinese employees who are paid in cash and not hired through a contract by their co-ethnic employers, and it is reported that it is a practice that seems to be justified due to their cultural expectations and economic vulnerability. Additionally, David's description evokes other contexts in which other behavioural characteristics, such as being hardworking, are exploited by employers. In a glass factory in England, MacKenzie and Forde (2009) reported the attitudes of employers towards migrant employees who were deemed "good workers". These were recently arrived central European employees who were willing to work hard for long hours at a pay rate unattractive for locals and who at times were rented out to other companies (Mackenzie and Forde, 2009). In this light, the defining cultural characteristics as well as the attitudes to which David refers are not unique of Latinos but the interactions described are framed within neoliberal work conditions.

As David continued to narrate, David said that they began to organise themselves to ask for their benefits and denounce abuse by the managers. They eventually obtained a London-living wage and the right to unionise and, after a week they had obtained them, David and other 20 irregular co-workers were called to a meeting by the company. David said that one of his co-workers felt suspicious about the meeting and feared that it could be a trap, a migration raid. David said he did not believe that that could happen since there were other workers in an irregular status who were the managers' protegees and who would attend the meeting. David did not believe that the managers could turn their backs on them.

Excerpt 21: "They used them as bait"

> cuando el tercer tema dentro de un salón como este que tiene dos entradas *exit* salidas de emergencia pero que dan acceso a la universidad y entran cincuenta oficiales de migración y se suben así así como están es el teatro allá y se paran en cada salida los muchachos cincuenta trabajadores habían ahí . . . se paran [oficiales de migración] ahí con casco con toletes con botas y se pusieron en la salida y les hicieron la redada "documentos" "nombre" y ahí comenzaron cogieron a nueve trabajadores el resto que no pudo entrar porque cuando justo como siempre uno queda atrasado . . .

Translation

> when they were addressing the third topic inside a lecture theatre like this, which has two entrance doors, emergency exits leading to the University, fifty migration officers entered and walked into the lecture theatre and blocked each emergency exit. the pals there were fifty workers there and they [migration officers] stood there wearing a helmet, boots, holding batons and they stood in the exit and the raid began "documents" "name" and that's how they started they detained nine workers the rest that could not enter because as usual they were running late . . .

David's account goes on.

> Ellos [la compañía] dijeron que tenían que cubrir con las leyes migratorias lo cual es mentira, ellos mismos los liaban a los trabajadores. Sabían quién era el jefe todo eso y lo más triste usaron para carnada a sus propios queridos hijos, sino nadie entraba. Los pusieron

como carnada porque sabían porque lo pusieron que no fue su culpa se pusieron los managers a llorar. Son latinos también los managers, colombianos que ellos no sabían nada de la compañía. ¡Mentira! Hasta lloraban porque la gente se les fue encima "ustedes sabían, traicioneros" y ellos hasta lloraban, pero muchos se quejaron de esa traición que nos hicieron . . .

Translation

They [the company] said they had to meet the migration law, which is a lie, they themselves set them upon the workers. They knew who was the leader and all that and the saddest thing was that they used their protegees, otherwise no one would enter the lecture theatre. They used them as bait because they knew it they said they did not have anything to do with it. The managers were crying. They are latinos as well, colombians and said they did not know anything about the company. That's a lie! They were even crying because people complained to them "you knew it, traitors" and they were even crying, but many complained about how they betrayed us . . .

In excerpt 21 David describes the moment when migration officers walked into the lecture theatre to undertake the raid. According to David, this was premeditated by the outsourcing company in connivance with the managers and thus portrays an event of tension in which partial interests undermine social and work relations. In this sense, his discourse brings about the topic of betrayal that he foregrounds through two lexical choices; *lie* and *traitor*. The former characterises managers as deceitful people who called workers to an enclosed space where they could be detained. The latter, on the one hand, reinforces a negative categorisation of managers as they used their protegees as *bait*, which produces a dehumanising metaphor whereby other workers are constructed as pray. On the other hand, David's discourse also becomes relevant since it allows us to catch a glimpse of subjective elements constitutive of their realities in this context. It implies that there were assumed commonalities such as being Latin American that may have organised their social and work relations. These are, nevertheless, fractured by the partial interests that the managers pursued as David's discourse suggests.

The descriptions presented so far through Sharon's and David's accounts respectively point to asymmetrical power relations that are seemingly predicated by the specific positions of power that the actors described occupy. However, it is pertinent to further explore such power relations among Latin American immigrants in the same context in order to obtain a better insight into them and examine how they are connected with other stories that are also situated within a larger neoliberal frame and socioeconomic class differences.

Diego: *"He started to take unfair advantage of them"*

My various interactions and conversations with other Latin Americans allowed me to negotiate access to more participants in various sites in north London. We would meet and talk no only in cafes but restaurants where Diego shared his life story with me. He was born in Ecuador and, at the time of the interview, had been in England for over sixteen years, a time span in which his migration status has gone through a refugee and undocumented status until finally getting British citizenship. In Ecuador, he used to be a sales agent for a transnational company in his country but he left it due to a combination of factors such as economic hardship and death threats. Upon arriving in Heathrow airport, he applied for political asylum, which was granted to him, and contacted an acquaintance's uncle already living in London. This last person provided him with accommodation before he was allocated with housing by the government and helped him expand his social network that, as he said, consisted mostly of Latinos. Their help was instrumental for Diego to get a job in the service sector through which he was able to remit money to his wife and sons in Ecuador and where at the time of the interview he still worked.

In the excerpt below, Diego recounts how he moved from one cleaning job to another and what his motivations were to make such decision. He relates how his supervisor began to assign him extra work given that he was an industrious worker, which Diego saw as unfair treatment. He did not complain but rather he kept silent and continued to work under the same person's supervision as he did not want to risk his three-hour job until he found a full-time job somewhere else.

Excerpt 22: "He was mmm, well, he robbed them literally"

> Él era colombiano, pero eh yo lo que veía era que mucha gente abusaba mucho. O sea, él lo que hacía, como supervisor, era meter gente con papeles así, no correctos. No les pagaba a tiempo. Empezaba a abusar de ellos. Le venía, mmm bueno, a robarle prácticamente el dinero y él abusaba de la gente y yo decía que por qué, pero a mí ya me empezó a ver con esa situación entonces yo dije "no, ya no, ya no voy a seguir más", me fui a trabajar el full time . . .

Translation

> He was Colombian, but what I saw was that many people took unfair advantage of I mean what he did, as supervisor, was to hire people like, under the table. He did not pay them on time. He started to take unfair advantage of them. He was mmm, well, he robbed them literally and he took unfair advantage of them and I would say why, but then he started to be wary of me so I said "no, that's enough, I will no longer work here", I moved to a full-time work . . .

In excerpt 22, Diego describes both illicit ways of hiring people in the service sector and practices of exploitation with which he seemingly disagreed since he decided to move to another job. However, unlike David who openly narrated a similar tense environment, negative attitudes and actions in the same context, Diego's account is characterised by discursive negotiations that hesitantly provide a picture of asymmetrical relations. On the one hand, Diego's reference to the supervisor's nationality, *colombiano*, both culturally differentiates him and characterises him as dishonest since this trait is emphasised as he describes the supervisor's recurrent behaviour through negatively connoted-verbs of which he is the agent, *he did not pay them on time, he took unfair advantage, he robbed them literally*. On the other hand, it appears that Diego intends to save face as though he did not want to depict the supervisor's attitudes negatively, and discursively hedges the supervisor's practices, *he hired people like under the table*, intended to function as a euphemism that attenuates unlawful hiring practices. In this sense, Diego's lexical choices pad his statement and obfuscate the manager's abusive practices that he undecidedly describes.

On the day of the interview, Diego and I met in a cafe but he decided to go to a Latin American restaurant where he said we could talk and he felt more comfortable. This was a place owned by an Ecuadorian family with whom Diego had a very good relationship and to which, according to our conversations and my observations, he would go and sing karaoke on either Fridays or Saturdays. In fact, he invited me to join him on a Friday night when he introduced me to his friends from Ecuador who also worked in the service sector as cleaners. This setting and the activities there on the day of the interview seemed to have had a particular effect on the language Diego employed.

The restaurant had just opened and the owners and one of the waiters were setting up the tables and chairs and were walking back and forth past the table at which Diego and I sat. As Diego touched upon events that he suggested as delicate such as his being undocumented and working without a permit more than ten years ago, he either spoke hesitantly, euphemistically or lowered his voice. This was a speech pattern that he also showed while he narrated the events in excerpt 22, which implied he did not want to talk about it openly before he changed the subject of his account. This illustrates a social space and environment unlike the more controlled conditions in which David openly talked about exploitation, and it also reminds us that language use is a practice co-constructed with the situatedness of the social environment in which the interaction occurs and that physical space is not neutral (Lefebvre 1974; Dong 2017). For Diego, the restaurant seemed to be a space of recreation rather than space of denunciation.

As the interview went on and approached to its end, Diego narrates another experience in a different site where the role of social capital also highlights strategies on which Latin American immigrants draw for accessing and keeping their jobs. A friend of Diego's asked him to fill in his cleaning job in a hospital while his friend covered for someone else's cleaning job in another site with a higher salary.

Excerpt 23: So, who benefits from that?

> había muchas personas latinas ahí. y lo que hacían es.era de recargarles trabajo recargarles el trabajo y la gente se iba y tenían que hacer el trabajo del otro por el mismo precio. Entonces ¿quién se beneficia de eso? Es el manager o el supervisor que está a cargo no le paga a la persona lo que debe ser . . .

Translation

> there were a lot of Latin American people there and what they did was to give them too much work, give them too much work and when people quit, they had to do somebody else's work for the same salary. So, who benefits from that? It's the manager or the supervisor in charge, they don't pay them what they worked for . . .

In this account, Diego points to the numerical presence of Latin American workers who are described as the recipients of unfair treatment due to which they left their jobs resulting in wards unattended to and tasks undone. This required that the latter activities had to be taken over by those who stayed in the job and for which they received no remuneration. In this context, Diego's description resonates with the description of David and also with other studies documenting London's migrant division of labour in which cleaners have to work long hours of overtime and are often underpaid (see Wills and Kavita 2009). I will elaborate on this below. As to Diego's discourse, it foregrounds the topic of exploitation that becomes the situational frame in which a person in a position of power performs unfair actions. Such practices are emphasised by the repetition of *give them too much work*, and by his use of *they don't pay them what they worked for*. Consequently, Diego's narrated experience exemplifies a discourse of polarisation indicative of vertical interactions that present Latin American employees as victims in contrast to the manager who is presented as an agent who deliberately exploits them as also the rhetorical question implies, *who benefits from that?* Nevertheless, the reference to either the manager or the supervisor in charge remained vague, and in order to understand his experience more closely in the interview I asked him if he knew the managers.

Excerpt 24: "They are Latinos themselves"

> ¡Son LATINOS! Son latinos mismos. Colombianos, ecuatorianos qué se yo . . .

Translation

> They are LATINOS! They are Latinos themselves. Colombians, Ecuadorians who knows . . .

Excerpt 24 exemplifies his direct and emphatic answer that carries overtones of frustration and disappointment. As we have discussed in chapter 1.3 and above, Latin Americans as many migrant groups rely on social capital as both the conduit to their inclusion in a new society and as a mechanism of job insertion that allows them to develop social relations through which they also generate interpersonal trust (Putnam 1993; Portes 1988). Diego's stress on the word *LATINOS* and his use of *themselves*, that also functions as an emphasiser of its precedent noun implies his own disbelief about exploitation among Latinos since it appears that his assumed cultural commonalities and relations of trust have been transgressed. Nonetheless, his answer containing disillusionment, as we noted above, is accompanied with vagueness and a face-keeping effort; his use of hedging as illustrated in the concluding phrase, *who knows*, discursively emerges as an attempt to point to neither a particular nationality nor a particular social actor, and after which he kept silent in the interview. I noticed certain discomfort in him that may have been explained by the conditions and environment of the interview that I described above. I attempted to follow up his account by mentioning that there was then a tense environment in which he worked, but he corrected me.

Excerpt 25: "they do anything to survive in this country"

> Bueno corrupción lo que hay es también entre mismos latinos porque la gente viene necesitada y hacen lo que sea por tener ingreso porque tienen que pagar. porque ellos hacen lo que sea por sobrevivir en este país. pagar renta comida qué sé yo transporte de aquí este país no es fácil de vivir económicamente es muy costoso . . .

Translation

> Well corruption is what there is among Latinos themselves because people come here in need and they do anything to have an income because they have to pay because they do anything to survive in this country to pay for rent food and whatnot transportation here this country isn't easy to live in economically it's costly . . .

Although Diego recognises a dishonest practice such as corruption among Latin Americans in London in the service sector, it gradually becomes backgrounded in what unfolded as a discourse of empathy. In Diego's account, *corruption* is nominalised given that the actors of it are not explicitly mentioned and seems to be implied as an understandable practice through which those in positions of power knowingly exploits the socioeconomic needs that Latinos in search of work face. Phrases such as *people come here in need, they do anything to have an income,* foreground the main monetary motivations of people to take up a job, which are in turn accentuated by Diego's pointing to how they struggle to make their ends meet, *they do anything to survive in this country*. He thus aligns himself with those in search of work and whose behaviour he seems to rationalise as exploitable and as generalised reactive practices due to the socioeconomic environment in which Latin Americans live. After telling me this, Diego once again changed the subject and I decided not to pursue his description of exploitation as he was noticeably not at ease talking about it.

Diego's narrated experiences are consistent with those of Sharon and David in the sense that their interactions with other Latin Americans suggest and reflect asymmetrical relations articulated by the positions of power that the actors involved in the accounts hold. It is also suggested that the industriousness of workers that their accounts depict is treated as exploitable. Nevertheless, it must be emphasised that the attitudes portrayed here, although they have been reported in previous studies of the same population (see McIlwaine 2011; 2014), go beyond conflict and asymmetries among Latin Americans and, as we have seen, they rather interrelate with wider practices of labour exploitation within other migrant groups. As I have said above, Diego's account is reminiscent of the discourse of the "good worker" (MacKenzie and Forde 2009), but it is also intertwined with what other researchers have identified as the unequal distribution of income and resources that have been exacerbated by "the uneven effects of globalisation" (Wu and Lie 2014: 1392). That is, the limited economic resources with which migrants move to a new society, and whose lives largely resonate with Diego's, point to issues of socioeconomic class differences and inequality rather than tensions or exploitation explained by national origin or ethnicity. The subsequent account of Alfonso, nonetheless, can offer us another window to the interactions that we have set out to explore in the same context where nationality and geographical origin are discursively presented as factors that influence how Latin Americans associate or dissociate with other Latin Americans.

Alfonso: *"Latinos outside their country are different"*

As I have mentioned, part of my fieldwork involved visits to NGOs, festivals as well as markets in Lambeth. This is one of the boroughs in which Latin Americans have obtained official recognition as an ethnic group (McIlwaine 2016; CLAUK 2015). Here I would meet with contacts from Colombia and Venezuela that I had made in my previous visits and who worked in either restaurants or informally selling home-made cheese to market goers. These contacts introduced me to Alfonso. His work was not based in the same site but his visits to it were more motivated by his circle of friends there as I was able to observe. Alfonso is a Venezuelan immigrant who has been living and working in London for over thirteen years. He was trained as a Telecoms Technician in Venezuela and practiced this training in the Dutch island of Aruba where he worked for an American company. At the time of the interview, he worked as a care assistant in a hospital in London that he described as the best thing that has happened to him since he came to London, and such a hindsight is illustrative of the nature and conditions of the various jobs such as cleaning that he has done in his time in London.

In the next excerpt, Alfonso attempted to describe his social activities in answer to my question about how he organised his social life. The question sought to understand his social interactions as well as events and places to which he could go with more Latin American people.

Excerpt 26: "I don't like relating to Latinos"

> Yo, mira, a ver. yo te voy a decir algo. Yo soy cien por ciento latinoamericano ¿verdad? No me gusta vincularme con latinos para serte honesto ¿verdad? Porque el latino fuera de su país es distinto desafortunadamente . . .

Translation

> Look I am going to tell you something I am a hundred percent Latin American, right? I don't like relating to Latinos to be honest, right? Because Latinos outside their country are different unfortunately . . .

Alfonso's account interestingly opens with a confession-like description through which different values are intimated and that seemingly influence his social relations. It is interesting to see his use of hyperbolic language to refer to his being Latin American since it emphasises an identity that he does not seem to treat as synonymous with the noun *Latinos* given that the latter is introduced through a phrase of affective distance epitomised by *I don't like*. As his narrative progresses, he euphemistically begins to distance himself from Latinos by defining them as *different*, a vague definition about which I asked him what he meant by it.

Excerpt 27: "Latinos here function like small clans"

> Es muy materialista, es excesivamente materialista y prácticamente yo creo que el dios de ellos es el dinero, ¿me entiendes? Y es bastante incomodo, en sí es bastante incomodo porque yo no soy así ¿veda? Yo entiendo que las personas e su tiempo es importante porque ellos lo necesitan para producir dinero para lograr sus metas. Todo eso yo lo entiendo. Me parece muy bien, pero en lo consiguiente me vinculo muy poco con latinos. O sea, poquísimo. Prácticamente porque los latinos aquí funcionan como pequeños clanes. Si tú no eres colombiano,

es muy difícil que entres en ese clan, imposible casi ¿me entiendes? Si no eres ecuatoriano, si no eres boliviano, ellos son muy muy cerrados en su situación ¿me entiendes? . . .

Translation

They are materialist, excessively materialist and literally money is their god, you know what I mean? And it's pretty uncomfortable pretty uncomfortable because I am not like that right? I understand that people er their time is important because they need it to make money to achieve their goals. I understand all that. I understand it, but therefore I socialise with Latinos very little. I mean very little. That's because Latinos here function like small clans if you are not Colombian it's very hard that you become part of that clan it's almost impossible, you know what I mean? If you are not Ecuadorian, if you are not Bolivian, they are very very close-knit, you know what I mean? . . .

In excerpt 27, Alfonso gives the reasons why he decides to socialise very little with other Latinos in London and justifies them by detailing their defining characteristics. Through hyperbolic language such as *excessively*, and a metaphoric representation of what dictates their lives, *money is their god*, Latinos are emphatically categorised as money-oriented individuals whose behaviour is directed to material gain, which does not reflect that of Alfonso. In addition, he argues there are other conditions that influence his infrequent interaction with them. The construct of national identity comes to the fore and appears by means of a simile, *like clans*, as a common ancestry that, for Alfonso, establishes and articulates rules of inclusion and exclusion among Latinos. By drawing on such simile, Alfonso represents them as culturally differentiated groups that socially organise themselves independent from one another, a practice of cultural segmentation that nonetheless discursively typifies Latinos.

In addition to Alfonso's narration of events, there are three intertwined elements that should not be disregarded in order to enrich our understanding of the social relations he depicts. The first one is the act of moving to another country and what this involves. As stated in chapter 1.3, people move for a number of reasons and the routes that they travel to a great extent influence both their social experiences and may impact their social identities. Also, they may mobilise their socioeconomic resources and social networks at both micro and meso level such as personal contacts and ethnic identity or nationality in order to make their move and their arrival less challenging. They provide information about where to live and work. Economic and social capitals are indeed relevant material and symbolic elements that affect and to a great extent organise the formation of cultural groups and thus their delimitation from others (see Castles and Miller 2009); In other words, these capitals help us gain insight into Alfonso's view of nationality as a factor that shapes social relations in migrant groups. It must be added that the description included above is not exclusive of Latin Americans in London, but rather reflects what other researchers have referred to as enclaves based on this symbolic element that may offer support or a respite from the challenges they may face in a new society (Portes and Bach 1985; Samers 2010). In this vein, it must be noted that moving to another country may create new conditions of existence such as economic pressure that indeed plays an influential role in migrants' experiences and ways of organising their lives in a new society (see Mahler 1995). We will see more of this below that relates to a highly important third element.

The second element pertains to what some authors call residual culture. A residual culture refers to "experiences, meanings and values which cannot be expressed or verified in terms of the dominant culture", in this case the receiving society, "but are nevertheless lived and practised on the basis of some previous social and cultural formation" (Williams 1977:122). In addition to this, in a residual culture there is also a "reaching back" to those meanings and values which were created in actual societies and actual situations in the past, which still seem to have significance because they represent areas of human experience (Williams 1977: 124). This means that migrants' experiences in their countries of origin may inform and articulate those in their new society. In this vein, Alfonso's view of Latinos as materialist and money oriented suggests traces of a residual culture by pointing to previous social relations with them opposed to material-based ones and oriented to and located in the homeland. Thus, Alfonso's discourse evidences an understanding that is rooted in a meaningful former social experience that, nonetheless, is not only an element of the past, but it figures as an active element of the here and now through which he makes sense of the attitudes that he discursively disqualifies (see Williams 1977). There is additionally a third element that intertwines with the two mentioned above. Alfonso's lexical choice, *different*, also leads us to think not only of elements of a residual culture where there is a disruption of his former social relations, but people's new conditions of existence. We should remind ourselves that Latin American migration is a South to North migration in the sense that, although not in all cases, people move to the UK in search of economic advance; an objective that people attempt to reach and that by implication influences their behaviour. Thus their being different in a new society conjoined with a material-oriented attitude that Alfonso describes are indexical of a behaviour that characterises neoliberalism in many societies. That is, a competition driven attitude comes forth and is suggested as a force that creates antagonism between Latin Americans. This has also been captured in other migrant groups who exhibit their disillusionment with fellow migrants whose behaviours and attitudes change when living in another country. Mahler (1995) documents how Salvadoran and Honduran immigrants in Long Island, USA describe their compatriots as jealous or competitive and find that they are victimised by their own. The economic pressures that they face such as the payment of travel debts, remittances, and rents result both in the suspension of social rules such as reciprocity that existed before migration and in an aggressive, competitive subculture where migrants exploit other fellow migrants (Mahler 1995). In the context of this study, we will continue to explore these socioeconomic factors and attitudes in Alfonso's penultimate excerpt in more detail.

It must be noted that the description that Alfonso provides, nevertheless, seems to be ambivalent due to his social practices that he also mentioned in the interview and that I was able to observe. Alfonso's preferred leisure activity was to play chess in the Elephant and Castle area where he had a close circle of friends with whom he would get together at the weekends and who would be from Latin America. As stated above, Alfonso visited a market in the borough of Lambeth where he would interact with other Latin Americans that introduced him to me and where through my observations and participations in their conversations I did not identify any confrontation among them. On the contrary, they talked, joked and interacted in amicable terms. Alfonso's actions thus contradicts his discourse and, although it is a type of contradiction that has also been recorded in previous studies of Colombians in London (see McIlwaine 2012; Cock 2011), still merits further examination. The recurrent topos of culture, that is the common-sense view that stereotypically aims to explain people's behaviour due to their geographic origin, and the construct of nationality keep being resorted to as a sense-making mechanism of Alfonso's experiences. Such topos and construct may background other larger socioeconomic factors that may impact the quality of Latin Americans' social or work relations which we will continue to examine below. As his narrative progresses, Alfonso he then touches upon his work experience with Latin Americans in a London-based hospital in an attempt to justify his previous description.

Excerpt 28: "the Colombians en bloc bullied us"

> A mí me toco una vez trabajar de supervisor en X hospital de cleaner donde el manager era colombiano. El noventa por ciento del staff era colombiano. El otro resto eramos yo venezolano boliviano y ecuatoriano y los colombianos en bloque nos hacían bullying a nosotros

Translation

> I happened to work as a cleaning supervisor in a hospital where the manager was Colombian. Ninety percent of the staff were Colombian. The rest was me Venezuelan a Bolivian and an Ecuadorian and the Colombians en bloc bullied us . . .

In excerpt 28, Alfonso describes the make-up of nationalities as well as the positions that each of them occupied in the workplace where he used to work as a cleaner. He also describes alliances that become manifest in in-groups vs out-groups with which he identifies. His discourse brings about the topic of intimidation of which he as part of the out-group was the object as his account suggests, and which presents him as the underdog. This is furthermore emphasised by his employment of a discursive strategy of numbers exemplified in the numerical superiority of the staff, *ninety percent*. However, such strategy of numbers has a hyperbolic vague effect since there is no mention of specific numbers of the people to whom Alfonso attributes a violent behaviour. The latter nevertheless becomes evident in his metaphorical use of the adverbial phrase, *en bloc*, which is followed by a negatively connoted action, *bullying*, through which Alfonso categorises Colombians' attitudes as systematically aggressive and who are thus presented as agents who deliberately intimidate co-workers who do not belong to the same nationality. The accusation that Alfonso's discourse produces in the above excerpt seems to be justified by way of examples:

Excerpt 29: "they were close friends of the manager's"

> A mí me tocó ser supervisor y habían dos colombianos. Llegaban a las once de la mañana y se iban a la una y media de la tarde cuando supuestamente tenían que llegar a las seis de la mañana e irse a las tres y media ¿verdad? Y eran amigos íntimos del manager. Yo no había dicho nada porque vamos estábamos en un buen rollo, estábamos todo bien, pero cuando el manager le hizo un complaint a un boliviano que llegó media hora tarde después de las seis, le hizo un *complaint* por escrito al boliviano. Ahí fue cuando yo dije "bueno, tú haces complaint por media hora, pues yo voy a hacer complaint por tus dos amigos que lo que trabajan son dos horas. Si acaso tres horas y y el pago es full time" . . .

Translation

> I happened to be a supervisor and there were two Colombians. They arrived at eleven in the morning and left at half past one when they supposedly had to arrive at six in the morning and leave at half past three, right? And they were close friends of the manager's. I had not complained because we were cool, we were ok, but when the manager filed a complaint about the Bolivian guy who got to work half an hour late, he filed a written complaint about the Bolivian guy. That's when I said "hold on, you file a complaint for half an hour, alright then, I am going to file a complaint about your two friends who work two hours. Maybe three and they get a full time salary" . . .

In excerpt 29, Alfonso details a work routine in another setting where two of his Colombians coworkers used to turn up late for work and still received a full-time job salary. They, as Alfonso's passage suggests, had a close friendship with the manager whose tolerant attitude to lateness was influenced by their common nationality. What his discourse produces is the topic of partiality as a top-down practice from which his Colombian co-workers benefitted and about which Alfonso complained. As he continues to describe these vertical work interactions, he produces discourses of both empathy and derogation that exhibit, as we have seen in the previous cases of Sharon, David and Diego, polarised and antagonistic work relations. On the one hand, a discourse of empathy is accorded to the non-Colombian group which is therefore represented as the victims of arbitrary rules that placed him in the out-group and that could threaten his own job. On the other hand, by mitigating a fault committed by his Bolivian co-worker he produces a discourse of derogation through which he foregrounds and stresses the others' dishonest practices to which he nonetheless decided to turn a blind eye initially.

The negative other-representation that we saw above is also best understood within a frame of time and productivity; while Alfonso obscures the agency of his Bolivian co-worker by only alluding to the timeframe, *half an hour*, he not only foregrounds their habitual unpunctuality but their leaving early and receiving a full-time salary. In this light, Alfonso's discourse implicitly categorises the Colombian workers as unprincipled whose practices are explained by cultural ties that seemingly justify partiality and strengthen power relations that lead to exclusion. The existing antagonism that Alfonso describes above by alluding to *your two friends* can still be further examined in the following excerpt and that figures as an organising topic that nevertheless backgrounds an economic phenomenon that transcends the construct of nationality.

Excerpt 30: "the problem is that they are friends of yours"

> Entonces yo le dije a él "el problema es que son amigos tuyos son de tu misma ciudad en Colombia. son casi de tu mismo barrio y son amigos desde allá", ¿me entiendes? . . .

Translation

> So I told him "the problem is that they are friends of yours from your own city in Colombia they are almost from the same neighbourhood and you have been friends since then", you know what I mean? . . .

Alfonso's short passage intends to re-enact his confrontation with the manager and narrates how he stood up against what he described as an injustice. Social capital in Alfonso's account is depicted as problematic since, as he has implied above, it generates partiality that he emphasises through the repetitive use of a possessive pronoun such as *yours, your*. In the interview, Alfonso told me that after a meeting with hospital administrators and the manager, he had one of the Colombian workers fired due to his recurrent unpunctuality whilst he helped the other stay and work a full-time schedule. He later learnt that they had three jobs in different sites across London, which, as Alfonso acknowledged in the interview, explains their lateness. In this sense, there is an interesting aspect. Having two or three jobs, as we were able to see in the previous chapter and above in

Miguel's and Diego's account respectively, is a practice found in migrants from many nationalities working in the service sector and it points to the migrant division of labour in London (Wills et al. 2009; Alberti et al. 2013). In addition, it must be noted that service sector jobs are usually underpaid, outsourced and require that employees work unsociable hours or commute by bus long distances from one work site to another (Ruhs and Anderson 2010; McIlwaine 2016).

The above observation is not to delegitimise Alfonso's view, as I did not have access to the experiences described here or more empirical evidence that could have greatly enriched an analysis of his experiences. It is rather an attempt to draw attention to a material reality that mainly affects a working-class migrant population of various nationality groups and to shed light on the economic and work conditions in which they find themselves in a receiving society that has been documented to show signs of growth in low paid-work (see Wills et al. 2009; Berg 2020). As stated above, this problem among fellow migrants has been studied and has been found in other contexts such as the USA (see Mahler 1995). However, this socioeconomic reality does not figure as the organising topic of Alfonso's discourse but what dominates his account is the construct of nationality. In order to pursue this last statement in the interview I asked him whether he thought that the geographic origin of people influences these interactions.

Excerpt 31: "I don't like Latinos, living with them? Not a chance!"

> Estoy cien por ciento seguro porque yo lo he vivido aquí. Por eso es que a mí no me gusta trabajar con latinos ni vivir con latinos. No ¿vivir yo? En la casa donde estoy viviendo, todos son ingleses ¿verdad? A mí no me gustan los latinos, ¿vivir con ellos? No, vamos, ni que me paguen. ¿Trabajar con ellos? Ni que me vuelvan a pagar otra vez, ¿me entendiste? . . .

Translation

> I am hundred percent sure because I have experienced it here. That's why I neither like working with Latinos nor living with Latinos. No, live with? In the house where I live, everybody is English, right? I don't like Latinos, living with them? Not a chance! Working with them? Not in my lifetime, you got me? . . .

Alfonso's answer to my question encapsulates two different domains of his social life such as his private life and his work life. The affective distance that his discourse exhibits in the repetitive negative use of the verb *like* seems to be informed by a discourse of evidentiality (see van Dijk 2006); that is, the hyperbolically emphasised negative experiences he describes he has had in the workplace with Colombian co-workers provide a justification for him to dissociate from them socially. Nevertheless, his account seems to typify Latinos and ascribe negative attributes to them indiscriminately. For instance, the implied comparison between the English and Latinos embedded in Alfonso's discourse produces a topos of culture to explain and contrast values and practices that define a particular social behaviour of what is conceived of as a clearly delineated and homogenised cultural group. Such comparison was also found in David's discourse about the Latino manager whose negative actions were emphasised by obscuring what seemed dishonest practices of the English manager and, in both comparisons, we find a negative generalised categorisation of Latinos.

In light of the above, a striking feature in both Alfonso's and David's representations of Latinos is their attempt to create a common-ground understanding of what Latinos are like. By turning to implications and rhetorical questions that aim to account for a seemingly defining ethos, I, as a Latin American researcher, was supposed to recognise how Latin Americans carry themselves, *"you know what we latinos are like"*, *"I don't like Latinos/ living with them? not a chance! Or working with them not in my lifetime, you got me?"* Therefore, the attitudes and practices of those who have access to power positions in the specificity of their work context where they are described are made sense of through topoi of culture; assumed traits that create expectations of social interactions that background neoliberal work practices that fragment social relations among the Latin Americans involved here.

The interactions among Latin Americans that I have described and analysed so far are not limited to one single work context such as the service sector. As I said at the beginning of this chapter, their interactions can also be located in the domains of language teaching and domestic work where cultural, social and economic capital seems to be mobilised as class distinctions and differentiations among them.

4.3 Social categorisations among Latin Americans

Linda: *"they have lost money, they have never gone back to their country and hate everything"*

Linda is a Mexican immigrant who I met through a snowballing process that developed as I met more Latin Americans in London. Emails and phone calls were the means through which we communicated and agreed to meet in central London. As I have stated elsewhere (Morales-Hernández 2023), Linda moved to England in 1989 and has inhabited diverse social spaces. She grew up in Mexico City where she obtained a degree in Psychology, and before she migrated to the UK she took English-teaching courses to become an English teacher. Her reasons to leave Mexico range an intricate and complex combination of factors that aim to a forward-looking life view. Her quest for her true sexuality that could be stifled by a regulatory Mexican society was a major incentive for her to discover it abroad. Also, domestic violence figures as a major catalyst for her to leave Mexico and improve her living conditions. Furthermore, she intended to improve her English and become an English teacher in the UK. Although she reached her goal, she narrated that it was not easily achievable as she explained that cleaning was one of the first available jobs to which she had access. Before leaving Mexico, she got in touch with an Irish woman through Linda's sister and who put her in touch with a group of English-speaking friends and who would provide her with accommodation and who became her social network. At the time of the interview, she was married to an English man who was part of the group of people that had welcomed her in the UK and with whom she had a daughter.

Among the many jobs that Linda had, she narrated that she also worked for other people from Latin America whose attitudes she depicted through a negative light.

Excerpt 32: "Latinos were my worst bosses"

> Los latinos fueron mis peores jefes. Principalmente dos de ellos ¿no? Un chileno. Él me mandaba a las oficinas de gobierno en español ¿no? Y él me pagaba ocho libras por hora y un día me manda con los invoice, y él cobraba treinta y cinco libras por hora para empezar, y él me pagaba ocho y de ahí me descontaba . . .

Translation

> Latinos were my worst bosses mainly two of them, right? A Chilean. He would send me to the government offices in Spanish, right? And he paid me eight pounds an hour, and one day he sent me with the invoices, and he charged thirty-five pounds an hour, and he paid me eight from which he made deductions . . .

In this account, Linda retrospectively assesses her experience working for a Chilean person who used to run a Spanish teaching school that offered language classes to London-based companies to which Linda was sent. As we have seen in the previous accounts of David and Diego, the organising topic of Linda's account is also that of deceit. This lack of transparency is instantiated by the underpayment that Linda reports she received and from which on top of that she was deducted. In this light, Linda's discourse categorises her boss as abusive and dishonest. As the interview went on, Linda recounts her experience with an Argentinian woman whose needs differ from those of Linda.

Excerpt 33: "I am doing you a favour by giving you a job"

> Ella me pidió que que siempre hablara español con la niña lo cual yo no quería porque yo quería aprender inglés ¿no? Este me pagaba, creo que me pagaba tres libras por día. No me acuerdo. O sea, no por día, por hora. Una cosa ridícula y vivía fuera de Londres.O sea, yo tenía que viajar un montón para ir a su casa y nunca me entendió que lo que me pagaba no me servía. Que además yo le estaba haciendo el favor de enseñarle a su hija español o sea igual ¿no? Y me contestó de una forma así de que "te estoy haciendo un favor de darte un trabajo" y..no sé . . .

Translation

> She asked me to speak in Spanish to the little girl which I did not want to because I wanted to learn English, right? She paid me, I think three pounds a day. I can't remember. I mean not a day, an hour. Something ridiculous and I lived outside London. I mean, I had to travel a long distance to go to her house and besides she did not understand that I was doing her a favour by teaching her daughter Spanish I mean and she said that "I am doing you a favour by giving you a job" . . .

Linda's account exhibits an interesting interaction with her Argentinian employee whose daughter Linda looked after and to whom she was asked to speak in Spanish, which seemingly Linda reluctantly did due to her interest in learning English. It must be noted that her reluctance to speak Spanish in England as well as other language ideologies that will continue to come up in her account and subsequently in that of Mayra will be, nonetheless, pursued in the following chapter in more depth due to the focus of analysis of this chapter. As to this interaction, the topic of language interest and job needs are foregrounded as the site of struggle that is redolent of two-way hierarchical attitudes from both parties. Through the phrase *I was doing her a favour by teaching her daughter Spanish*, Linda indexes her language capital as a valuable asset that empowers her and that, although is presented as underestimated, is needed by her employer. The latter is in turn discursively placed in a position of power as the individual who can give Linda a job but is discursively categorised as unappreciative and condescending, *she said "I am doing you a favour by giving you a job"*. The description that Linda provides is consequently illustrative of conflictive power relations as the interactants in the event narrated seem to exploit the language and economic needs each of them sought to meet.

In addition to the injustices and tensions that Linda narrates, her migration experience also instantiates a process of declassing that to some extent resembles that of David as she was also undocumented for a time due to her overstaying her passport. This led her to job exploitation in hotels and forced her to leave the country to re-enter it through France. After this, she and her now husband decided to get married and she no longer risked entering on an irregular migration status. She also recounted that once they were married, they faced economic problems and thus decided to move to Mexico and teach English in language schools and universities. Furthermore, her story also echoes that of Alfonso, Miguel and Diego in the sense that the jobs available to newcomers are at the lower echelons of society or are found in a context of informality which are usually poorly paid (McGregor 2007). However, her experience contrasts with those above due to two main interrelated elements. The first one is her language capital aspiration that appears as one of the main drives to be in the UK and not necessarily an economic one as she said she did not have to remit money back to her family. The second one pertains to her and her husband's moving to Mexico. Linda stated that relocating their lives to Mexico in order for them to teach English for three years enabled them to save more than enough money and return to England where they for a time would live in her mother-in-law's house. In this sense, there are social as well as language capital and socioeconomic class differences that index a reality that reflects neither the pressing economic living conditions nor the precarity that an irregular migration status may bring about and in which other migrants such as Miguel, Diego, Irma and David found themselves respectively. This allows us to gain insight into and reminds us of the material conditions of migrants' lives (see Block 2017; 2018) since they exhibit both how migration is experienced and how social relations may be narrated and constructed.

The interview with Linda went on and I asked her about her relationship with more Latin Americans and her views on their presence in London.

Excerpt 34: "they are very unpleasant"

> Mi relación con gente de latinoamérica mmm. Veo un grupo de gente latinoamericana que vino con aspiraciones de hacer mucho dinero, que han trabajado como burro enormemente, que han perdido la salud, han perdido el dinero, nunca se han regresado a su país y odian todo ¿no? Y son muy nefastos. Veo a otro grupo de gente que vino con aspiraciones, que no aprendió el idioma, pero que, aunque no aprendió el idioma ha luchado y han logrado y tienen algo. Tienen su casita, que es gente que ya conocí hace diez años cuando yo comprendí que ya podía hablar español sin tener miedo a no aprender ingles, ¿no? Y es gente muy positiva, muy luchadora y es gente que, aunque no se ha podido integrar, no es gente que se esté odiando el sistema. Como si el sistema no es el que no les permitiera ser, ¿me entiendes?

> Su recuento continúa.

> y hay otro grupo de gente que es mucho más positiva, que viene con aspiraciones, que lucha como loco por esas aspiraciones. Entre ellas conozco una dentista colombiana que fue la primera odontóloga latina habilitada para trabajar aquí y tiene su consultorio en la calle de los dentistas más famosos. La pobre, o sea, su renta la está matando y los gastos, pero esa gente que viene enfocada, de esa gente que hace todo lo posible por quedarse en ese nivel [académico], o sea, yo podría decir que yo fui así . . .

Translation

My relationship with people from Latin America mmm. I see a group of Latin American people who came here with money-making dreams, who have worked like an ox and who have lost their health, they have lost money, they have never gone back to their country and hate everything, right? And they are very unpleasant. I see another group of people who came with aspirations, who did not learn the language but despite that, they have fought and have managed to have their house. They are people that I met ten years ago when I understood that I could speak English without fearing not to learn English, right? And they are very positive people, very hard-working and they are people who even though haven't been able to integrate, they are not people who hate the system. Like it was the system that did not allow them to live, you know what I mean?

Her account goes on.

And there is another group of people that is much more positive. They come with aspirations and fight with energy for those aspirations I know a Colombian dentist who was the first Latina dentist licensed to work here and she has her office in a street where the most famous dentists are. The poor soul, I mean, the rent and the expenses are killing her, but those kinds of people who are focused and that do anything to keep their [academic] level, I mean, I would say I was like that . . .

As we can see in interview excerpt 34, Linda demarcates three different groups of Latin Americans in London. The first group is referred to as people whose economic aspirations seem to be the main drive to relocate their lives but whose plans of economic advancement despite their industriousness seem to have fallen through. The other two groups are depicted in a more positive light. The second is characterised as mentally positive, hardworking people who despite speaking no English still have managed to become property owners while the third one with whom she identifies is depicted as people who have set their mind to achieve their clearly identified academic and professional goals.

In light of the above, the discursive subdivision of groups she made marks the group in excerpt 34 as losers. Their losses, *they have lost their health, they have lost their money,* are accentuated by the simile, *they have worked like an ox,* which illustrates that her industriousness was to no avail. Furthermore, this simile carries a heavy cultural meaning with an implicit top-down categorisation. An ox is culturally depicted as a beast of burden that although works incessantly is also forced into heavy labour usually by means of a yoke. Through such a simile in this context, Linda seems to subsume both industrious behaviours and relegate them to a social hierarchy of symbolic subjugation. Additionally, her lexicalisation and the indicative tense of her statements *"they hate everything"*, *"they are very unpleasant"*, characterises the behaviour of those Latinos to whom she refers as factually disagreeable. Thus, Linda's discursive choices exhibits an evaluative social distance that places them beneath her at the same time that, as we saw above, evidences an ideology of neoliberalism in which the individual self-constructs as successful or unsuccessful.

The depictions of the participants' experiences with more Latin Americans that I have so far analysed shed light on interactions that seem to be accounted for by topoi of culture and by ideologies that focus on the achievements or failures of the individual. These interactions also point to social class differentiations and stratification among Latin Americans that could be further probed outside the settings narrated above as I now introduce Mayra from Ecuador and then Jazmin from Colombia.

Mayra: *"that's simply ignorance"*

I was able to get in touch with Mayra through another participant from Ecuador who I met in the Elephant and Castle area. Mayra and I met in a cafe in central London and although she greeted me effusively, she did not seem to open up as the interview progressed. Her attitude can be explained by the limitations that a one-time encounter can produce as she and I had not interacted with each other before the interview and thus I must acknowledge that this limits a more in-depth analysis of her discourse. However, her life story contains relevant information that can be linked to my observations and visits to various sites in London during fieldwork and that I will incorporate in this discussion to understand her discourse and situate it within a larger group of people with whom she interacts.

Mayra's migration to the UK was motivated by her husband's need for professional development. He holds a degree in architecture that he studied in England where they have now lived for four years. Mayra recounts how her initial experience in the UK led her to depression due to both a lack of a social network and the fact that her husband would spend most of the day at work. She eventually realised there was a presence of Latin Americans coming from Spain mainly and with whom she would get involved. She would fill in forms in English and would work as a translator for them, work that was free of charge as in the interview she stated that she did it as a contribution to her community. At the time of the interview, she held a part-time job at the embassy of her country in London and had her own business that I will describe below.

Due to her voluntary work experience mentioned above, Mayra said she also befriended many people who told them how people from their own community treated them. She narrated how a friend from Latin America living with another Latin American woman used to rent her one side of the bed for fifty pounds a week. Mayra refers to this attitude as follows:

Excerpt 35: "The ones who segregate you are those from your own community"

> Los británicos no te segregan. Los que te segregan son los mismos de tu comunidad y había como muchas personas que querían aprovecharse de ellos . . .

Translation

> The British do not segregate yo. The ones who segregate you are those from your own community and there were like a lot of people who wanted to take unfair advantage of them . . .

Mayra, in excerpt 35, refers to segregationist attitudes among Latin Americans as in the interview she said that recently arrived Latin Americans are subject to exploitation and abuse by their same community members to whom they initially resort for help. She categorises them as discriminatory and sly, *segregate* and *take unfair advantage*, which are practices that her use of the generic object and possessive pronoun, *you* and *your*, in the present tense interestingly presents them as facts. I asked Mayra why she thought this problem happens, and in the following excerpts we see how Mayra positions herself and categorise other Latin Americans.

Excerpt 36: "The people perish from lack of knowledge"

> Es por falta de conocimiento. El pueblo perece por falta de conocimiento. Es muy claro que las personas vienen acá y piensan que, porque les falta el idioma, no les queda otra que ser humillados que no les queda otra que dejarse someter por otras personas que ven en ellos una oportunidad de enriquecerse o de hacer dinero extra. Es simplemente ignorancia . . .

Translation

> It is due to lack of knowledge. The people perish from lack of knowledge. It is very clear that the people who come here think that because they can't speak the language, they don't have a choice but to be humiliated that they don't have a choice but to be subjected by other people who see in them an opportunity to become rich or make extra money. That's simply ignorance . . .

This very categorical explanation about the problem of abuse among Latin Americans that Mayra gives points to what she claims is the main core of the issue. Ignorance comes up as the organising topic of her discourse that is foregrounded by a noteworthy feature of her account such as the phrase, *the people perish from lack of knowledge.* The latter leads us to pose the question, where does it come from? It appears to be a biblical reference from the book of Hosea 4:6 where *the people* are cut off by their god as punishment for rejecting knowledge. In other words, their punishment is a consequence that they have brought upon themselves. In Mayra's account, such phrase instantiates an interdiscursive practice that promotes a view of a hierarchised social order and functions as an argumentation strategy of generalization. That is, she resorts to it as a maxim that is proverbially to explicate a behaviour and the lack of knowledge which is allegedly typical and by extension predictable of the people with whom she indirectly associates Latinos. Interestingly her account does not concentrate on the abusers of the practices above but on those who suffer them and who exhibit cognitive and linguistic characteristics presented as deficiencies that the lexical item *lack* evidences. In this light, Mayra's explanation places the responsibility on those who suffer exploitation as a result of their ignorance and thus describes such asymmetrical interactions as facts, truth values that she emphasises through an adverbial of manner such as *simply*.

In addition to this representation of Latinos, there also seems to be another non-linguistic aspect that may influence how Mayra voices her opinion and that to some extent resembles the self-presentation of Marcia and Karla in the previous chapter. That is, a socioeconomic position from which Mayra speaks as well as an ideology on which I will elaborate below as I describe what her work involved. As her account goes on, Mayra touches upon why in her view people from Latin America are not culturally visible and politically organised to claim their rights like the Muslim community in London.

Excerpt 37: "They come with a submissive attitude, well, beyond submissive"

> La mayoría de los latinos que se asentaron aquí son latinos que ya tienen formado su carácter en su país de origen. La mayoría entonces tú sabes que como latinos, hubo una época en la que se traía como ese yugo ¿no? La esclavitud de, de haber sido conquistados y entonces yo considero que muchos de esos latinos vinieron acá y vienen con la actitud de que aquí están los patrones, aquí están los reyes, los que nos conquistaron. Entonces, vienen agachados ¿me entiendes lo que te digo? Vienen con una actitud, ser sumisos, bueno, con una actitud de más allá de ser sumiso . . .

Translation

> Most of the Latinos who settled down here are Latinos whose character was formed in their home countries. Most of them then you know that as Latinos, there was an age in which there was like that bondage, right? Slavery to to have been conquered so I believe that many of those Latinos came here and come with the attitude that here is where the bosses are, here is where the kings are, the ones who conquered us. So, they bow and scrape, you know what I mean? They come with a submissive attitude, well, beyond submissive . . .

As we have seen in excerpt 37 Mayra produces a categorical assertion about the defining behaviour of the Latinos to whom she refers and which has prevented them from establishing themselves as a politically present community. She characterises them as subservient, and she accomplishes the above characterisations by the argumentative strategies of the topos of culture and the topos of history as a lesson since her discourse is located in spatiotemporal frames such as their geographic origin that interacts with the memory of colonialism in Latin America. As to the topos of culture, it is employed to categorise most Latinos' behaviour as a fixed attribute, *whose character was formed in their home countries*, explained by their geographic origin.

As to the topos of history, it is introduced by the assumed socioculturally shared knowledge in *you know*, whereby she not only intends to create a common ground with me as a Latin American researcher aware of this historical event, but justify her previous claim and support her subsequent negative categorisation of Latinos as subjects. Her word choices *bondage, slavery* and *conquered* are illustrative of the topos of history, but they also carry a denotational meaning that intertwines with what Bourdieu (1986) and Block (2017; 2018) have referred to as the embodied manifestation of habitus and body language respectively contained in *bow and scrape*. This last phrase indexes a negatively evaluated behaviour since it acts in opposition to the positively evaluated demeanour of holding one's head up resembling confidence and, in this sense, this way of behaving ascribed to Latinos exploits the idea of servitude and diffidence that the adjective *submissive* further underscores.

In light of the above, Mayra's categorisation of Latinos points to a particular social space and lifestyle from which she makes sense of the attitudes she evaluates. As noted above and at the time of the interview, Mayra worked part-time at the embassy of her country and said that she had her own business which enabled her to travel to other European countries. According to her description, her work consisted of training people how to obtain their financial freedom and it aimed to recruit people who are willing to mentor themselves as well as go the extra mile. Additionally, she also described that her social network encompassed people who she called entrepreneurial and who would have monthly meetings in different venues across London. As part of my fieldwork, I was able to visit two of these meeting points, which were conference rooms in hotels in central and north London and thus I was able to talk and interact with the attendees and potential study participants. Most of them were Latin Americans who either had recently arrived from Spain or had been working in the service sector as cleaners. They were being encouraged to become part of a network-marketing group to widen their contacts and thus sell dietary supplements, the type of job that is commonly known as pyramids and that, as I was able to learn through my conversations with them, promotes the financial responsibilisation of the individual.

In this context, Mayra's account seems to be illustrative of two intertwined aspects. The first one points to a relative socioeconomic position that, akin to

Linda, allows her to gain social distance from the Latinos who she evaluates. The second one is the ideology of neoliberalism in which the individual is held accountable for their own success or failure and which comes through her identity as an entrepreneurial individual. As the interview progresses, she subsequently attributes people characteristics that are also worthy of scrutiny.

Excerpt 38: "they feel they are the working class"

> Un ejemplo, los ecuatorianos que estaban en España dos o tres meses, te hablaban con un español más marcado que los mismos españoles. Es una falta de identidad, es un miedo, es una manera de reaccionar para tratar de ser aceptados. Y eso es lo que pasa, la gente, esa generación antigua que está presente, tiene ese esos paradigmas de que se sienten tal vez menos, de que se sienten la clase trabajadora . . .

Translation

> For example, the Ecuadorians that spent two or three months in Spain spoke with an accent that was stronger than the Spanish themselves it's a lack of identity it's fear it's a way to react to try to be accepted and that's what happens that old generation that is present has that those paradigms that perhaps they think little of themselves that they feel they are the working class . . .

As an attempt to bolster her previous claim of Latinos as subservient and insecure, Mayra provides an example that aims to contextualise the behaviour of her countrymen who she evaluates. However, the level and degree of detail in which she describes this outgroup exemplifies a discourse of negative other representation that categorises them as linguistically inauthentic and socially diffident individuals explained by their socioeconomic class. In this manner we see the intersection of two ideologies. By employing the phrase, *spoke with an accent that was stronger that the Spanish themselves*, Mayra's discourse conjures up what seems an ideology of linguistic authenticity. As we saw in chapter 2.4, Woolard (2008; 2016) has explored such an ideology in which speech varieties are perceived to be socially and geographically rooted in a territory so that they can have value. This means that the authenticity of a speech variety rests in its local origin where ways of speaking are identifiable as legitimate and natural (Woolard, 2016). In this sense the "strong accent" to which Mayra refers, on the one hand, points to a seemingly iconic way of speaking imagined as the Spanish accent. On the other hand, such a reference delegitimises their countrymen's way of speaking by suggesting they do not sound authentic, and represents them as linguistically insecure individuals with an inferiority complex who faked an accent so they did not stand out and thus allegedly went culturally unnoticed.

Additionally, Mayra's account is informed by an ideology of social class. Through the demonstrative pronoun, *that*, conjoined with *old generation*, Mayra's account exhibits a social distance reflected in an ageist discourse. Subsequently she attributes them cognitive characteristics and ways of behaving that, although she intended to hedge, still categorise them as an outgroup, *those paradigms that perhaps they think little of themselves*, whereby she reveals contrasting social values evidenced in *they feel they are the working class*, and thus she positions them beneath her. Her account, in this light, confirms what other researchers have drawn attention to: class distinction appears as a relevant construct in the choice of and dispositions of social relations in migrant groups. In his work on Latinos in London, Block (2006; 2008) also analysed both how a well-educated Colombian immigrant led a middle-class life. Even though his work was located in the service sector, Block's participant's social class affected his work relations and sense of place since his participant was never comfortable in his workplace or with his colleagues. The class-based discourse and attitude that Mayra openly discloses is also illustrative of a hierarchical sense of place and space and it points to ways of behaving with which she disassociates herself and thus her discourse draws social boundaries. As the interview went on, we touched upon how migration trajectories could shape people's worldview and I asked her whether she perceived a difference between Latin American people coming to the UK from Spain and those directly from Latin American countries.

Excerpt 39: "he comes in search of benefits"

> El que viene de España, la mayoría vienen a buscar protección del gobierno. Viene en busca de los beneficios que da el gobierno. El que viene de latinoamérica no porque nosotros no sabemos que existe eso en Latinoamérica. No existe protección del gobierno. Entonces, como no estuviste expuesto a esa información, vas al otro país y ni sabes que hay beneficios. Te enteras porque alguien te cuenta, pero, ¿así como voy de latinoamérica en busca de beneficios en UK? No. Los que vienen de españa sí, porque Europa, por mucho tiempo, ha sido bastante paternalista, no tanto como este [país] pero han sido. Entonces, te acostumbras y vienes a buscar lo mismo . . .

Translation

> The one who comes from Spain, most of them are looking for protection that the government provides. He comes in search of benefits that the government gives. He who comes from Latin America doesn't because we don't know that there is such a thing in Latin America. Protection from the government does not exist. So, since you're not exposed to that information, you move to another country and you don't even know there are benefits. You learn about them because someone tells you, but say do I move from Latin America in search of benefits in the UK? We don't do that. The ones coming from Spain do because Europe for a long time has been very paternalistic, not as much as this [country] but it has been. So, you get used to it and come in search of the same . . .

The topic of benefits in the UK has been widely promoted by media discourses as a problem. Benefits are allegedly an incentive that attracts enormous numbers of European immigrants who are escaping unemployment in their country of origin and purportedly expect the government to provide them with money, care and housing. As we saw in Marcia's and Karla's accounts in the previous chapter, such discourses have contributed to the representation of immigrants as lazy and dishonest since they are in the UK to exploit the local society's welfare. In this light, expressions such as the *one who comes from Spain comes in search of benefits* and *we don't*, bring about a discourse of polarisation in which Mayra clearly contrasts values that distinguish them from her collectivity and that unfolds in a discourse of neoliberalism. That is, this us vs them representation is further enhanced by, *we don't know that such a thing exists, you're not exposed to that information,* through which she locates herself with an ingroup coming to the UK directly from Latin America. By doing this, she distances herself from those who have been in Spain and who she tacitly categorises as immoral since it is suggested that they relocate their lives in full knowledge of and with the goal of obtaining benefits. Mayra, in this sense, reproduces a discourse of neoliberalism; the Latin Americans to whom she refers seek to depend on the state and are thus implicitly depicted, as Brown (2005: 42) has stated, as lacking "the ability to provide for their own needs and service their own ambitions".

The generalisation that Mayra makes in excerpt 39, nonetheless, provokes scepticism about people's working conditions and motivations to relocate their lives and that should be contextualised. In chapter 3, we saw the case of Miguel who moved from Spain and who worked in a restaurant and a storage house six days a week, which contests the view that Mayra expresses categorically. That is, Miguel did not depend on benefits and these were not his main motivations to move to England since, as I learnt through my conversations with him, he needed to remit money back to his family in Venezuela. Furthermore, other studies document that 89% of all Latin Americans in the UK are employed and that among those who came from Spain in recent years, around 22,000 people, 6% claimed an out of work benefit (McIlwaine and Bunge 2016). Additionally, Mayra's discourse may also suggest a degree of ambivalence. Latin American people who were part of her network, as stated above, had arrived in London after having lived in Spain for years and thus it is worth asking whether they fall into the same category. The insight that we can gain into this categorisation of Latin American immigrants is that the above views and experiences index different socioeconomic conditions from which emigration and immigrations occurred and that, at the same time, seem to shape their social relations; ideologies of self-responsibilisation that are worth perusing by returning to Sharon's case.

As stated above, Sharon is of Colombian origin and had been in England for more than twenty years. At the time of the interview, she had an export bussiness and was part of a network marketing company to which she recruited other Latin Americans. She said that working with them presented her with some challenges, one of which was to change their employee-like mentality to an entrepreneur one and convince them that such a change requires effort and time to improve oneself. In the next excerpt, we can analyse the ideology that underlies her discourse.

Excerpt 40: "if you haven't got good results, it's no one's fault, but yours only because you haven't made an effort"

> el trabajar aquí es diferente porque es trabajar consigo mismo ¿si me entiende? O sea, aquí no tienes un jefe, aquí tienes alguien, tú tienes un mentor, pero tú no tienes un jefe ¿sí? Y si tú no tienes resultados, no es culpa de nadie. Simplemente es culpa tuya porque no has hecho un esfuerzo suficiente. Hacemos un plan de trabajo, pero siempre y cuando funciona si tú lo pones a prueba ¿me entiendes? Si tú lo ejecutas, pero si no, no. Hay. O sea, la gente también está acostumbrada al trabajo fácil, al trabajo mecánico, al trabajo de que te doy cinco [pounds] por esto y tú me das tanto, al trabajo fácil, el esfuerzo se pierde . . .

Translation

> Work here is different because you work with yourself, you know what I mean? I mean you haven't got a boss here you've got someone, you've got a mentor, but you haven't got a boss, right? And if you haven't got good results, it's no one's fault, but yours only because you haven't made an effort. We lay out a work plan, but it works if you try it, you know what I mean? If you put it into practice, but if you don't, it doesn't. There is. I mean, people are used to easy money, mechanical work, the type of work where you get five [pounds] in exchange for what I give you, easy work, there is no effort . . .

In excerpt 40, Sharon's discourse describes the activities that characterise her work and points to an individual's expectations and responsibilities. On the one hand, the phrase *work with yourself* places the invidual as the object of one's work and who is to improve themselves in a work environment with no hierarchies, which is suggested by the phrase *you haven't got a boss*. On the other hand, her discourse indexes an economic elite-promoted ideology. The individual is placed within a bussiness, goal-oriented environment, *results*, in which success or failure are not only outcomes for which they are held responsible but derived from hard work as implied in *it's no one's fault but yours only*. Furthermore, the idea of self-responsibilisation that Sharon's discourse promotes is foregrounded through the implicit construction of a rational individual, *we lay out a plan*, who anticipates and predicts an outcome of their own making, *it works if you try it*. In this sense, her discourse points to what von Mises stated (2007: 290): "the entrepreneur is always a speculator. His success or failure depends on the precisión of his prediction about uncertain events. If he fails in his understanding of what it is to come, he is doomed". That is, Sharon's discourse categorises an individual as an entrepreneur who is the architect of their destiny.

In addition, Sharon's discourse not only points to desirable characteristics of an entrepreneur, but it employs a discriminatory categorisation about other Latin Americans who, as mentioned before, she recruits to her network marketing job by stating what type of people they are not. The social values and attitude of those people accustomed to what she called *an easy job* are implicitly contrasted with those of the figure of the entrepreneur in that the latter is a risk-taking individual; that is, those who are used to getting a salary in exchange for their work are not entrepreneurs. The implication derived from this discourse that delegitimises their work choices is that they do not know how to deal with uncertain economic conditions. In this light, the self-responsibilisation and entrepreneurship discourse that Sharon reproduces hierarchises and discriminates against other Latin Americans; categorisations in which, as we will see below, social class issues also matter.

Jazmin: *"For me, the connection with Latinos is always important"*

As I previously have noted, NGOs were sites that I visited and talked to volunteers and staff in order to invite people to participate in this study. Jazmin volunteered and we met in a cafe near her workplace in central London. Jazmin was born in Colombia and has been in England for nearly thirteen years. She currently works for a concierge that promotes tourism to Latin America. In Colombia, she would work for a travel agency and she came to England to better her English. After a year in London, she met and married an English man with whom she had a child. Unfortunately, their marriage failed due to domestic violence that she experienced for one and a half year. I will return to this experience in the next chapter. She managed to redo her degree in tourism as her previous college degree was not recognised in the UK and, at the time of the interview, she was about to finish her MA in Transport Management. She said that she frequently becomes nostalgic of Colombia and that she identifies with Latinos.

Excerpt 41: "where I dance salsa, there are no many Latinos"

> Para mí, la conexión con los latinos siempre es importante, estar conectada de alguna manera. Trato de ir a eventos, a donde bailo salsa no hay muchos latinos porque a donde yo voy son como clases diferentes, son como diferentes estilos de salsa. Entonces, no hay muchos . . .

Translation

> For me, the connection with Latinos is always important, to be connected in one way or another. I try to go to events, where I dance salsa, there are no many Latinos because the places I go to there are like different lessons, they are like different salsa styles so there aren't many . . .

In this account, Jazmin narrates the relevant role that her ties with Latin American people play in organising her social life in London. However, it is interesting to see that her connection and identification with Latinos, as she put it, is mediated by an activity, *I dance salsa*, rather than a direct interaction with them, which is explained by the little presence of Latinos in the places that she visits. As her account went on, she mentioned that she is aware of places and events such as the Latin American annual festival in the Elephant and Castle area where she has interacted with more Latinos.

Excerpt: "they don't have a good education"

> ese tipo de eventos no. Ya no me gusta, es muy lleno de gente y a veces la gente es grosera. No es la mejor gente en términos de que, de pronto no tienen educación, no se comportan de una manera que uno como que eso no me identifico. Me identifico más con gente como yo que ha estudiado ¿me entiende? . . .

Translation

> I don't like that type of events anymore. It's overcrowded and sometimes people are rude. They are not the best people in terms of, they don't have a good education, they do not bear themselves in a way that, like, I do not identify with that. I identify more with people like me who have studied, you know what I mean? . . .

As Jazmin continues to explain her affective distance with the festivals in that area, she draws a symbolic boundary through which she demarcates a social space inhabited by a collectivity whose behaviours and attributes she presents as dissimilar from hers. That is, politeness appears as the organising topic of her discourse given that she brings to the fore an outgroups' differentiating behavioural characteristics, *rude, they are not the best people*, that point to social attributes and values that she implies she does not embody. As she continues her description, she resorts to the phrase, *they do not have a good education* whereby she accomplishes a social demarcation that is confirmed in the phrase *I do not identify with that*. She, nonetheless, attempted to hedge her statement by the use of *like* in order to save face but her pointing to her education capital further differentiates the outgroup by implying it is a capital they lack as the concluding rhetorical question implies.

The social differentiation that emerges through Jazmin's discourse has also been reported in other migrant groups in the UK in which cultural capital may serve as common and bonding characteristics. Ryan (2011), for instance, documented the case of educated Polish migrants who sought to form networks and social relationships with people from the same social and educational background and not necessarily from the same ethnicity or geographic origin. Interestingly Ryan's participants mobilised their education capital as a valuable and distinctive trait even in the absence of economic capital (ibid). This study along with Jazmin's social positioning resonate with what Bourdieu termed habitus, a sense of space and place on which I will elaborate below where we can peruse how Jazmin further demarcates other Latin Americans into subgroups.

Excerpt 42: "they do not, do not make a good impression"

> gente que sabe lo que es vivir acá con ese tipo de gente yo me conecto. es que aquí hay mucho latino que ha vivido toda su vida aquí que. desafortunadamente no, no dan la mejor imagen...

Translation

> People who know what to live here is like. I socialise with that type of people because here there are many latinos who have lived their entire lives here and who unfortunately, they do not, do not make a good impression...

In this very short passage, Jazmin attempts to provide a justification why she relates with a particular group of people in London. As we have seen above, she differentiates the good social behaviour of her ingroup from the outgroup by pointing to the former's cognitive properties, *people who know what to live here is like*, that distinguish them from the outgroup who are in turn implicitly categorised as lacking a type of social knowledge of what it is to live in their receiving society despite the length of their stay. The representation of Latinos in this context, nonetheless, begs the question: what does knowing how to live in the UK mean? Although we cannot address this question directly since Jazmin did not state it explicitly, we can still attempt to examine it by drawing on Bourdieu's concept of habitus.

Habitus, as we saw in chapter 1.5, refers to the physical embodiment of cultural capital "turned into a permanent disposition, a durable way of standing, speaking, walking and thereby of feeling and thinking"; it is to have a "feel for the game" (Bourdieu 1990b: 69). These characteristics are situation-based ways of behaving that are deemed either appropriate or inappropriate social practices that hinge upon the social places or spaces that particular groups of individuals build. Within this logic, Jazmin's evaluation of those Latinos with whom she does not identify produces a lower-class distinction that does not resemble her values. In addition to this, her categorisation and social demarcation goes on and is euphemistically expressed in *they do not make a good impression* whereby, as we have seen above, not only she attempts to save face and distance herself from her statement but implicitly disapproves of their behaviour. Thus, Jazmin hierarchises their social identities and attributes them qualities that seem to be informed by an ideology of a superior social class that she justifies via the capital with which her academic education provides her.

The above description is reminiscent of the relevance of class distinction in migrant groups as it suggests that their relations are stratified. Such stratification in the context of the discourses examined here reflects social values that both demarcate ingroups from outgroups and point to the multi-layered social spaces and relations that the participants evaluate and hierarchise.

Summary

In this chapter, we have seen how the participants describe their experiences working and interacting with other Latin Americans in contexts such as the service sector, language teaching, and domestic work, and outside them such as volunteer work, network marketing and cultural events. The various categorisations that the participants produce interestingly pointed to ambivalences and contradictions as well as divergent and at times conflictual interests in the social spaces in which their accounts are situated. The latter suggest work conditions and ideologies of neoliberalism that index the precarity of their jobs and depict success or failure as the sole responsibility of the individual and that also intersect with social class distinctions; views through which they vertically evaluate and demarcate their social groups from other subgroups.

Chapter 5
Latin Americans' multi-sited ideologies

5.1 Introduction

In this chapter, I concentrate on language ideologies and, in this analysis, I look at the metaphors, implications and implicatures in the participants' descriptions. I begin with an examination of a participant's accounts, Linda, which begins to provide us with a window into her perceptions of language. Firstly, I concentrate on ideologies of linguistic assimilation, which in turn will lead to an examination of ideologies of accents, followed by ideologies of authenticity. In the same section, I move on to the case of Sonia from Ecuador whose (meta) linguistic comments suggest ideologies of Standard English as well as ideologies of language superiority and assimilation, which interestingly interact with ideologies of social class and neoliberalism. Both cases will then transition to those of Victor and Andres, section 5.3, whose accounts respectively suggest neoliberal ideologies of self-disqualification and language as an added value to socioeconomic mobility. In section 5.4, Julia's, Sarah's and Jazmin's experiences point to the one nation one-language ideology in institutional sites such as hospitals, a town hall and the court. Their analysis points to the power of language associated with the social positions of the participants that in turn have faced asymmetrical power relations. In these experiences, I take into account material and symbolic characteristics of social class such as the role of social capital as well as funding cuts that have affected interpreting and translation services in state institutions. In a multilingual society that is not impregnable from a neoliberal ideology, their discourses show the relevance of language ideologies when people along with their language and economic capitals traverse national boundaries motivated by specific circumstances.

5.2 Assimilation, authenticity and superiority

Linda: *"NO, I am Turkish"*

As I noted in the introduction to this book, the use of life stories allows for the identification of complex topics and discourse units that arise in the participants' narrated migration experience. The life story of Linda is a case in point since ideologies of language began to emerge as she narrated her experience interacting and working with more Latin Americans. As we noted in the previous chapter, one of the major motivations for Linda to move to the UK was to improve her English in order to become an English teacher (see Morales Hernández 2023). Linda arrived in the UK with the help of an Irish woman who she met in Mexico and put her in touch with English-speaking friends, one of whom became her husband. Although she accomplished her goal, her trajectory towards it is illustrative of language assimilation strategies that influenced and constituted her social relations in the different social spaces where she entered. In the previous chapter, Linda talked about working with an Argentinian woman in a context where she described a reluctance to speak in Spanish, an attitude that in the following excerpt we can follow up as Linda narrates how she refused to speak in Spanish while she was taking English-language teaching certification courses.

Excerpt 43: "because I wanted to learn the language, I refused to speak Spanish for years"

> Linda: había tantos españoles estudiando en las clases estas que se la pasaban hablando español. Entonces yo decidí que yo no iba a hacer eso. Y a mí me decían "!EY! ¿por qué? Tú eres latina" y yo decía "NO, yo soy turca" ¿no? Yo siempre fui turca para ellos
>
> Daniel: ¿a poco?
>
> L: Y ya cuando ellos vieron en la lista que mi apellido era Ramírez, me mandaron a la mierda (risa) y ya nadie se me acercaba, pero fue mi forma de aprender inglés, el negarme realmente a negarme a hablar español ¿no? Hablaba inglés con mi esposo, tenía todavía el círculo de amigos de mi esposo mmm, yo seguía limpiando cuartos de hotel y como limpiaba cuartos de hotel, yo siempre traía mis audífonos escuchando bbc. Era mi forma de aprender. Entonces, precisamente por aprender el idioma, yo por años me negué a hablar español . . .

Translation

> Linda: there were many Spaniards taking those classes and they would speak Spanish. So, I decided not to do that. And they told me "HEY, why? You're *Latina*" and I would say "NO, I am Turkish" right? I was always Turkish for them
>
> Daniel: really?
>
> L: And when they saw in the student list that my surname was Hernandez, they told me to fuck off (laughter) and then nobody would come up to me, but it was my own way of learning English, to refuse to speak Spanish, right? I would speak in English with my husband, I still had my husband's circle of friends and . . . I kept cleaning hotel rooms and when I was doing the cleaning, I would always wear my headphones to listen to the BBC. That was my learning method. So, because I wanted to learn the language, I refused to speak Spanish for years . . .

In the above sequence, Linda provides a depiction of the linguistic interaction that she avoided and about which in hindsight she laughs. She also relates that she had an English-speaking circle of friends who, as stated in the interview, has proved durable. This carries interesting connotations that suggest an intricate relationship between a notion of language interference leading to an ideology of linguistic assimilation in which social capital plays a significant role. Her reported refusal to speak Spanish to the extent that she denies her geographic and cultural origin that could give her away as a Spanish speaker seems to index a valorisation of her social relations. That is, the interaction with other Spanish speakers is implied as a type of company that would allegedly be an obstacle to her learning English, which seems to indicate that her decisions to speak only English point to a common-sense ideology of linguistic assimilation. The latter, nonetheless, involves social and linguistic interaction with English speakers in a work context that Linda depicts as little conducive to a constant interaction with English to which, as her account suggests, she listened on the radio. In this vein, her work-related experience, on the one hand, resembles that of many Latin Americans working in the service sector in the sense that such a sector most of the time does not lend itself for language opportunities (McIlwaine 2016). However, on the other hand, Linda's experience contrasts with other cases and studies that document ethnic ties, family or friends from the home country as the main networks that could provide support before or after the migration experience given that her social network encompasses an English-speaking social capital (see Haug 2008; Heering et al. 2004; McIlwaine 2011). This has proven to be both influential in the development of her social relations and instrumental in the access to a particular linguistic resource. Within a logic of linguistic assimilation, Linda's social relations and language use opportunities are constructed on a linguistic capital that she aspired to obtain. In the following sequence, Linda relates her work experience in a language-teaching institute where she worked as an English teacher in London.

Excerpt 44: "I never intended that the students repeated after me"

> L: a mí una cosa que me dijeron cuando yo empecé a dar clases fue que si podía tratar de imitar un poco el acento inglés "sería un poco más conveniente ¿no?". Yo dije "sí sí lo voy a intentar" pero yo dije "por qué mierda" ¿no? Si me están dando el trabajo se joden porque o sea ellos saben que hay algo bueno que yo puedo ofrecer
>
> D: ¿entonces no cediste?
>
> L: NO ¿POR QUE? Incluso me pagaron clases de dicción y "si tú quieres dar clases de inglés" me decían "siempre tienes que tener los músculos de las mejillas arriba y como decir *hello my name is Linda*" y "siempre tienes que hablar así (modifica su postura corporal y cambia expresión facial apretando las mejillas) para hacer una mejor entonación del idioma". ¡Yo que voy a estar haciendo eso!

D: ¿pero te lo dijeron ahí?

L: ¡Ah! me lo sugirieron. Claro que me lo sugirieron y me me me sugirieron clases de dicción que tomé o sea pero me fui a tomar clases de fonética porque a fin de cuentas la irlandesa que me animó a hacer el curso y todo y ella sabía de todo eso y ella me decía "tú no te preocupes con que tu sonido fonético sea lo más cerca y lo más acertado es suficiente". Y fue suficiente y yo nunca pretendí o sea yo no puedo hacer un acento inglés, no. Yo siempre tuve problemas porque en la escuela, en mis clases siempre metía fonética y metía gramática y en mis clases de fonética, yo jamás pretendí que los alumnos repitieran tras de mi. O sea, yo siempre tenía casetes con *native speakers*.O sea, aprenden lo que tienen que aprender . . .

Translation

L: One thing that they told me when I started teaching was if I could ty to imitate the English accent a little bit "it would be a bit more convenient, right?". Then I said "yes, yes, I will try" but then I said "why the fuck should I?" right? If they are hiring me then they deal with it because I mean they know there is something good I can offer

D: so you did not give in?

L: NO, WHY? They even sponsored diction classes for me and "if you want to teach English" they would tell me "you always have to have your cheekbones up and say 'hello, my name is Linda' and you always have to speak like this (she modifies her body posture and changes her facial expression by puckering) to speak the language with a better intonation". Why on earth I would do that!

D: but, they told you to do it there?

L: Ah! They suggested it. Of course, they suggested it and they suggested that I should take diction classes that I took I mean but I took phonetics classes because in the end the Irish girl who encouraged me to take the course and whatnot and she knew all that. She would say to me "don't you worry, as long as your phonetics is as close and accurate, it will be enough" and it was enough. I never intended I mean I can't do an English accent, no. I always had problems because at the school in my classes, I would always teach phonetics and grammar and in my phonetics classes, I never intended that the students repeated after me I mean I had tapes with native speakers I mean they learn what they have to learn . . .

Here we see how Linda's accent seemed to have been regulated by a series of interconnected ideologies in different work-related situations in which an Irish colleague showed her support. Firstly, we see that speaking with an English accent that generates problems of representation by concealing the variety of accents associated with different regions and social classes among other variants, indexes a social construct in which the individual is expected to speak with the "right" accent and points to a model of linguistic authenticity. The latter reflects an ideology in which the value and legitimacy of a language must be associated with an identifiable social and geographical space to be perceived as genuine (Woolard 2016). That is, Linda's accent did not seem to have indexed the "authentic" pronunciation of what English is supposed to sound; it is not the "right" accent for the type of job she performed and that therefore had to be corrected.

What also comes forward in Linda's description in relation to the classes she had to take is both a prescription of her body language and an ideology of accent reduction. Such prescriptivism and the accent reduction ideology depict a process of linguistic purification (Blommaert 2010); that is, it is implied that she had to take diction and phonetics classes that would dispose of pollutant and foreign elements. Although Linda suggests that she did not give in to the above-mentioned attitudes and that she kept her job, as it is implied in *it was enough*, and stated in the interview, a number of studies about language ideologies confirm that the latter can be a mechanism of social discrimination and job selectivity (see Lipi-Green 2012; Piller 2016). In previous studies, for instance, about the relationship between accent and employability in the UK, Ashley (2010: 722) reported that a group of lawyers of ethnic minorities educated in private institutions faced minimum discrimination in the job market since they spoke with the "right" accent (cited in Timming 2016: 412). Similarly, Creese and Wiebe (2009) and Garrido and Codó (2017) have documented the accent discrimination experiences that well-educated immigrants from sub- Saharan and African countries have encountered in both Canada and Barcelona, which affected their ability to become employed. These accounts index homogenisation processes that ideologically delegitimise other language variants and their speakers and may economically affect their lives in a context of migration.

In light of the above, it is also interesting to see how Linda implicitly assesses her own accent when she reports that she did not intend to model pronunciation in class. Her description seems to suggest a teaching practice that promotes the ideology of the native speaker in which the pronunciation of the latter acts as the only language model and norm to follow (Holliday 2005; see Jenkins 2009). It must be noted that audio material is used as support materials and that is widely employed in language classes; however, in this context it is worth posing the questions, why did Linda not intend to model the pronunciation? Moreover, what do the phrases *I always had problems* and *they learn what they have to learn* index? The event narrated in this way implies that Linda appeared to have given in to an ideology that disqualified her accent and qualified it as inauthentic. Taken all together, the ideologies that Linda's experiences evidence are reminiscent of what we discussed in chapter 2.4, that language ideologies are contextual, multiple and necessarily built from the sociocultural experience and orientation of the speaker (Kroskrity 2004). Likewise, it is pertinent to take on board what Bourdieu (1977) stated as to social judgements and valorisations of language, "speech always owes a major part of its value to the value of the person who utters it". Ideologies of language are not strictly associated with language but with the search and exercise of power (Woolard 1988).

Linda's recounted experience shows normative language regimes that occur in many parts of the world (see Piller 2016; 2001). That is, her account points to what is also known as native speakerism in which so called native speakers of English are benefited in both English and non-English speaking countries over teachers who are non-native speakers. Indeed this is problematic due to its discriminatory effects and it should be a reminder that no accent is neither better than nor superior to another one.

However, even though the description above is implicitly presented through a negative light, the prescriptions that Linda relates should also be viewed from a different angle and consider other factors that may allow us to understand Linda's complex socioeconomic needs and experience better. Linda found herself in an institutional context that offered language classes to a diverse group of people. They were from different countries and class backgrounds whose language needs, aspirations, ideas about language and expectations in a receiving society should also be taken on board when analysing Linda's decision to not model pronunciation. In addition, we should not lose sight of the social relevance and value that society and people attribute to certain language variants, which matter in the every day social experience of individuals. That is, although problematic and as an ideological process that often has a gate-keeping function that should be challenged, people and institutions still place some language variants and accents in a higher social scale. In this logic, Linda's accent reduction experience by taking phonetics classes and her intent to not model pronunciation in an institutional setting also suggest how she negotiated her own social position, which was not entirely conducive to a negative result given that she was able to keep her job. The language ideologies so far examined illustrate experiences of social hierarchisation and valorisation that, in order to understand them better, it is necessary to keep scrutinising them in contextualised situations where different notions of social class and alignments emerge.

Sonia: *"you have to keep up appearances"*

As I have mentioned in previous chapters, I visited a number of events and places in London such as the Elephant and Castle area where there is a shopping centre that houses restaurants and coffee shops in which many Latin Americans congregate to socialise, find out about job offers or learn about flats to rent. In one of these coffee shops, I met Sonia who I introduced in the introduction to this book. Sonia is a black woman who was born in Ecuador but moved to Spain with her family at age of sixteen due to economic problems in their home country, and lived in Spain for more than 11 years. As her life progressed she married a Spanish man and in 2009 she and her husband decided to come to the UK as their economic situation in Spain was not promising. Since their arrival, she has done various jobs such as volunteer work for law firms and NGO's that work closely with Latin American people in London. Before the interview, I talked to and interacted with her a number of times and she told me that she worked in network marketing to which she recruited more Latin Americans to sell dietary supplements and for which they would hold monthly meetings in London-based hotels. In one of our meetings in the Elephant and Castle shopping centre, we had the interview in which she touches upon her language challenges and aspirations in London. She also offers an account of her social life where she interacts with different groups of people who seemingly influence her behaviour.

Excerpt 45: "if I have to be with the British then I become British"

Sonia: no soy tan british, pero si tengo que estar con british, pues me hago british ¿no?

Daniel: ¿Y cómo es eso? ¿Cómo que te haces british?

S: pues es muy fácil. O sea porque por ejemplo eh. Pues los latinos somos más expresivos, más apasionados a la hora de hablar, de decir las cosas el tono de voz es más como cantadito ¿no? Y claro, pues cuando estás con la cultura inglesa, muy *quiet* todo. Muy tranquilo. No puedes estar allí como que los ojos están bailando como. No, no. O sea, todo tiene que ser mmm, guardar mucho las formas . . .

Her account goes on.

S: pero si tienes una postura tranquila tu tono de voz es normal ni tan bajo ni alto, si tu si tu mirada no es como, como somos los latinos o las latinas, como más, como más *quiet*

D: mmm

S: entonces si hablas un inglés y de por sí ya tienes un acento inglés, ¡guau! O sea, lo has hecho

D: ¿el acento [es]?

S: [es] importante. Es importante porque en cuanto te escuchan hablar ellos sienten que tú eres parte de ellos. O sea, hablar un inglés súper *hard*. O sea, está bien porque ellos te entienden. Ellos prefieren entenderte a no entenderte que hables con *hard*, pero te entienden a que intentes hablar con acento y que no te entiendan entonces.. Pero si hablas con acento, es mucho mejor . . .

Translation

Sonia: I am not that British, but if I have to be with the British then I become British, right?

Daniel: And how is that? What do you mean you become British?

S: Well, it's very easy. I mean because for example er, we Latinos are more expressive, more passionate when talking. The tone of voice is more like singsong, right? And obviously, when you are with the English culture, it is very quiet. Everything is very quiet. You can't be unfocused like. No, no. All has to be mmmm, you have to keep up appearances . . .

Her account goes on.

S: but if you are composed, your tone of voice is normal neither so low nor high and if your look is not like we latinos or Latinas like more like more quiet

D:mmm

S: so if you speak English and if you have an English accent, wow! I mean, you've made it

D: Accent [is]..

S: [it] is important. It is important because when they hear you speak, they feel you are one of them. I mean, to speak super hard English. I mean, it's ok because they understand.They prefer to understand you than not understand you, but to speak hard but they understand when you try to speak with an accent and then they will not understand you, but if you speak with an accent, it is much better . . .

In excerpt 45, Sonia describes how she adapts her behaviour depending on the people with whom she interacts; while she describes Latinos as more expressive than the English when talking, she presents the latter group as reserved and concerned with social norms to which she appears to orient herself. For Sonia such behaviour is accompanied with ways of speaking such as the tone of voice, which she defines as normal. Also, it is interesting to see her statement, *if you speak English and if you have an English accent, wow! I mean you have made it*, which indexes a type of language identified as the representative model of a culture that, in this light, is depicted as uniform and that characterises a particular way of speaking. Furthermore, both the interjection and the concluding phrase of such statement are worth analysing. They point to a social recognition and praise attributed to the speaker whose pronunciation reflects what she calls the English accent.

Additionally, the comparisons that she makes, *super hard* and *with an accent* also deserve attention since they point to an evaluation of these perceived manners of pronunciation in which the former, although conditionally acceptable, is hierarchised and subjected to the latter. In this sense, her statements become ideological. As we saw in chapter 2.4 accent is a manner of pronunciation and given that it is impossible to speak without pronunciation, accent is a property of individuals (see also Andersson and Trudgill 1992; Hughes et al. 2012). Likewise, accent points to language variations which is not strictly limited to a geographic region since, as we also mentioned in the discussion of Linda's case, it also becomes manifest in dynamic social groups of speakers. Thus, the belief that there is only one English accent that provides the speaker with prestige seems to reflect a social construct in which a language variant is objectified as a higher value vehicle to social acceptance and inclusion. In this context, Sonia's account seems to be informed by the ideology of the standard language in which a language is imagined or idealised as homogenous and which is often the language model of the higher social class (Lipi- Green 2012).

It must be added that Sonia's metalinguistic account is not limited to the context of the UK. Similar ideologies have been documented in Latin America, particularly in Mexico and Ecuador that help us explain and understand the accent-based social distinctions that speakers make as well as their relevance for the formation and selection of social relations. In the context of Mexico and Ecuador, language hierarchies and the evaluation of accents are articulated in terms of a rural-urban divide accompanied with evaluated ways of behaving that suggests social class distinctions. A study that concentrated on speakers' attitudes towards variants of Mexican Spanish documents that accents associated with Mexico city are viewed as either unmarked or as more prestigious than other dialects particularly from rural areas (Stockler 2015; see Hidalgo 1986). These, in turn, are categorised as uncouth, uncultured, uneducated and often associated with the term *ranchero*, hilbilly in English, whose ways of speaking are often attributed notions of backwardness and are labelled as noise from which the participants distance themselves (Stockler 2015). Also, Flores Mejia (2014) documents the social prestige attributed to variants spoken in Ecuador. She refers to the negative attitudes of speakers from the capital city of Quito towards the Spanish spoken in Guayaquil and who state that they speak without accent (Flores Mejia 2014), unmarked as in the case of the Mexico study. Furthermore, her participants draw relevant distinctions not only in terms of accents that are unpleasant for speakers from the capital city, but in terms of behaving that to some extent also echo those that Sonia described above. That is, proper ways of speaking should be accompanied with "being polite and courteous" and "with a use of language that should not mix words with others from indigenous languages" (Flores Mejia 2014: 435). Both studies stress the social prestige assigned by speakers to urban variants where the standard variety is allegedly encountered and practised. In this sense, they both resonate with Sonia's views of the English accent that, although it differs from the perception of the unmarkedness of accents registered in these studies, is also located in an urban setting such as London and exhibit the delineation of and orientation towards higher social class positions that promote class divisions.

The analysis of Sonia's orientation towards the standard ideology, nonetheless, is not to suggest that abiding to it is condemning her. Rather it is an attempt to understand it in a context where other non-linguistic identity traits may also play a role in the constitution of her social relations as she seeks social mobility.

As stated at the beginning of this section, Sonia is a black, Ecuadorian immigrant that has experienced discriminatory attitudes and, as we will see this in more detail below, not only speaking English but also doing it with what she implies as the standard accent may be mobilised to contest and counteract the identity hierarchisation that she experienced and that her discourse suggests. In the following excerpt, Sonia continues her account and describes what it is required to be able to speak English.

Excerpt 46: "in order not to lose out, I have to have MY relationships to keep my English up to date"

> S: cualquiera que quiera aprender sale del círculo latino o se mete a clases de inglés siete u ocho horas al día mínimo al menos los adultos. Mira los niños cuando vienen, se meten siete horas al día y en un año siete meses te hablan un mejor inglés que nadie, con acento y todo porque el medio te empuja y están como una esponja. Entonces todo está a favor para que ellos aprendan, y en cambio uno adulto que viene ya con las estructuras mentales y habla poco inglés y estudia poco inglés, ¿el resultado cuál va a ser? Pues poco o ¡NADA! Entonces, una persona para que tenga un buen inglés, mínimo son dos horas al día o sea ¡MINIMO! Y aquí, como ves, todo el día, hoy un ejemplo tan claro, es español y si me quedo aquí toda la noche, seguiré hablando español
>
> D: mmm
>
> S: entonces para no perder YO tengo que tener MIS relaciones para mantener mi inglés al día..

Translation

> S: Anyone who wants to learn (English) must leave the latin circle he either takes English classes seven or eight hours a day at least adults. Look at the kids, when they come, they study seven hours a day and in a year seven months they speak English better than anybody, with an accent and whatnot because the environment pushes you and they are like a sponge. So, the odds are in their favour so they learn and on the other hand adults with mental structures and speak little English and study little English, what will the outcome be? A little or NOTHING! So, for someone to speak good English at least two hours a day I mean AT LEAST! And here, as you can see today, for example, it's Spanish and if I stay here all night, I will continue speaking Spanish
>
> D: mmm
>
> S: so in order not to lose out, I have to have MY relationships to keep my English up to date..

The social assessment of accent that we saw in excerpt 45 continues to organise Sonia's account. In it, she mentions practices and activities as well as decisions to make that must be conducive to what is suggested as speaking good English. Nevertheless, it is left unstated to what end or in what context the good English to which she refers must be spoken. We must remind ourselves that the context of the interview is a place where various Latin American-run businesses such as cafes and restaurants are located and that other Latin Americans attend to socialise and learn of job opportunities and flats to rent. It is in this setting in which her statement, *here, as you can see today, for example, it's Spanish and if I stay here all night I will continue speaking Spanish*, gains social significance and points to two socially significant aspects. The first one indicates the evaluation of Spanish and English in which the former is suggested as a disadvantage while the latter is implied as an advantage. However, her phrase seems to go beyond the description of a language choice; that is, the loss of linguistic capital that Sonia attempts to avoid indexes evaluated social identities at the same time that it implies that social relations are constructed as investments of a language capital that she aspires to obtain. The latter argument is an implication contained in her phrase *so, in order not to lose out*, which emphasises social values that foreground the speaker's individual aspirations. Such social values can be better understood when they are connected to the second socially significant aspect.

The second socially significant aspect pertains to ethnographic notes. As stated in the introduction to this book, ethnographic notes were taken after our meetings and conversations prior to the interview in the same area and in which I asked her how often she visited the Elephant and Castle shop centre. She said that she did not organise her social life around that area and that her visits were job-motivated.

Excerpt 47: "they do not make an effort to improve their life opportunities"

> Notas de campo: En el centro comercial de elephant; "si la gente decide quedarse en su ghetto porque es aquí donde pueden hablar español, no hacen ningún esfuerzo por mejorar sus oportunidades de vida y inglaterra es una tierra de oportunidades" (Notas del 4 de julio, 2014)

Translation

> Fieldnotes. At the Elephant and Castle shopping mall, "if people decide to stay in their ghetto because it is here where they can speak Spanish, they do not make an effort to improve their life opportunities and England is a land of opportunities" (Field notes July 4th, 2014)

In this context, Sonia's views may help us understand the constitution of Latin Americans' social relations in which ideologies of social class, as we previously saw in Mayra's, Jazmin's and Linda's cases, interrelate with their views of language and their speakers. That is, while English is perceived as the language of progress and mobility, Spanish seems to be associated with an area labelled as a social space of seclusion and regress, attitudes and behaviours that allegedly characterise each group of speakers. As the interview went on, Sonia touches upon the relevance of English inside or outside England, and she said that she could even speak it in Latin America if she wanted to and I asked her whether she would do it.

Excerpt 48: "They regard you more intelligent when you speak the language"

>S: Quizás sí. Yo he ido a barcelona y a algunos así yo les hablaba en inglés y ya está porque no me apetecía hablar en español
>
>D: ¿a poco?
>
>S: y tú ves la reacción es diferente
>
>D: ¿qué reacción has tenido?
>
>S: la reacción cuando te escuchan hablar inglés dicen "uy es extranjera", pero cuando hablas español "anda mira esta qué se cree, latino no sé qué"
>
>D: ¿a poco?
>
>S: ¡CLARO! Por eso te digo es muy diferente es cuando tú hablas *English property* (sic) *English* a cuando hablas un inglés *hard* cuando hablas inglés ¿sí te das cuenta?
>
>D: mmm
>
>S: Pero para eso hay que vivirlo. Te consideran más inteligente cuando hablas el idioma
>
>D: ¿Cuando hablas inglés?
>
>S: Claro. Es, es que tienes más posibilidades. Es que es así. Es que las mejores obras literarias vienen en inglés, las mejores cosas vienen en inglés, todo lo que tú quieras viene en inglés. El español está muy limitado en todo . . .

Translation

>S: Perhaps. I would I have been to Barcelona and to some I would speak in English because I did not feel like speaking in Spanish
>
>D: Really?
>
>S: And you see a different reaction
>
>D: What sort of reaction have you had?
>
>S: The reaction that when they hear you speak English, they say "wow, she is a foreigner", but when they hear you speak Spanish "who does this Latina think she is?
>
>D: Really?
>
>S: OF COURSE! That is why I am telling you that. It is different when you speak English property (sic) English than when you speak hard English, when you speak English, you know what I mean?
>
>D: mmm

S: But that is why you have to experience it. They think you are more intelligent when you speak the language

D: When you speak English?

S: Of course! you have more opportunities. That's the way things are. The best literary works are in English, all the best things are in English, you name it. Spanish is very limited in everything . . .

Through the interactions that Sonia describes, we can both draw conjectures of her language choices in different domains and the interaction of various ideologies and identity attributions. On the one hand, the ideology of cultural superiority with which a language allegedly endows an individual comes forward in this narrated event. For instance, it is interesting to see the higher social and cultural value that Sonia attributes to the term *foreigner*, which here is understood as an English-speaking person and that in Sonia's words enjoys a de-territorialised social prestige. In this sense, Sonia's description about speaking English in a situation where there is an implication of a pejorative attitude towards her Spanish, *who does this Latina think she is?* seems to be motivated by two interrelated aspects. That is, the belief that English helps her counteract a suggested diglossic situation between two Spanish variants through which speakers evaluate themselves and hierarchise their social relations, and, as stated above, that seems to contest a possible top-down racialisation for being a black Latin American immigrant. This, although it is not made explicit in the narrative of Sonia as an ideology that may have informed the attitudes that she describes, is also worth considering given that it has also been documented in the context of Barcelona where Latin American immigrants have faced discrimination and have been positioned in terms of race meaning that they do not look European enough (see McIlwaine 2016; Block and Corona 2014).

On the other hand, it is also noteworthy the ideology of intellectual superiority of an individual by speaking a language such as English. That is, speaking English is implied as a cognitive quality of an individual who is characterised as educated and progressive and who in turn is socially lifted and differentiated from speakers of other languages. Such an ideology should be understood in the specific context where Sonia is situated and where, as stated above, she may have reproduced it to contest the hierarchisation of her identity; that is, a Latin American immigrant who seeks a higher social status and upward mobility. Nonetheless, as her narrative goes on, Sonia's description of English versus Spanish, *Spanish is very limited in everything*, still indexes what Mocek (1999) calls social Darwinism. As stated in chapter 2.4, this is an ideological depiction of English as naturally better equipped for the technological demands of our times and not as a consequence of political or economic processes (Milroy and Milroy, 2005; Moreno Cabrera 2008). All of the above reminds us of the ideology of English as an indispensable and fundamental skill conducive to social mobility that, as we will see in Mario's case below, also resonates with a neoliberal discourse and worldview to which individuals must orient themselves. The ideologies thus far analysed seem to reflect what I previously established; these are notions, beliefs of a language with specific cultural and political constructs that seek the exercise of power (Del Valle 2007; Woolard 2016). The interview went on and Sonia emphasises the social relevance of English.

Excerpt 49: "we have to speak English and, for people, that is very difficult to understand"

> S: tú sabes que cuando hablas en inglés, es como aprender eso a leer, a aprender a hablar. Es que es vital, es vital en un país donde se habla inglés es vital
>
> D: ¿para tu trabajo, para tus relaciones?
>
> S: Para todo, para todo, para todo, para todo, para lo que me pongas. Es vital. El inglés es importante. Estamos en Inglaterra, hay que hablar inglés y eso les cuesta mucho a las personas no entender porque.. las personas lo entienden, pero no quieren y a eso se debe muchas veces el fracaso de la educación, el fracaso profesional. El fracaso personal muchas veces tiene que ver con el idioma. El idioma y con el cambio de hábitos, de no querer salir a veces de su comodidad . . .

Translation

> S: you know that when you speak English, it is like learning how to read, or learning how to speak. It's vital, it's vital in a country where English is spoken
>
> D: for your work, for your relationships?
>
> S: for everything, for everything, for everything, for everything, you name it. English is vital. It's important. we re in England, we have to speak English and, for people, that is very difficult to understand because. People understand, but they do not want to and that many times explains education failure, professional failure. personal failure many times has to do with the language. It has to do with language and change of habits, with sometimes not wanting to leave their confort zone . . .

In excerpt 49, Sonia discursively presents English as an indispensable instrument in every aspect of people's social life or as she emphatically put it, *for everything*. It must be noted how such emphasis is accompanied by lexical choices that denote specific systems of social values. Sonia's statement: *we are in England we have to speak English*, apart from pointing to the one-language one-nation ideology in which English is assumed the *de facto* language, conjures up a prescription of linguistic assimilation that is presented as both people's obligation and as the common-sense strategy to take on in order to succeed academically and workwise. Following this line of argument, the one-language one-nation ideology seems to be reinforced by the implicit mention of its educational institutions. Such ideology not only instructs future generations through a specific linguistic vehicle but functions as a mechanism of a social reproduction such as keeping a socioeconomic order in a London society where more than 300 languages and their variants are spoken (see Vertovec 2007; Piller 2016). Linguistic assimilation, according to Sonia's description, is therefore an unquestionable norm and a rational decision in which personal failure is explicated by an individual's will.

In light of the above, Sonia's account also points to what other studies have identified as the neoliberal discourses of responsibilisation. As I noted above, Ullman (2012), in a study of narratives of Mexican immigrants that explored emergent ideologies in the USA, found that the participants oriented themselves to ideologies of personal responsibility to educate themselves in English and ideologies of an acceptance that one must learn English to become successful. That is, notions of success that are often associated with social inclusion through language and with economic advancement that the individual has achieved after hard work and self-discipline. Thus, as we have also seen in the previous chapters, what comes to the fore is an ideology of neoliberal values in which success is recognised as the sole responsibility that an individual must take on.

It must be noted, nevertheless, that the attitudes that Sonia shows also merit more scrutiny in order to not contribute to the promiscuity of neoliberalism as the term upon which all blame is put or where individual responsibility is reduced to a neoliberal-self (see Clarke 2008). In order to understand this better, a pertinent comment is that individual responsibilisation predates the times of neoliberalism, but there are present political and economic conditions that should also be considered. For instance, in an interesting discussion of the historic evolution of the meanings of social class, Skeggs (2004) notes that the the notion of individual self constructed as responsible of their own economic progress dates back to post Civil War times in England (1642–1648). Here the emergence of an "economic man" is documented and is depicted as a figure upon whom all economic responsibility is transferred (Day 2001 in Skeggs 2004: 33). In a similar vein, Block (2018) makes reference to Smith's writings in which an individual-oriented attitude is also found. He notes that Smith sees human beings as "naturally self-interested individuals" whose need of support from others is not explained by a gregarious nature or a need of collective support but by the pursuit of his/her self-interest (Block 2018:107). What characterises neoliberalism, we must remind ourselves, is the dismantling of labour rights and, among many other top-down actions, the reduction of public funding in domains such as health, education and even, in the context of the UK, in the provision of language classes for immigrants. It has been documented how the British government initially funded English for Speakers of Other Languages (ESOL) classes to address the linguistic and educational needs of migrants in the 1960s but eventually, in 2007 and then in 2011, it cut funding in ESOL classes (Granada 2013; Williamson 2009). This resulted in the withdrawal of automatic fee remmissions, the introduction of fees for these courses and limited eligibility requirements to a certain category of students or migrants (Granada 2013; Hubble and Kennedy 2011). In this context, Sonia's words referring to why people fail in a new society exhibits a neoliberal logic not only because they concentrate on individual responsibilisation but on the individual's lack of decision and, as she put it, will to change their *habits* and *leave their comfort zone* in adverse economic circumstances where state support is increasingly being reduced.

The ideologies that we have analysed so far point to divergent interests that are motivated by language ideologies that construct social relations based on a sought-after linguistic capital. Furthermore, social capital and notions of higher social class also figure as highly influential aspects in the constitution of social relations, the top-down construction of identities and in the interpretation of sociolinguistic realities of Latin American immigrants. Their lives thus exhibit differential access to sociocultural resources, social class inequalities that can be further pursued below where language is also depicted to play a major role in the socioeconomic reality of Andres.

5.3 Socieoconomic mobility

Andres: *"At the beginning, the language was a very big obstacle"*

As I have stated in chapter 1.3, Latin Americans are dispersed throughout London. Such dispersion is evident not only in the physical places on which their work sites are based but in the cultural activities they organise and perform such as folk dances. These are a clear manifestation of festivals such as *Fusion de los Pueblos* and, as the name suggest, it attracts people from various nationalities and different age groups such as children, teenagers and adults. This festival that I also attended was open to everyone and took place in central London where people wore typical Bolivian, Mexican, Chilean, Ecuadorian and Colombian outfits as they danced or played music on stage for nearly four hours. The organisers, as I was able to observe and learn from my conversations with them, are volunteers whose roles involve promoting the event on social media, handing out leaflets on site, setting up the venue, selling tickets for the festival, etc. Andres was one of the volunteers that I met and with whom I was able to have a conversation as I bought a ticket for the festival. From the moment we started talking in Spanish, he was friendly and open and, as he described the programme of the festival, he exhibited excitement about it. He later on told me that folklore was something he was passionate about. He also asked me where I was from and what I was doing in London. We talked at length about Mexico and touched upon some its traditions and music that he said he loved. After a trust-building process, he volunteered to talk to me in one of his workplaces.

Andres is a Colombian immigrant who has been in the UK since 2000. He left his country with his brother when he was nineteen years old to help his family improve their economic situation. Since his arrival, he has done all types of jobs, cleaning included as he said that this is the type of job where every Latin American starts working. After a number of years in London, he met a Colombian woman who was a British citizen and with whom he got married and eventually became a British citizen as well. At the time of the interview, he worked as a care assistant but also taught salsa-dancing classes in the evening in a south London pub where people from Chile also worked as bar tenders. Although he had these two jobs, he said that his economic situation was not good enough to have his own home; he and his wife lived in a small room with other people and he was considering moving back to Colombia. In the interview that took place in the pub I mentioned above, he and I talked about the difficulties he encountered in London upon his arrival, and language came up as an issue.

Excerpt 50: "you can't communicate. It binds you"

> e mira que fue complicado. Es complicado por lo menos para nosotros porque llegamos y no había muchos latinos. O sea, sí había, pero no habíamos tantos como los habemos ahora. La comunidad latina no era tan grande entonces. Fue difícil porque primero para empezar a trabajar demoré cuatro meses ¿sí? Porque decía "¿ahora qué hacemos?" No sabíamos dónde movernos. O sea, fue difícil, fue difícil porque económicamente no teníamos. Al principio el idioma fue un obstáculo muy muy grande porque lógico, no te puedes comunicar. Te ata las manos. Entonces fue muy difícil.. Después sí empecé a estudiar, a adaptarme un poquito mejor . . .

Translation

> Erm well it was complicated. It is complicated at least for us because we arrived and there weren't many latinos. I mean, there were some, but not many like there are now. The latin American community was not so big back then. It was hard because first, it took me four months to get a job, right? Because I thought "what do we do now? We did not know where to go. I mean, it was hard. It was hard because we did not have money. At the beginning, the language was a very big obstacle because of course, you can't communicate. It binds you. So it was very hard.. Then I started to study to adapt a bit better . . .

In excerpt 50, Andres narrates how complicated his and his brother's arrival in England was and points to the uncertainty that they faced by not knowing what to do or what places they could go or how to get around in London. Likewise, he also depicts a place in which there was not a strong Latin American presence on which he could count. In these adverse circumstances that he describes, two interesting representations of language emerge. First, the phrase *the language was a very big obstacle*, produces a metaphorical portrayal of language as personified and characterised as emphatically problematic due to its silencing effect that he narrates. In addition, the phrase *it binds you*, also evokes the metaphor: language is a physical force that, as we have seen above, is represented as having a disabling effect on the person who does not speak it. This description becomes highly relevant due to the immediate socioeconomic conditions and challenges that he relates he faced and that he attempted to overcome. We must remind ourselves that Andres moved to England motivated by economic needs at a young age and with no connections that could allow him to obtain a job and thus ease his integration into a new society. In this context, Andres' inability to speak English seems to be accompanied with a sense of frustration that in the absence of a strong economic and social capital may have forced him to a marginal social position. The frustration that Andres expresses also echo Linda's job experiences that we saw in the previous section and who below relates her job aspirations upon her arrival in the UK.

Excerpt 51: "The language can cripple you"

> al principio ni siquiera para aspirar a un trabajo en Tesco ¿no? De cajero o de limpieza o sea..no yo nunca lo vi como una posibilidad. Yo nunca lo vi como una posibilidad. Entonces es importante, es bien importante aprender el idioma. El idioma te puede hacer un invalido. Yo estoy convencida de eso..

Translation

> at first it was impossible to aim for a job in tesco, right? As a cashier or in cleaning I mean I never saw that as a chance. I never saw that as a chance. So it's important. It's very important to learn the language. The language can cripple you. I am convinced of that . . .

We must remind ourselves that Linda holds a B.A in psychology and that experienced a downward social mobility. How she makes sense of her narrated experience draws attention to how she conceives of language. The personification of language as in *language can cripple you* points to the metaphor language is a physical force since it seems to act upon Linda's reality and, by implication, it can be interpreted that for Linda it has agency that undermines her ability to seek a better job. We can still peruse this metaphorical representation of language in Alfonso's experience in which he describes his job aspirations.

Excerpt 52: "when you don't speak the language, you have to take the job they give you"

> es un poco complicado. Entonces cuando tú no hablas el idioma, tienes que agarrar el trabajo que te den. No puedes exigir. Tú no puedes decir NO, yo no quiero hacer esto, yo no quiero lavar platos, yo no quiero trabajar de kitchen porter, no quiero trabajar de *cleaner*..

Translation

> It's a bit complicated. So, when you don't speak the language, you have to take the job they give you. You can't be demanding. You can't say NO, I don't' want to do this, I don't want to wash dishes, I don't' want to work as a kitchen porter, I don't want to work as a cleaner . . .

As we saw in the last chapter, Alfonso was trained as a Telecoms Technician in Venezuela and at the time of the interview he worked as a care assistant in a London-based hospital after working as a cleaner in various other schools in the same city. In this description, Alfonso's inability to speak English is accompanied with topics of frustration and resignation. Like Linda's representation of language, the metaphorical depiction of language as a physical force implicitly resonates in Alfonso's discourse given that it seems to be portrayed as materialised in the silencing and marginalising effect that it has on his decision to choose what job to do or apply for. According to these depictions, language is presented as having a discriminatory effect by deskilling, declassing and excluding them from a job market where English is implicitly represented as the *de facto* language and the language capital to be attained and perceived as the language of progress.

Following up Andres' experience, he then recounted that he was able to adapt to his new social environment by gradually studying the language. Although he did not narrate how he learnt English in detail, he said that he began to study grammar and eventually began to speak the language fluently through the interactions with other people in the various jobs he has done. Indeed, before and after the interview, I observed his interactions with his salsa-class students, most of whom were English and Polish, and he greeted them and gave them instructions in English fluently and he seemed confident while speaking it. However, his ability to speak the language has not allowed him to have the economic mobility that he initially sought when he moved to England as we will be able to observe in more detail below.

Excerpt 53: "I want to get (language) certificates for teaching English"

> algo me está dando vueltas en mi cabeza. No sé si sea una buena idea, no sé si lo vaya a realizar, pero tengo la idea de como dentro de dos años regresarme ¿sí? Quiero sacarme los certificados para enseñar inglés. Tal vez sea una manera de tener un trabajo allá y no sé, tener una mejor calidad de vida. No sé de qué. Bueno, eso depende de mí, pero bueno, lo estoy cocinando ahí . . .

Translation

> Something is going on on my mind. I don't know if it's a good idea, I don't know if I'll do it, but my idea maybe in two years' time is to go back, right? I want to get (language) certificates for teaching English. Maybe that's a way of getting a job there and I don't know, maybe getting a better quality of life. I don't know doing what. Well, that is up to me, but well, I'm thinking about it . . .

In excerpt 53, Andres expresses his thoughts about where he could move and what to do in the future since he suggests that he is concerned with his lifestyle and living conditions in London. As stated above, he and his wife were living in a small room that they shared with other people and were paying six hundred pounds a month for rent. His description very much resembles the reality of many Latin Americans in two interrelated aspects. The spatial conditions of living that he describes are due to economic constraints that prevent them to rent a flat on their own and often find themselves sharing a room with people they do not know or live in overcrowded conditions. In addition, many also share a living space in order to save money that they can remit back to their families in their home countries (McIlwaine 2016; Ramos 2017).

In the case of Andres, his aspirations to improve his living conditions are based on language, and it is in this context where a neoliberal ideology of language is implied. English is presented as the vehicle that could enable him to improve his economic situation since he, although hesitantly as it can be seen in hedging phrases such as *maybe* and *I don't know*, discursively constructs it as the necessary skill to get him a job. Furthermore, such a skill, as he suggests, must be complemented by a language certification that is to legitimise his knowledge of English and that should equip him to teach it in Colombia. His discourse, as we saw in chapter 2.4, resonates with Duchêne and Heller's (2012) argument in the sense that ideas about language are framed in economic terms as a matter of added-value, an investment that people are interpellated to make and from which they are to reap the profits.

However, the reality described by Andres also foreground other factors that could present him with obstacles. The acquisition of cultural capital such as a language certification, which requires a significant economic investment (see Heller

2018; Grin 2015), to a great extent involves freedom from economic constraints, which I have established Andres is not free from. Rather, having two jobs and struggling to pay a high rent for a shared room bring to the fore his economic pressures. In addition, his current cultural capital may provide him with differentiated access to the mobility he wishes to obtain given that he has a high school diploma and no degree. This is neither to suggest that Andres' aspirations are unjustified nor underestimate his cultural capital. It is rather a statement to stress the ideology of English as the language of economic progress that is to some extent equated with a better job and thus a better lifestyle that nonetheless masks socioeconomic inequalities. In this light, Andres' aspirations may be undermined by the lower-class structure in which his economic, cultural and social capital are located. Issues of social and cultural capital will continue to appear as a valuable resource as we analyse the following case of Mario whose reasons to be in the UK are also economically motivated.

Mario: "*it is not that I've wanted to travel and learn English*"

After having paid a visit to a Latin American-oriented NGO in Lambeth, I met Mario. He is from Peru and arrived in England in 2015 after having lived with his wife and son in Spain since 2004. His wife first moved to Spain in 2003 since his sister in-law was able to get her a job as a domestic worker. A year later, they would reunite. He decided to leave Peru due to a lack of job opportunities and ageist job policies in his area of expertise. He is 55 years old and holds a degree in accounting. Mario has been declassed and deskilled in both Spain and England. That is, although he has a B.A in accounting, he has not practiced his degree in neither country but has done a number of different jobs that could help him pay the bills and that eventually led him to run his own delivery business in Madrid.

Due to the economic crisis that hit Spain in 2008, Mario began to lose his customers, his own delivery business and his house in Toledo. He attempted to get back on his feet by working in delivery again but now for a company that eventually went bankrupt. He later on worked as a night watchman in a complex of buildings for sale in Spain, but they never got sold and he did not get paid. After all these misfortunes, he decided to come to England in search of a job, as he eventually intends to bring his wife and son. They all have EU citizenship. At the time of the interview, Mario had been in England for two months and was renting a flat that he shared with four more Latin American people who worked in the service sector.

Upon his arrival in England, Mario encountered a number of communication challenges that contributed to a sense of loneliness and limited his social and language interaction opportunities. Mario described himself as the type of person who likes going into the shop and striking up a conversation with people; activities that he could no longer perform due to his inability to speak English.

Mario's discourse casts light on how people could be interpellated by ideas of what skills and what language are allegedly desirable and valuable. Such interpellation becomes problematic given that, as we can gather from other migration stories outside London (see Garrido and Codó 2017), it erases people's job experience and their academic credentials. Mario's plan to bring his son to the UK and then move to the US illustrates his views of English as a guarantee to have socioeconomic mobility. He refers to this plan as follows:

Excerpt 54: "it's not like bringing a degree from Peru"

> M: mi hijo que está estudiando allá en España, que haga su maestria acá. Ojalá que se pueda tener una beca ¿no? Que haga su maestría acá y ahora, mira bien, en españa la gente termina su carrera y no consigue trabajo. Entonces, yo tengo entendido que si que aquí sí, ¿ves? Entonces, si va a estudiar, si va a egresar de la universidad y va a tener un título para que pueda trabajar acá, hermano, ¿para qué va a estudiar, si no va a poder trabajar en España?
>
> D: mmm. Si no tiene trabajo alla
>
> M: Claro ¿ves? Ahora, una maestría inglesa, en Estados unidos le abrirá las puertas pues porque yo no creo que Inglaterra sea cualquier cosa, ¿no? No es como traer un título de Perú a Estados Unidos. Sin embargo, llevándole un título de Inglaterra ya las cosas cambiaran ¿no? Entonces si ya va a poder trabajar y con el idioma, va con todo eso, todo eso es ya una cosa muy buena, muy buena ¿no ves? Hay un montón de esperanzas cifradas en este viaje mío en esta aventura no es solamente que yo haya querido viajar y aprender inglés pa mí. No, no. Es un programa de familia es un proyecto de familia este que, queremos salir a delante. Que mira, estamos dando manotazos de ahogado ahorita allá abajo. Mira yo, con cincuenta y cinco años . . .

Translation

> M: my son who is studying there in Spain should do his MA here. I hope he can get a scholarship, right? I want him to do his masters here and, look, in Spain, people finish their degree and don't get a job. So, I assume that people here do. So, if he is going to study, if he is going to finish university and have a degree so he can work here, mate, why is he going to study when he won't be able to find a job in Spain?
>
> D: mmmmm if he does not find a job there
>
> M: That's right, see? Now a masters from England will open doors for him in the US because I think that an English degree must worth something it's not like bringing a degree from Peru to the US, however, things will be different with an English degree, right? So, if he is able to work and speaks the language all that is very good right? There is a lot of hope in my journey in this adventure it is not that I've wanted to travel and learn English. No, no. It is a family plan, it is a family project because we want to make progress because we are in a dire economic situation and with me, in my mid-fifties . . .

In excerpt 54, Mario describes the job prospects that his son could explore if he obtained a degree from Spain where Mario implies there are few job opportunities. For Mario, earning a postgraduate degree in England will open doors and lead to promising job opportunities in both England and the US, which figures as the final destination in Mario's family project. In this light, Mario's discourse conjures up two interrelated ideologies. On the one hand, English is represented as the desired resource, a skill that will lead to socioeconomic mobility since it is assumed that knowing how to use it will qualify his son for a well-paid job as it is implied in *if he is able to work and speaks the language all that is very good, right?* In this manner, his perception of English reproduces a widely spread ideology of language and progress in which the former is subsumed with education. On the other hand, his phrase *it's not like bringing a degree from Peru* reproduces a topos of culture by assuming the superiority of English institutions and education over those of Peru that do not guarantee a job abroad, *things will be different with an English degree, right?* In this light, the ideology of English as the language of progress intersects with a neoliberal ideology in that Mario's discourse indexes a market logic in which he self-disqualifies as he implies that his credentials along with his son's linguistic capital are devalued and insufficient to secure a job. Thus, Mario's discourse is structured by and structuring a price formation of symbolic resources that can be used to obtain material gains (Bourdieu 1991).

However, Mario's hopes should also be accounted for in a socioeconomic reality from which he speaks. As he said, *we are in dire economic situation* since he was still looking for a steady job and struggling to pay for rent in a flat that he shared with four more people. These, as I have stated above and elsewhere (see Morales Hernández 2023), were people from Latin America who worked in the cleaning sector and who got him a job as a late shift- cleaner. He also worked as a kitchen assistant, which required Mario to work from two o'clock in the afternoon to past midnight since he had to clean up the kitchen of the restaurant that closed at half-past ten. He quit both jobs due to the long hours and exploitative conditions in which he was forced to work. In this ligh, issues of social class matter as they explain the resources with which Mario sought socioeconomic and geographic mobility, where and with whom he lived. Mario's unemployment in Spain, spatial conditions of living, lack of property and income as well as limited contacts in England foreground the absence of economic and sociocultural resources. In other words, his experience and hopes index what other scholars call "the hidden injuries of class"; "the feeling of not getting anywhere" despite his efforts to get a well-remunerated, steady job, "the buried sense of inadequacy" that he resents himself for feeling (Sennet and Cobb 1972: 58).

5.4 Language ideology in institutional sites

Julia: *"I say to her 'no speaking English'"*

I met Julia through another London-based NGO, but arranging to meet with her brought me closer to people's complex life stories. After three failed attempts to meet, Julia and I talked in a coffee shop in north London. Julia is a Chilean mother who has been in England for two years with her son and husband. The family lived eight years in Spain where Julia, her husband and son got Spanish citizenship. They left Chile due to their son's illness, cystic fibrosis that could not be treated in Spain, as they did not want their son to die like their younger son who had died of the same disease in Chile years before. Julia relates that she and her husband who used to be a blacksmith sold their house in Chile to move to Spain where their son's disease was treated but eventually, he needed more advanced medical treatment that he could only get in England. Julia's husband works as a cleaner in London and she looks after her now sixteen-year-old boy whose health requires that he be frequently hospitalised. This is the reason why we could not meet before. Julia's son is the only one in her family that can speak English. In her narrative, she states that she has received support from other Latin Americans who have proved to be a strong network; while going to the hospital for the first time, a Colombian woman interpreted for her and helped her get the medical attention her son needed. However, in her narrative she describes discriminatory attitudes that she has faced in the hospital where her son was treated.

She recounts that her sixteen-year-old-son's medical treatment is rigorous. He needs to be hospitalised for intravenous detoxification regularly apart from the physiotherapy he needs to do, as well as the medicine he takes at home. In addition, he always carries an oxygen tank wherever he goes. According to Julia, her son is at an awkward stage and was not following his treatment as he should, which caused his lung capacity to be low. She and her son went for his check up to the hospital where they were usually provided with an interpreter but on that visit, they did not get one. She describes an interaction with a doctor as follows.

Excerpt 55: "this is the age when kids commit suicide"

> le pregunta "¿por qué está tan bajo?" y yo le digo "porque se ha vuelto desobediente" mi hijo traduciendo "se ha vuelto desobediente con las fisioterapias no cumple con su tratamiento está un poco rebelde" y le dice "mano, ah, eso no se hace". Le empezó a decir cosas y mi hijo escuchaba, yo el inglés lo entiendo, me dice "esta es la edad en que los hijos se suicidan y no vengas tú apuntándome a mi llorando" y diciéndome "yo te lo dije" y mi hijo traduciendo y los médicos adultos que estaban ahí le dicen "¿por qué le dices eso?" Entonces,

me chocó, me chocó lo que me dijo. Y yo le dije bueno pero "¿por qué se expresa usted de esa manera? ¿Por qué me dice eso?" Yo en castellano y mi hijo traduciendo . . .

Translation

He asked him "why is it so low?" and I said "because he has become disobedient" my son was translating (sic) "he has become disobedient as to the physiotherapy he does not follow his treatment, he is a bit rebellious" and he said to him "you shouldn't do that, mate". He started to say a few things to him and my son was listening, I understand English, and he told me "this is the age when kids commit suicide and don't come to me crying" and he said to me "I told you so" while my son was translating (sic) and the doctors that were there asked him "why are you saying this to her?" So, I hated it, I hated what he told me. And I said "why are you saying these things? Why are you saying these things?" I was speaking in Spanish while my son was translating (sic) . . .

According to Julia, her son had learned English through the various interactions he had had with nurses throughout their stay in England and he is who translates and interprets for her and her husband in shops and, as we see above, in hospital. As to excerpt 55, the physician's attitude that she describes is, although mediated by her son, directed to her, and it is located in a physical site where a language and institution element merits to be examined in order to gain insight into how Julia could have perceived its social impact. As stated in chapter 2.5, Bourdieu (1977b; 2003) reminds us of the power of language that is not strictly an inherent feature of it, but it is associated with the social position of the speaker as well as the situation in which the communicative event occurs. In Julia's description, a setting such as a hospital is identified as an institutional space in which there is a hierarchisation of identities characterised by the roles of the actors here described. It is also the site in which the physician holds a position of authority. This is highly significant given that it also seemed to have been deployed in the physician's utterance at two interrelated levels, one of which is the language of the interaction that seemed to have put Julia at a disadvantage due to her inability to contest such attitude directly in English. The other is the implicature of *this is the age when kids commit suicide* given that it seems to function as a diagnosis of her son's health. Both suggest the exercise of power in an ideological site, a field where they seemed to have had a downward and discriminatory effect on Julia and have silenced her voice.

The asymmetrical interaction that Julia recounts does not seem to be isolated from similar experiences that deserve attention in a state-sanctioned environment. Studies by Phillimore et al. (2010) and Johnson (2006) have also documented insufficient translation and interpreting support for non-English speakers as well as cultural insensitivity of health providers in the UK. Similarly, Julia's related experience resonates with other studies in which immigrants accessing health services face a form of gender or language related discrimination and where their medical issues and those of their children are disparaged (see Lonergan 2015; Moyer 2013). In the following excerpt, Julia touches upon another experience.

Excerpt 56: "you have to learn English"

> llevábamos como un mes en el hospital, estaba una máquina ahí en la que le sacan a mi hijo el azúcar y me dice, se expresa conmigo en inglés y yo le digo "no speaking english" me dice, según mi hijo me dice, "tienes que aprender a hablar inglés" y yo toco el computador de mi hijo que tenía abierto yo pongo las manos en el computador de mi hijo y cierra el computador así de bruces y dice "TIENES QUE APRENDER INGLES". Eso me pasó con una enfermera. lloré como una magdalena porque no era justo que, la acusé. Sí la acusé porque no, hizo llorar a mi hijo también . . .

Translation

> we had been like a month at the hospital, there was a machine that they use to draw sugar from my son and she says, she addresses me in English and I say to her "no speaking English" and she says, according to my son, "you have to learn English" and I rest my hands on my son's computer that was open and headlong she slams the computer close and says "YOU HAVE TO LEARN ENGLISH". That happened to me with a nurse. I cried because it was not fair that, I reported her. I reported her because, that made my son cry as well . . .

Julia's above account depicts another incident in a different hospital but this time with a nurse when her son was to have his blood-glucose monitoring. As we saw above, her son interpreted this interaction for Julia who later on in the interview clarified that she was yelled at and told she had to learn English. She reported the incident to the hospital staff and requested that she and her son did not see the nurse anymore. Her related experience, nevertheless, indexes an ideology that, although it has been widely studied, does not cease to be relevant for our discussion due to the self-righteous and at times violent attitudes that it may trigger or legitimise (Billig 1995). The one nation one-language ideology promotes the idea that linguistic boundaries coincide with the political boundaries of the nation state (Piller 2016) and regulates as well as produces identities in an idealised monoglot state (Blommaert 2006). It also implies that immigrants have the moral obligation and responsibility to learn the language of their new environment. That is, if people are in England, they have to speak English. Within this logic, Julia is expected to learn English in a nonetheless multilingual society, and it is an expectation that, according to the interview, she had been trying to fulfil. However, due to her son's illness that required her to be with him at all times and her family being relocated a number of times to different London boroughs, her attempts to enrol in English classes provided by a Latin American-oriented NGO had failed for nearly two years.

It must be said that learning the *de facto* language of the host society is neither negative nor an undesirable practice since it may bring benefits for immigrants who seek integration that may also be conducive to a better lifestyle. Indeed, Julia, in my conversations with her and as I was able to observe, expressed a desire and need to learn it due to her inability to communicate with people and her frustration with merely pointing to objects that she wanted to buy when she was in shops. Learning the language of her new context may provide her with more choices and alleviate social isolation and exclusion in sites and contexts where she may need to have a voice. What is problematic is the means and, as stated above, the circumstances in which she intends to learn English that are often obscured in views of why immigrants do not learn the language of their receiving society and that directly affect her English-learning opportunities.

Researchers have discussed the challenges and diverse needs that may motivate or hinder immigrants' language learning. In the context of the USA, McHugh and Doxsee (2018) draw attention to immigrants' and refugees' family responsabilities and changeable work schedules that limit class attendance and participation and that hinder their opportunities to become proficient in English. In England, the Department for Communities and Local Government (DCLG) has also made a similar report. The DCLG stated that the Government has wanted to offer new ways to teach basic English courses to people facing integration challenges. However, it has been reported that these courses are often "not suited to their needs" as "they may be either too far from home or lack the adequate infrastructure that lead to an impractical learning environment" (Foster and Bolton 2018: 9). In addition to this, English language-learning opportunities for Julia are also very limited. Latin American-oriented NGOs, about which I will say more below, offer free English classes, but these take place two times a week (Latin American House 2018). Thus, learning English for Julia involves dealing with a series of personal circumstances as well as political, material and structural factors that hinder her language learning and impact her life.

It is also worth emphasising that Julia's account exhibits that she sought to meet their language needs through the help of NGOs that cater for the various needs of Latin Americans in London. As I mentioned in the introduction to this book, I visited a number of places among which there were NGOs that offered IT and English classes as well as employment rights workshops, and they were the sites through which I got to meet and contact more Latin Americans in London. The role of NGOs has proven to be a valuable source of information, and they function as a type of social capital since they also offer immigration, housing and social welfare advice in Spanish. The latter, as a vehicle of communication, could be helpful in clarifying information for many Latin American immigrants who are not only unable to speak English but who are unfamiliar with rules and policies implied in a specialised language that we can continue to examine in the following case.

Sarah: *"Back then, I was not fluent in the language to defend myself"*

Through a Kilburn-based NGO I met Sarah with whom I met and talked in London a number of times before the recorded interview. We would meet in Victoria train station, but our conversations took place either in coffee shops or in her social housing flat. The life story of Sarah resembles the complexities of citizenship and the motivations as well as the circumstances in which she immigrated to London. Sarah met an English man in Mexico and had a daughter with him. After a five year-marriage, the couple divorced but their daughter obtained dual citizenship while living in Mexico. Sarah relates that her daughter began to experience health problems that were too costly for her. A cousin of hers took care of her daughter's medical treatment for three months, but he was unable to support her more as it was economically onerous. She also recounts that she did not receive economic help or moral support from her father due to Sarah's decision to renounce Catholicism. At the time of the interview, Sarah and her father had begun to repair their relationship. As she kept looking for help, she went to the British consulate in Mexico City where she was advised to move to England where her daughter's illness could be treated.

Before moving to England, Sarah had a fair knowledge of English but no contacts that could inform her of either immigration laws or her rights. She recounted that her daughter received the medical treatment of which she came in search, but they did not have a permanent place where they could stay. She and her daughter would live in hostels or in a living room of newly made acquaintances from Spain. However, these acquaintances would then return to their country, which forced Sarah and her daughter to sleep on the streets. Below I include her account that will help us contextualise her life story and understand the subsequent analyses of language ideologies as well as their consequentiality better.

Excerpt 57: "They always told me that the girl was English and that I was Mexican"

> yo pedí ayuda a social services, pero me lo negaron. Siempre me hablaban con leyes, siempre. no encontré apoyo como una madre sola en este país, aunque sabían que ya estaba mi aplicación en migración. No me fue nada fácil. Siempre me decían que era la niña inglesa y yo mexicana . . .

Translation

> I asked for help to social services, but they did not help me. They always told me about the law always. I found no support as a single mother in this country, even though they knew my application was in process. It wasn't easy. They always told me that the girl was English and that I was Mexican . . .

In excerpt 57, Sarah describes the experience she had when asking for social housing assistance that she eventually obtained while, through the help of one her Spanish acquaintances, she was applying for a visa on compassionate grounds that after five years she was granted. Her depiction, nonetheless, is illustrative of an experience of exclusion. Although not all cultural distinctions are essentially exclusionary, in this context, her account both points to the contemporary complexity of nationality and to delineation of borders between citizens and noncitizens that differentiate who have rights and who do not. Her depiction portrays, and as later on she found out, that she could have been legally separated from her daughter due to the precarious situation in which she relates she lived. Moving to a new country involves learning new rules, and her limited knowledge of English seems to have affected her experiences.

Excerpt 58: "They did not offer me a translator"

> tuve que luchar por mi niña físicamente y no dejé que me la quitaran. Ya estaban llamando a *social services* que porque decían que si yo también estaba poniendo en riesgo a mi hija al no estar yo bien, al no darle una buena casa, alimento y todo ¿no? Ellos tenían que asegurarse que la niña no estaba siendo afectada con nada, y que yo le estaba dando los cuidados tenía que como una niña e. cubrir todo lo que tengo como madre de cuidarla. Entonces yo ya no sabía qué hablar ya no sabía yo qué decir qué cosas me perjudicaban. Yo no tenía la facilidad del idioma para defenderme, para poder explicar las cosas correctamente. No me, AHORA sé que hay traductores. No me ofrecieron traductores ni nada. Entonces, yo traté de defenderme con lo que yo sabía de inglés en ese entonces ¿no? Y era muy frustrante . . .

Translation

> I had to fight for my daughter and did not let them take her away from me. They were calling social services because they said I was risking my daughter's wellbeing by not providing her with a house, feeding her, right? They had to make sure that the girl was not in danger, and that I was looking after her properly, and that I was being a responsible mother looking after her. So, I did not know what to talk about, I had no idea what to say, what things could affect me. Back then, I was not fluent in the language to defend myself, to be able to explain things correctly. They didn't, NOW I know there are translators (sic). They did not offer me a translator (sic) at all. So, I tried to defend myself with the English I knew back then, right? And it was very frustrating . . .

In excerpt 58, Sarah describes an asymmetrical linguistic interaction with the council. She narrates that she did not have access to interpreters who could help her explain why she was asking for social housing in a situation where she recounts that a female staff member attempted to take her daughter from Sarah and told her that she would put her in a foster family. In these circumstances, Language is represented by Sarah not only as a vehicle of communication but also as an instrument to fend off what she describes as an aggression. For instance, the metaphorical representation of language as a shield, *I was not fluent in the language to defend myself*, gains social significance in the situations described given that it points to the knowledge of language as a tool to protect herself and her daughter in an event which she implies as threatening due to her fear of losing her.

Additionally, for Sarah to be able to explain her situation and need for social housing 'properly', in a language that she did not 'master' also carries implications of the context-based use of language. This is what it has been interpreted as communicative competence (Rampton 2006; Agha 2007) in which speakers choose particular ways of speaking with specific social functions whose impact and end also hinge on the spaces that the interactants inhabit. That is, describing an illness to either a friend or a doctor involves the use of a particular register and the result will therefore vary. In a state-sanctioned space and with a liminal migration status, the appropriateness of Sarah's discourse is crucial given that her ability to explain things in English did not seem to be strictly associated with her knowledge of the language. Rather, her narrated frustration of describing things inappropriately in conjunction with *I had no idea what to say what things could affect me*, implies that she may not have had access to the contextual meaning of a particular register that articulates and that could materialise in rules enforced in her new social environment that could have separated her from her daughter.

Her account thus suggests that Sarah seems to have been faced with a top-down specialised monolingual ideology that placed her in a disadvantaged social position and that may have aggravated her sense of frustration at the time. Later on in the interview, she stated that she eventually got social housing benefit for her and her daughter but her visa application was still being processed and, as mentioned above, such application process took five years, time during which social services would send her letters annually to notify her that she was going to be withdrawn from benefits. She would initially explain to social workers that her visa was still being processed and which by then she had not been denied. She then would be called to meetings with the managers to whom she would try to explain that she would not leave the country until immigration issued her with a deportation letter.

Excerpt 59: "Everything was in English, everything was in English"

> Todo en inglés, todo en inglés. También ellos tienen la facilidad del traductor (sic). No me lo dieron y este, y ellos decían que me podían entender bien, pero yo sé que cometí muchos errores y que no pude expresarme como yo me hubiera gustado expresarme. Yo tenía muchas dudas, muchas preguntas que hacer y yo no no, no podía hacerlo ¿no? . . .

Translation

> Everything was in English, everything was in English. They can also provide you with a translator (sic). I was not provided with one and erm, they said they could understand me well, but I know that I made a lot of mistakes and I could not express myself the way I would have liked to. I had many doubts, many questions to ask and I could not do it, right? . . .

In excerpt 59, Sarah responds to my question about the language of the interviews with the managers and, as we saw in the above passage, she reports not having been provided with an interpreter. The lack of access to an interpreter seems to have had a downward effect on Sarah's social identity articulated by two intertwined aspects in a situation that points to a situation of inequality. The first one, her inability to communicate her ideas, *I could not express myself the way I would have liked to,* points to both how her agency is undermined and how her communicative needs appear to have been silenced in an office of social services. The latter is a site where the power of language, as we saw in Julia's case, is enforced by the social position of the interactants implicitly described. In other words, the event is located in a state institution and thus politically and legally sanctioned in which, as Bourdieu noted, "the use of language, the manner as much as the substance of discourse depends on the social position of the speaker, which governs the access he/she can have to the language of the institution" (2003:109).

As to the second one, a monoglot ideology in which a language is treated as homogenous, uniform and that encompasses all the social domains as "a neutral vehicle of communication" (Spotti 2011: 40; see also Anderson 1991), is suggested in Sarah's phrases such as *I had many doubts, many questions.* Both seem to index both the variations in meaning as well as the social function of a particular register, which, as we saw above, Sarah may have sought to clarify in the absence of an interpreter, and whose consequentiality transcends a communicative event in a politically charged site. Her experience echoes those of other women reported in various institutional sites in the UK. Blackledge (2000), for example, reports how Bengali-speaking Bangladeshi mothers in school felt embarrassed to approach English-speaking teachers. Moreover, the consequentiality of such a monolingual ideology was that their language was not accommodated in the school when one of them received a letter about the need of remedial classes for her daughter (Blackledge 2000).

Sarah narrated that she was finally granted a six-year visa on compassionate grounds and that when this time elapsed, she subsequently applied for indefinite leave to remain in the UK. However, her application fell through since the lawyer that assisted her submitted the wrong application about which she only found out through a letter from the immigration office. In her account, Sarah said that her lawyer did not keep her informed of the visa application process even though she tried to stay in touch with her through telephone calls, text messages and emails, which her English educated daughter helped her write to avoid any misunderstandings. At the time of the interview, Sarah had applied for a visa extension and was still expecting an answer from the Home Office, an immigration process she was undertaking through the help of a Spanish-speaking lawyer volunteering in a London-based NGO.

Excerpt 60: "he helps me write the letters and everything else"

> llegué a esta ONG y conocí a Marcos que conoce de migración y me comenzó a dar consejo migratorio, pero prácticamente yo soy la que me estoy representando sola ante migración. Él me aconseja, me ayuda, me guía, me ayuda a escribir las cartas y todo y entonces ya tengo un poquito más de conocimiento. Y todo gracias a ese apoyo que encontré ahí, que ayudan a los latinos y sentí que se me quitó así totalmente un peso de encima porque me sentía totalmente sola. Pero con este tipo de organizaciones que yo no sabía que existían, si te ayudan emocionalmente, te ayudan mucho, te cambia mucho mentalmente también y, yo he contado con la bendición de que es una persona, Marcos, que en cualquier momento que yo lo necesite, él siempre está ahí para aconsejarme. A veces quiero hacer algo para migración porque a veces siento que no hago lo suficiente y él me dice "no espera a que ellos te contesten espera" y sí me ha ayudado mucho ¿no? . . .

Translation

> I went to this NGO and met Marcos who knows about migration (laws) and he started to give me migration advice, but I am representing myself before the Home office. He gives me advice, he helps me, and guides me, he helps me write the letters and everything else. So, I have a little bit more knowledge. And thanks to the support that I found there where they help Latinos and I felt a burden off my shoulders because I felt absolutely helpless. But with this type of organisations that I did not know they existed, they help you emotionally, they help you they help you a lot mentally, and I have been blessed by Marcos' help, he is a person who I can count on at all times. He is always there to give me advice. Sometimes I want to do something migration-related because sometimes I feel that I am not doing enough and he tells me "no wait until they get back to you" he has indeed helped me a lot, right? . . .

In our conversations in coffee shops and her home with her daughter prior to the interview, Sara exhibited an ability to communicate in English. Nonetheless, Sarah's account, despite the circumstances of her migration status, reveals a sense of relief in which language appears to function as a sense-making instrument when she is confronted with the exclusive and specialised discourse of the law. In this context, her receiving help to write letters to the Home Office continues to point, on the one hand, to the above-mentioned monoglot ideology in which a state's institution glosses over the linguistic diversity of its society and permeates all the social domains as a neutral vehicle of communication (Blackledge 2009; Spotti 2011). On the other hand, the specialised register in which she is not fluent and to which she has no access, continues to appear as socially meaningful and politically consequential. The specificity of legal language, as we saw in David's case of removal in chapter 3, influences social behaviour, and lack of access to it may obscure entitlements or may have marginalising effects.

For Sarah, to be able to receive information and legal advice in Spanish has enlightened her understanding of migration laws and by extension of her situation that in this context strikingly contrasts with and thus helps us get a better insight into those that she previously depicted. In addition, lack of access to translation and interpretation services for Sarah also draws attention to neoliberal policies that have affected both state institutions and individuals like her. Gentile (2017) explains that the UK government began to outsource Public Service interpreting to a for-profit company called Capita since 2012. This company "downgraded fees for interpreters" who have been forced to either leave the profession or "have been unwilling to work for low pay such as £13.32 a day before tax" (Gentile 2017: 73). Outsourcing has proven detrimental for the sustainability of the public service profession and for the delivery of justice (Slaney 2012) as there have been concerns about the increase in ineffective trials as a result of non-attendance of interpreters (Justice Committee 2013). In my last contacts with Sarah, the Home Office had neither denied nor confirmed her visa extension yet.

The role of Latin American-oriented NGOs is also worth highlighting. The information and courses they provide interestingly coincide across their sites in London, which to some extent allows us to place Julia's and Sarah's linguistic, metalinguistic and migration stories as well as their capital in a larger social reality in which Latin Americans in London live. The latter argument is not to be treated as a generalising or reductionist statement through which I intend to say that their needs and realities are easily identifiable or even predictable. Rather it is to argue that these NGOs function as a type of social capital that may be made accessible to those who cannot afford it and have come to take on the responsibility of the state. This has failed to address civil society's needs due to funding cuts and outsourcing logics that accentuate a neoliberal regime of austerity (see Garrido and Codó 2017). NGOs' roles, however, also deserve more attention as they may also function as sites where the ideologies identified above also circulate. In a survey obtained from London-based NGOs users from Latin America, McCarthy (2016) documented that one of the main reasons to learn English pertains to job improvement aspirations and because it is the language of their country of residence; that is, monoglot ideologies that keep reinforcing the *de facto* language. As stated above, learning the majority language may have a positive impact on people's lives in a destination society that, nonetheless, should recognise and embrace its multilingual composition across all institutional levels where migrants interact and seek services under circumstances specific to their trajectories as we will see below.

Jazmin: *"I made a lot of mistakes in my application"*

As we saw in chapter 4, Jazmin is a colombian woman who emigrated to the UK to improve her English. Although she accomplished her academic goals, she also faced institutional challenges that draw us closer to monoglot ideologies in the legal system that, as we saw in Sarah's experience, may have exclusionary effects. Due to domestic violence, Jazmin divorced her husband with whom she had a child. As they both sought the custody of their son, the case went to court in 2005. This is a context where she locates her description of the language difficulties she encountered.

Excerpt 61: "I needed someone to help me express myself"

Jazmin: cometi muchos errores en mi aplicación tras de que yo no tengo conocimiento legal pues requeria un soporte no? "Pues digame, vengo a hacer esto". Pero yo todo lo tenía que hacer "voy a hacer esto" bueno de alguna manera lo logré, pero siempre a ellos se les olvidaba algo porque yo quería que tuvieran un traductor porque a pesar de que yo hablo inglés porque como es un caso tan delicado bueno yo a veces me ponía muy nerviosa y, en otros casos que hemos tenido con mi ex, yo me ponía a llorar. Entonces yo necesitaba a alguien que me ayudara como a expresarme.

Daniel: ¿ningún interprete te proporcionaron?

Jazmin: No, nunca me lo reservaron y luego para poder sacar al niño, ellos la corte te pide un reporte a como se llama esto? (inaudible) Que es como quien cuida el *welfare el wellbeing* del Reino unido. Igual, súper lentos, super mal organizados, no tenían mi historial. O sea, ¡una cosa impresionante! Muy ineptos, muy ineptos. Yo hubiera hecho un trabajo mil veces mejor. Falta de experiencia de niños o yo qué sé. Pésimo! Yo era la que tenía que enviar mi historial "mira hay que hacer esto, mira está la visita ¿cuándo voy?" El caso estaba ya frustrándome esto no va para ningún lado el papá . . . no se qué. Fue muy estresante y pasé un tiempo muy difícil hasta que dije: "esto se acabo". . .

Translation

Jazmin: I made a lot of mistakes in my application since I have no knowledge of the law and needed support, right? "Well, tell me I am here to do this". But I had to do everything "I'm going to do this" well, somehow I managed to do it, but they always forgot something because I always wanted them to provide me with a translator because despite the fact that I speak English and because it was such a delicate case, I sometimes got nervous and, like in other cases that we had to deal with my ex, I started crying. So I needed someone to help me express myself . . .

Daniel: Did they not provide you with an interpreter?

Jazmin: No, they never provided me with one and then to be able to have the custody of the child, the court asks you for a report, what do you call it? (inaudible) Which is like something about welfare o wellbeing in the United Kingdom. The same, they were super slow, they were poorly organised, they did not have my records. I mean unbelievable! They were incompetent, very incompetent. I would have done a better job and they lack experience with kids, heavens know. Terrible! I was the one who had to send in my records "look, you have to do this, look I have an appointment to make, when is my appointment?" The situation was frustrating, it was going nowhere. The father, heavens know. It was frustrating and I had a very hard time until I said: "this is it" . . .

In excerpt 61, Jazmin depicts her anxiety caused by the lack of familiarity with legal proceedings. By referring to her need of a *translator*, her discourse brings about the one-nation one language ideology that is articulated through the law as an official institution of the monolingual state. That is, the court, as Jazmin's discourse implies, did not address her linguistic needs that could have been conducive to a better understanding of the legal implications affecting the outcome of her application. As in the case of Sarah, language seemed to have been treated as homogenous, uniform and as a neutral vehicle of communication and thus Jazmin was put in a social and legal disadvantage that could have ended in her being separated from her son. Jazmin's limited competence of a legal register of a language that she knew had the potential to restructure her social reality.

Jazmin's account also shows how discourse and society are dialogically interrelated in the sense that her depicted reality indexes larger political structures that further expose the one-nation one language ideology. In 2005, there was record of an increased demand for interpreters in British courts, which had the legal obligation to provide interpreters (Summers 2005). These, nevertheless, were often untrained, underpaid and their skills were regarded as unimportant (Summers 2005). In a factual multilingual society such as London, the shortage of interpreting services in state institutions sugggest the disregard for other languages and their speakers' needs; a monoglot ideology that also informs legal practices in other multilingual societies. In the United States, Abel (2009) reports the case of child whose grandparents needed a court order to enroll her in school and get health care for her. The grandparents had limited English proficiency and were unable to describe their situation accurately. After a long wait, they then learned they were not pursuing the right order. As the school year was coming up and the child's health was getting worse, "they nearly gave her up to foster care", but they were able to get the proper court order with the help of an interpreter (Abel 2009: 3–4). In this vein, the one nation one language ideology organises state institutions in a way that could structure exclusionary practices against migrants' families; it hierarchises people's civic participation and threatens their integrity by neglecting their linguistic needs.

Summary

This chapter has offered an analysis of various context-based (non) linguistic ideologies that intersect with social class and an economic model that affects people's subjectivities and relations. For instance, ideologies of socioeconomic mobility, the standard language and self-disqualification are expressed as the participants seek social inclusion and a way out of economic adversity. The socioeconomic and sociocultural resources that they have at their disposal foregrounds inequality and divergent needs in a destination society. Here, the one nation one language ideology becomes manifest in institutional places where the participants are not only hierarchised but where a neoliberal economic model has undermined translation and interpretation services whose cuts index a neglect of people's linguistic needs and family unity.

Chapter 6
Conclusion

This book opened with an account of my own social trajectory to acknowledge my motivations to undertake this study as well as reflect upon my positionalities in relation to the sociolinguistic experiences here explored. A social trajectory, as noted above, is neither travelled alone nor is it an isolated experience. In other words, the personal is dialogically connected with larger historical, sociopolitical contexts that influence what one decides to research. Researcher subjectivity should thus be acknowledged as an act of reflexivity. As some scholars have noted, reflexivity should not be limited as the mere self-reflection of the researcher (May 1997) but as an active involvement with the social and "historical structures that condition one's thinking and inner experience" (Emirbayer and Desmond 2012: 591). Being of working-class extraction and witnessing how inequality motivated and influenced migration decisions and channels respectively have shaped my interests in the experiences, the discursive events and ideologies analysed here.

In addition, one's sociopolitical contexts also influence how one experiences reality and how one tells it. Life stories are also both personal and social as their subjective element inflects their meaning in relation to people's living conditions and the social and political structures that people may be able to navigate. Thus, life stories can have an instructive (Herbert and Rodger 2007) and political function in that they can explain and can have the potential to defy assumptions of the constitution of societies. For instance, the often-unproblematised depiction of illegal immigration exhibits interdiscursive elements that should be historically located to understand how it contributes to a social order of hierarchies and exclusion. As we saw in chapter 3, to talk about illegal immigrants is antonymous with undocumented or irregular immigrants and, although both are loaded with issues of (im)morality, it is necessary to employ critical sociolinguistic tools to continue to challenge the discursive normalisation of identity ascription categories that may perpetuate the stigmatization of people. By pointing to and scrutinising a subtle distinction between removal and deportation and their concomitant consequences, the discursive analysis of "illegality" intends to bring about awareness and a better understanding of the social identities and relations that such a discourse constructs and may perpetuate.

A focus on discourses of illegality may also encourage us to keep criticising and questioning current depictions and characterisation of migration since the figure of the migrant has continued to be used as the scapegoat of the economic malladies in Western societies. In continental Europe, some authors have noted that the economic difficulties of the late 2000s produced both rising unemployment and right-wing support to restrict immigration (Greven 2016). In the UK, right-wing populism has also arisen due to structural economic changes that have negatively impacted working-class people who have felt politically unrepresented (Ford and Goodwin 2014; Gill and Good 2019). Media outlets and political speeches have fuelled xenophobic attitudes that threaten people's integrity. For instance, the fact that migrants have increasingly been the object of overt racist slurs after Brexit (see Booth 2019; Fernández-Reino 2020; Rzepnikowska 2019) stresses the need to take on a more militant role that counteracts processes of social exclusion, disenfranchisement and self-disqualitification. As sociolinguists, we find ourselves in the need to keep challenging dehumanising discourses and encourage informed views of society since "one way to think of the society in which one would like to live is to think of the kinds of voices it would have" (Hymes 1996: 64).

Migrant communities are not homogenous, sociocultural groups whose realities, experiences and interests could be easily identifiable. Migration "is more than the summation of a balance sheet between a set of push and pull factors delineated by origin and destination countries", but, as analysts, it "involves a critical engagement with social axes of differentiation" such as social class (Samers 2010: 119). Indeed, social class differentiations emerge and explain how the participants self-present, categorise others and themselves. That is, the participants' discourses evidence social alignments and distancing that have allowed us to gain insight into the inner social layers that constitute the Latin American community. The material as well as the symbolic construct of social class foregrounds the distinctions and divisions that affect and hierarchise their relations as well as how they make sense of the realities they describe. Although socioeconomic differences in other studies of the same population have been pointed to (see McIlwaine 2015), the incorporation of social class into sociolinguistic discussions lends itself to a more in-depth analysis of people's migration trajectories in order to understand them holistically.

Social class issues matter and their incorporation in the study of language in society could shed a wider light on people's identities and the everyday material conditions in which they live. As he makes the case for a more class-based analysis in sociolinguistics, Block (2014) writes:

> Class is a difficult construct, both in conceptual and research terms. However, it holds the promise of helping us develop better understandings of a range of issues related to language and identity in the midst of the current crisis of capitalism, which engulfs and affects us all, albeit in a very different and unequal ways. And that is something for all language and identity researchers to bear in mind (Block 2016: 251).

It is indeed a difficult construct due to the dynamic transformation of societies and people's variegated practices that may make it an elusive concept to capture. However, its complexity has valuable analytical purchase in explorations of language and identity issues. As stated in chapter 2.2, social class may be regarded as one's relational identity in the sense that other people may recognise one's symbolic and material resources and thus sanction them as belonging or not to a particular group when entering a social space or interaction; the question about "who" we are hinges upon the relation to and interaction with other social actors (Joseph 2004) situated in social, political and cultural contexts. Therefore, the construct of social class could be a lens whereby we incorporate understandings of socioeconomic stratifications and declassing as we explore people's subjective representations of their experienced reality through discourse.

In addition, social class can also allow us to address sceptical views about its analytical usefulness. We should remind ourselves that the construct of class is typically conceptualised in nationally contained spaces and has been claimed to be dead as well as has been suggested as insufficient to account for inequalities outside so-called Western societies (Pakulski and Waters 1996). On the one hand, the cases of Mario, Julia, Irma, David and Andres exhibit that social class still matters, and it does transnationally. By migrating, they have sought socioeconomic mobility as a way of improving their material living conditions in their countries of origin. That is, they have experienced social class inequalities in origin, transition, Mario's case, and destination societies where they have varied language-related aspirations and differentiated sociocultural and economic resources that affect their life chances and social identities. On the other hand, the cases of Marcia and Karla provide us with insights into the importance of social class matters that explain divergent alignments from the figure of the migrant. Thus, social class, language and identity could be integrated as analytical tools that could help us develop a more critical stance towards inequality.

The ideology of neoliberalism also affects and inflects the participants' relations and realities. As it emerged in the discourses analysed, the ideology of neoliberalism offers us both a view of individual-oriented values that some of the members of the Latin American community have (re)produced and the evaluative way in which they build their social relations. An attitude of self-responsibilisation not only intersects with the participants' different capitals and aspirations, but it is discursively mobilised implicitly and explicitly to explain the socioeconomic realities in which the participants live or deserve to live, which further underscores the hierarchisation of Latin Americans' relations. In this context, the neoliberal winner-loser dychotomy constructs polarised relations at two interrelated levels. At a first level, a rationalist view becomes prominent in that it blames the other for their own misfortunes or incapacity to lift themselves out from economic precarity.

At a second level, the figure of the entrepreneur emerges. This has been described as a characterisation that has a converging set of capitalist values by being conceived of as "the motor of economic development and as a unique being in possession of the right innate characteristics" (Block, 2018: 18). As observed in the discourses of Mayra and Sonia, the figure of the entrepreneur evidences an individualist ideology that reduces the other to an immoral destitute whose alleged lack of understanding of what the world offers them and how it functions is a fact of nature.

As it has been oberserved and criticised in many societies, neoliberalism has perpetrated many domains of our social lives, one of which is the work domain through a business-inflected practice. Outsourcing, in the context of cleaing services, provides the socioeconomic conditions in which the discourses of David, Alfonso and Diego are located and which negatively affect their work and social relations. Why immigrants change in a new country, or in Alfonso's words *they are different*, casts a wider light on how a neoliberal logic of competition is a major factor in the problem of social injustice in immigrant communities as they seek to meet their economic needs at the expense of fellow immigrants (see Mahler 1995). Nonetheless, people's economic pressures such as the payment of rents and remittances should play a more prominent role in our analysis to explain and criticize how a South to North migration has contributed to the migrant divison of labour in which material conditions of living result in rapacious attitudes among working class co-ethnics. In this sense, it is worth reminding ourselves what Marx stated:

> Within the capitalis system all methods for raising the social productivity of labour are put into effect at the cost of the individual worker . . . they become means of domination and exploitation of the producers; they distort the work into a fragment of a man, they degrade him to the level of an appendage of a machine . . . they deform the conditions under which he works, subjecting him during the labour process to a despotism more hateful for its meaness; they transform his life-time into working time and drag his wife and child beneath the wheels of the juggernaut of capital (Marx, Capital, Volume 1, Chapter 2).

Although the working conditions of which Marx talked are located in XIX century Europe, one cannot ignore work sites such maquiladoras in the US-Mexico border or factories in India that reflect current means of domination that sustains a system of labour exploitation. In the context of this study, outsourced work also illustrates contemporary forms of economic gain at the expense of individuals. The fragmented schedules in which many Latin Americans work not only feed a so-called economic logic of efficiency from which other institutions such as universities benefit, but degrade their living and working conditions to relations of exploitation and the precarisation of their realities. Thus, a focus on people's material living and working conditions becomes socially pertinent when the participants' accounts point to conflict, exploitation and discrimination practices as fixed cultural traits that we saw in chapter 3. That is, an essentialising view of people's behaviour that is allegedly predictable and explained by their geographic origin to which I was also interpellated to agree. Being a Latin American myself, I was assumed to know, and perhaps embody, those defining characteristics of dishonesty and slyness that shape social relations. Thus, it is my intent that this study contributes to a critical attitude towards a neoliberal work scheme that may background the inequalities and processes of exclusion that Latin Americans and other immigrant groups face or may assume to be the natural state of things.

In addition, outsourcing has badly affected the provision of translation and interpretation in legal settings with wider social consequences. Although specialised interpretation and translation exist, outsourced language service providers have proven to undervalue translators' and interpreters' jobs by 40% wage-cut and appointing non-professionals (often at lower pay rate) to perform specialised legal interpretation in the UK (Moreno 2020). In this sense, outsourcing creates an environment of economic hostility towards interpreters and translators whose expertise and wages are reduced to the deteriorisation of their profession in a factually multilingual society. Speakers like Sarah and Jazmin whose limited knowledge of a specialised legal register that could determine their migration status and family's wellbeing, are affected by an economic logic that interacts with a monoglot ideology in a way that access to a fair legal process is not guaranteed.

The detailed exploration of the complexity of language ideologies has enabled us to gain insight into the constitution of Latin American immigrants' social relations and experiences. Such ideologies intersect with social class. On the one hand, the study of language ideologies in relation to English as a vehicle to socio-economic mobility and inclusion allows us to see that members of the Latin American community construct and value their social relations as investments. Language has been reconfigured as an economic resource and "helps us understand part of what people are trying to do with language, not just in how they think of it but in how they concretely try to turn it into an exchangeable resource with measurable value in economic terms" (Heller and Duchêne 2016: 144). The varied and divergent social and linguistic interests that some Latin Americans have expressed and that have assumed to be common-sense views are shot through by profit-seeking discourses. On the other hand, as we have seen in chapters 4 and 5, ideologies of the standard accent, authenticity and the one language one nation have exclusionary effects on the participants who have experienced them. The standard language ideology also appears not only as a monolith but as a cultural capital that grants status and may counteract race-based ideologies that speakers like Sonia may face. Thus, the complex (re)production of language ideologies in a neoliberal context exhibits the differentiated distribution of economic, social and cultural capital to which the participants have had access and that are (un)able to mobilise according to their migration and social trajectory.

In light of the above, one can state that language is a major constituent of people's ways of being and acting in the world. Heller et al. (2018) have stressed the importance of language in a number of contexts such as education, language policy and migration as they state that:

> [language] is connnected to how we construct social differences and how social and political life is organised around them. These differences (whether understood as national, ethnolinguistic, racialized, gendered, sexualized or anything else) are bound up with the processes through which we make and rationalize inequality. We conceptualize and make sense of the world around us though language, and we negotiate our relationships with others through language. Who we are considered to be, and who we can become, are language matters. And who we can become is all about our access to things that matter: political power, economic resources like jobs, education, social status or cultural resources like stories, songs and art (Heller et al. 2018: 1).

Their argument about the permeability of language in social life resonates with the migration trajectories and experiences discussed here. It also puts power and inequality at the centre of a critical sociolinguistic perspective. This, in my view, is an attitude that we as sociolinguists should embrace in order to challenge and counteract marginalisation processes that we observe across societies, and that many times we may reinforce.

To understand people's experiences better and connect their discourses to the economic system that may structure their lives and relations, it is necessary to incorporate a more ethnographically informed work from a critical perspective. As Fitzpatrick and May (2022: 15) have noted, critical ethnography could be understood as a "form of ethnography with an orientation to the political and to justice". That is, our observations and interactions with the people whose realities we seek to understand, could benefit from a more active and critical engagement with the sociopolitical and economic environment within which we find ourselves. As a number of scholars have also stated, an engagement with the economic and material bases of human activity and social life in Applied Linguistics and sociolinguistics has been scant (Ricento 2012; Block, Gray, and Holborow 2012; Block 2014; 2018). Thus, a critical ethnographic stance may allow us to recognise and interrogate how wider power relations operate to frame knowledge, create subjectivities and affect people's lived realities (see Fitzpatrick and May 2022).

A critical ethnographic attitude is consonant with those taking on a Marxist stance to inequality (Simpson and O'Regan 2018). This may affect people's experiences and opportunities to access language classes, translation and interpretation services in institutional sites as well as material living and working conditions in the service sector. In this context, Latin American managers' voice and discourses of working with other Latin Americans should be taken into account for a more in-depth examination and description of their work interactions with other Latin Americans and immigrants from the so called global South. The rationale to scrutinise their accounts lies in the motivation to shed a wider light on how they account for them and the extent to which such descriptions may be influenced by an exploitative economic system that constructs migrants as "good workers". These, as we saw in chapter 4, must have defining characteristics such as being willing to work long, fragmented hours for low pay and possessing personal behaviours needed to effectively perform a role that helps companies and businesses meet their strategic objectives (see Lucia and Lepsinger 1999). What managers have got to say about these characteristics may allow us to see how an economic logic may continue to dehumanise social and work relations by turning them into opportunities of personal economic gain; rapacious attitudes that pit one individual against the other. In a capitalist system, such attitudes could index that the workers may have no choice but to sell their labour as the only way whereby "they can access money to buy what they need to live, feed themselves and provide a roof over their heads" (Holborow 2018: 60). This is not to justify exploitation, but to continue to encourage a critical sociolinguistic take that enables us to look at uneven material realities from which people speak and that, when work and life conditions are increasingly unequal, could raise a call for a more militant attitude towards social justice and change as we attemtp to account for issues of language and society.

Finally, the ideology of self-responsibilisation calls for counteraction by considering and practising the social meaning of such words as community with which many Latin American migrants identify and that of solidarity. As to community, it evokes a place where we may find values of commonality and the empathy of people who disinterestedly help one another (Bauman 2001). In other words, the *feelings* of community bring people together and, in times of fierce competition and the connivance of states with capital, have the potential to encourage collective practices that benefit us all and that may construct solidarity. Like many other terms, solidarity is indeed a polysemous and contested concept (Wilder 2022), but one that could lend itself to building alliances among heterogenous sociocultural groups across regional and national boundaries as demonstrated in the political movements of the 1960s. Solidarity carries the potential to stimulate political action as we take sides and seek to change the structures of social injustice.

Appendix A

Transcription conventions

Transcription conventions used in interview excerpts (adapted from Jefferson (1984)):

¿?	indicates question;
,	indicates micropause;
.	indicates long pause;
¡!	indicates interjection/exclamation;
[text]	indicates the end and overlapping of words between interactants;
. . .	indicates edition/omission of text;
CAPITALS	indicates rising intonation/emphasis;
"text"	indicates words in an indirect style (quotation);
((text))	indicates non-verbal activity (body language; laughter);
Italics	indicates English (interview excerpts) or Spanish words (analysis).

Appendix B

Table of participant information

Pseud-onym	Nationality	Gender	Age (app-rox.)	Education	Race	Length of stay in the UK	Marital status	Job/ occupation
Marcia	Brazilian-Italian	Female	45	M.A in Arts M.A in education	Mixed	23 years	Married to an English man	Language teacher
Miguel	Venezuelan-Spanish	Male	44	High school	Mixed	3.5 years	Married (wife and daughter living in Venezuela	Worked in a storage house and restaurant
Karla	Chile	Female	36	B.A in Journalism M.A in Anthropology	white	3	Engaged to a Scottish man (she held a spouse visa)	Volunteer and secretarial job at NGO
David	Ecuador	Male	38	B.A in Physical Education	Mixed	15	Married to Ecuadorian-British woman	Outsourced Cleaner in a London-based University
Irma	Ecuador	Female	36	High school	Mixed	16	Single	Ran her own event-management business directed to Latin Americans
Sharon	Colombian-British	Female	36	B.A in Business and Finance	Mixed	20 years	Married to Colombian-British man	Import and export business/ network marketing

(continued)

Pseud-onym	Nationality	Gender	Age (approx.)	Education	Race	Length of stay in the UK	Marital status	Job/occupation
Diego	Colombian-British	Male	40	High school	Mixed	17 years	Married to high school educated, Colombian-British woman	Cleaner in Hospital
Alfonso	Venezuelan-British	Male	38	College (Technician)	Black	14 years	Divorced	Care assistant in hospital
Linda	Mexican-British	Female	45	B.A in Psychology	Mixed	26 years	Married to an English man	English teacher and ran her own antique bussiness
Mayra	Ecuadorian	Female	35	B.A in international relations	Mixed	4 years	Married to Ecuadorian man	Part-time job at Ecuadorian embassy and Entrepenuer
Jazmin	Colombian-British	Female	36	M.A in Transport Management	Mixed	13 years	Divorced	Worked at tourism-promoting concierge
Sonia	Ecuadorian-Spanish	Female	33	High school	Black	6 years	Married to Spanish man	Network marketing
Mario	Peruvian-Spanish	Male	55	B.A in accounting	white	2 months	Married to Peruvian-Spanish woman living in Spain	unemployed

(continued)

Pseud-onym	Nationality	Gender	Age (approx.)	Education	Race	Length of stay in the UK	Marital status	Job/occupation
Andres	Colombian-British	Male	35	High school	Mixed	16 years	Married to Colombian-British woman	Care assistant and salsa-class instructor
Julia	Chilean-Spanish	Female	40	High school	white	2 years	Married to Chilean-Spanish man	Housewife
Sarah	Mexican	Female	38	High school	white	14 years	divorced	unemployed

References

Aalbers, Manuel B. 2013. Neoliberalism is Dead . . . Long Live Neoliberalism! *International Journal of Urban and Regional Research* 37(3). 1083–1090.
Abel, Laura. 2009. *Language Access in State Courts*. New York University School of Law: Brennan Center for Justice. Available at: https://www.brennancenter.org/sites/default/files/legacy/publications/154142_LangWhite.pdf (accessed 18 december 2022)
Abrams, Lynn. 2016. *Oral history theory*. Second edition. London: Routledge.
Ager, Alastair & Alison Strang. 2008. 'Understanding Integration: A Conceptual Framework', *Journal of Refugee Studies* 21(2). 166–191.
Agha, Asif. 2007. *Language and Social Relations*. UK: Cambridge University Press.
Ainsworth, Susan & Cynthia Hardy. 2004. Critical Discourse Analysis and Identity: why bother? *Critical Discourse Studies* 1(2). 225–259.
Al-Ali, Nadje & Khalid Koser (eds.). 2002. *New Approaches to Migration? Transnational Communities and the Transformation of Home*. London: Routledge.
Alan, Kori &Bonnie McElhini. 2017. Neoliberalism, Language and Migration. In Suresh Canagarajah (ed.), *The Handbook of Migration and Language*, 79–101. London: Routledge.
Alba Monteserin, Susana, Ana Fernandez Asperilla & Ubaldo Martinez Vega. 2013. *Crisis Económica y Nuevo Panorama Migratorio en España* [Economic crisis and new migration overview in Spain]. Centro de Documentación de las Migraciones de la Fundación 1o de Mayo. http://www.1mayo.ccoo.es/nova/files/1018/Estudio65.pdf (accessed 15 april 2015)
Aldridge, Hanna, Sabrina Bushe, Peter Kenway, Tom MacInnes & Adam Tinson. 2013. *'London's Poverty Profile 2013'*, Trust for London: London.http://www.trustforlondon.org.uk/wp-content/uploads/2013/10/LPP_2013_finalReport_Web.pdf (accessed 20 may 2016)
Alberti, Gabriela, Jane Holgate & Maite Tapia. 2013. Organising migrants as workers or as migrant workers? Intersectionality, trade unions, and precarious work. *The international journal of Human Resource Management*, 24(22). 4132–4148.
Allen, William. 2016. *A Decade of Immigration in the British Press*. The Migration Observatory at the University of Oxford. https://migrationobservatory.ox.ac.uk/wp-content/uploads/2016/11/Report-Decade_Immigration_British_Press-1.pdf (accessed 15 november 2017)
Althusser, Louis. 1971. Ideology and ideological state apparatuses. In Louis Althusser (ed.), *Lenin and Philosophy*, 85–126. New York: Monthly Review Press.
Althusser, Louis. 2014. *On the Reproduction of Capitalism: Ideology and Ideological State Apparatuses*. London: Verso.
Anderson, Benedict. 1991. *Imagined Communities. Reflections on the Origin and Spread of Nationalism*. London: Verso.
Andrews, Molly, Corinne Squire & Maria Tamboukou. 2008. *Doing Narrative Research*. London: Sage.
Andujar Castillo, Francisco. 2017. Gobernar por decreto y sin Consejos en el reinado de Carlos II. Patronazgo, venalidad y corrupción [Governing by decree and without councils in Charles II's reign. Patronage, venality and corruption]. In Michel Bertrand, Francisco Andujar Castillo & Thomas Glesener (eds.), *Gobernar y reformar la monarquía. Los agentes políticos y administrativos en España y América (siglos XVI–XIX)* [Govern and reform the monarchy. Political and administrative agents in Spain and America in XVI–XIX], 171–186. Valencia: Albatros.
Antaki, Charles. 1994. *Explaining and arguing. The social organization of accounts*. London: Sage Publications.
Antaki, Charles & Sue Widdicombe (eds.). 1998. *Identities in Talk*. London: Sage.

Appadurai, Arjun. 1996. *Modernity at Large. Cultural Dimensions of Globalization*. USA: The University of Minnesota Press.

Arnorsson, Agust & Gylfi Zoega. 2018. On the causes of Brexit. *European Journal of Political Economy*, 55. 301–323. https://doi.org/10.1016/j.ejpoleco.2018.02.001

Ashley, Louise. 2010. 'Making a difference? The use (and abuse) of diversity management at the UK's elite law firms. *Work, Employment and Society* 4. 711–727.

Atkinson, Robert. 2002. The Life Story Interview. In Jaber F. Gubrium & James L. Holstein (eds.), *Handbook of Interview Research. Context and Method*, 121–140. London: Sage Publications.

Austin, John L. 1962. *How to Do Things with Words*. Oxford: The Clarendon Press.

Augustine-Adams, Kif. 2015. Hacer a Mexico: La nacionalidad, los chinos y el censo de población de 1930 [Making Mexico: nationality, the chinese and the population census in 1930]. In Pablo Yenkelevich (ed.), *Inmigración y Racismo: Contribuciones a la historia de los extranjeros en México* [Immigration and racism: contributions to the history of foreigners in Mexico], 155–194. Mexico: El Colegio de Mexico.

Baer, Werner. 1972. Import Substitution and Industrialization in Latin America: Experiences and Interpretations. *Latin American Research Review* 7(1). 95–122.

Bailey, John. 2014. *Crimen e Impunidad. Las trampas de la seguridad en México* [Crime and Impunity. The traps of security in Mexico]. México: Random House.

Basch, Linda, Nina Glick-Schiller & Cristina S. Blanck. 1994. *Nations Unbound; Transnational Projects, Postcolonial Predicaments and De-territorialised Nation-states*. Amsterdam: Gordon Breach.

Bakhtin, Mikhail M. 1981. *The Dialogic Imagination: Four Essays*. USA: University of Texas Press Slavic Series.

Bamberg, Michael. 2006. Stories: Big or small: Why do we care? *Narrative Inquiry*, 16(1).139–147.

Bamberg, Michael & Alexandra Georgakopoulou. 2008. Small stories as a new perspective in narrative and identity analysis. 28(3). 377–396. https://doi.org/10.1515/TEXT.2008.018

Bansel, Peter. 2007. Subjects of choice and lifelong learning. *International Journal of Qualitative Studies in Education* 20(3). 283–300.

Baran, Dominika. 2017. *Language in Immigrant America*. UK: Cambridge University Press.

Barat, Erzsébet, Jiří Nekvapil & Patrick Studer (eds). 2013. *Ideological Conceptualizations of Language: Discourses of Linguistic Diversity*. Volume 3. New York: Peter Lang GmbH, Internationaler Verlag der Wissenschaften.

Barker, Chris & Darius Galasinski. 2001. *Cultural Studies and Discourse Analysis. A Dialogue on Language and Identity*. UK: Sage Publication.

Barlán, J. 1988. *A system approach for understanding International Population Movement: The role of Policies and Migrant Community in the Southern Cone*. IUSSP Seminar, Genting Highlands, Malaysia. September 1988.

Barth, Fredrik. 1969. *Ethnic groups and Boundaries: the social organisation of culture difference*. Boston, MA: Little, Brown and Company.

Bartram, David, Maritsa V. Poros & Pierre Monforte. 2014. *Key Concepts in Migration*. London: Sage Publications.

Batalova, Jeanne & Jie Zong. 2017. Cuban Immigrants in the United States. Migration Policy Institute. https://www.migrationpolicy.org/article/cuban-immigrants-united-states-2016 (accessed 14 august 2022)

Bauman, Zygmunt. 1998. *Globalization: The Human Consequences*. Cambridge: Polity Press.

Bauman, Zygmunt. 2001. *Community. Seeking safety in an Insecure World*. Cambridge: Polity Press.

Bethell, Leslie. 2018. *Brazil: Essays on History and Politics*. London: Institute of Latin American Studies.

Berg, Bruce L. 2004. *Qualitative Research Methods for the Social Sciences*. 5th Edition. Boston: Pearson.

Bermudez Torres, Anastasia. 2003. *ICAR Navigation Guide. Refugee Populations in the UK: Colombians*. Information Centre for Asylum and Refugees. London. http://www.icar.org.uk/?lid=260 (accessed 23 march 2015).

Benwell, Bethan & Elizabeth Stokoe. 2006. *Discourse and Identity*. Edinburgh: Edinburgh University Press.

Billig, Michael. 1995. *Banal Nationalism*. Great Britain: Sage Publications.

Birch, Kean & Vlad Mykhnenko (eds). 2010. *The Rise and Fall of Neoliberalism. The Collapse of an Economic Order?* London: Zed Books.

Blackledge, Adrian. 2000. Monolingual Ideologies in multilingual states: Language, hegemony and social justice in western liberal democracies. *Estudios de sociolinguistica* 1(2). 25–45.

Blackledge, Adrian. 2005. *Discourse and power in a multilingual World*. Amsterdam: John Benjamins Publishing Company.

Blackledge, Adrian. 2009. Being English, speaking English: Extension to English language testing legislation and the future of multicultural Britain. In Clare Mar-Molinero, Patrick Stevenson & Gabrielle HoganBrun (eds.), *Testing Regimes: Critical Perspectives on Language, Migration and Citizenship in Europe*, 83–108. Amsterdam: Benjamins.

Blackledge, Adrian & Angela Creese. 2017. Translanguaging in Mobility. In Suresh Canagarajah (ed.), *The Routledge Handbook of Migration and Language*, 31–46. London/New York: Routledge.

Blinder, Scott & William Allen. 2016. *UK Public Opinion towards immigration: Overall Attitudes and Level of Concern*. The Migration Observatory. Oxford University. http://www.migrationobservatory.ox.ac.uk/wp-content/uploads/2016/04/Briefing-Public_Opinion_Immigration_Attitudes_Concern.pdf (accessed 19 september 2016)

Blinder, Scott. 2016. *Deportations, Removals and Voluntary Departures from the UK*. The Migration Observatory. Oxford University. http://www.migrationobservatory.ox.ac.uk/resources/briefings/deportations-removals-and-voluntary-departures-from-the-uk/ (accessed 19 september 2016)

Blinder, Scott & Lindsey Richards. 2020. *UK public opinion toward immigration: Overall attitudes and level of concern*. Migration observatory briefing. https://migrationobservatory.ox.ac.uk/resources/briefings/uk-public-opinion-toward-immigration-overall-attitudes-and-level-of-concern/ (accessed 16 September 2021)

Block, David. 2006. *Multilingual Identities in a Global City*. Basingstoke: Palgrave Macmillan.

Block, David. 2008. Spanish-speaking Latinos in London: Community and language practices. *Journal of Language, Identity and Education* 7(1). 5–21.

Block, David, John Gray & Marnie Holborow. 2012. *Neoliberalism and Applied Linguistics*. Routledge, UK.

Block, David. 2014. *Social Class in Applied Linguistics*. New York: Routledge.

Block, David & Victor Corona. 2014. Exploring class-based intersectionality. *Language, Culture and Curriculum* 27(1). 27–42.

Block, David. 2016. Class in language and identity research. In Siân Preece (ed.). *The Routledge Handbook of Language and Identity*, 241–254. London: Routledge.

Block, David. 2017. Social class in migration, identity and language research. In Suresh Canagarajah (ed.), *The Routledge Handbook of Migration and Language*, 133–148. London: Routledge.

Block, David. 2018. *Political Economy and Sociolinguistics. Neoliberalism, Inequality and Social Class*. London: Bloomsbury.

Block, David. 2018b. What would Karl say? The entrepreneur as ideal (and cool) citizen in 21st century societies. *Language Sciences* 70. 16–25. https://doi.org/10.1016/j.langsci.2018.04.006

Block, David. 2019. What on earth is 'language commodification? In Barbara Schmenk, Stephan Breidbach & Lutz Küster (eds.), *Sloganization in Language Education Discourse. Conceptual Thinking in the Age of Academic Marketization*, 121–141. Bristol: Multilingual Matters.

Block, David. 2022. *Innovations and Challenges in Identity Research*. London: Routledge.

Blommaert, Jan & Jef Verschueren. 1998. The role of language in European Nationalist Ideologies. *Pragmatics* 2(3). 335–375.

Blommaert, Jan. 1999a. The debate is open. In Jan Blommaert (ed.), *Language Ideological debates*, 1–38. Berlin and New York: Mouton de Gruyter.

Blommaert, J. 1999b. The debate is closed. In Jan Blommaert (ed.). *Language Ideological debates*, 425–438. Berlin and New York: Mouton de Gruyter,

Blommaert, Jan. 2001. Context is/as critique. *Critique of Anthropology* 21(1).13–32.

Blommaert, Jan. 2003. Commentary: A sociolinguistics of globalisation. *Journal of Sociolinguistics* 7(4). 607–623

Blommaert, Jan. 2006. Language policy and national identity. In Thomas Ricento (ed.), *An introduction to language policy: Theory and method*, 238–54. Malden, MA: Blackwell.

Blommaert, Jan. 2010. *The Sociolinguistics of Globalization*. New York: Cambridge University Press.

Blommaert, Jan &Jie Dong. 2010a. Language and Movement in Space. In Coupland, Nicholas (ed.), *The Handbook of Language and Globalisation*, 366–385. Oxford: Blackwell Publishing.

Blommaert, Jan & Jie Dong. 2010b. *Ethnographic Fieldwork. A beginner's Guide*. Multilingual Matters. Bristol. UK.

Blommaert, Jan &Jie Dong. 2009. Space, scale and accents: constructing migrant identity in Beijing. In James Collins, Stef Slembrouck & Mike Baynham (eds.), *Globalization and Language in contact. Scale, Migration, and Communicative Practices (Advances in Sociolinguistics)*, 42–61. London: Continuum.

Blommaert, Jan & Ad Backus. 2011. Repertoires revisited: 'Knowing language' in superdiversity. *Working Papers in Urban Language and Literacy*. 67. https://www.kcl.ac.uk/sspp/departments/education/research/Research-Centres/ldc/publications/workingpapers/abstracts/WP067-Repertoires-revisited-Knowing-language-in-superdiversity.aspx (accessed 15 august 2017)

Blommaert, Jan. 2013. Citizenship, Language, and Superdiversity: Towards Complexity. *Journal of Language, Identity & Education* 12(3).193–196.

Bhopal, Kalwant & John Preston (eds.). 2011. *Intersectionality and race in education*. London: Routledge.

Boas, Taylor C. & Jordan Gans-Morse. 2009. Neoliberalism: From new liberal philosophy to anti-liberal slogan. *Studies in Comparative International Development* 44(2). 137–161.

Bonilla Silva, Eduardo. 1999. The Essential Social Fact of Race, (Reply to Loveman, ASR, December 1999). *American Sociological Review* 64(6). 899–906.

Booth, Robert. 2019. Racism rising since Brexit vote, nationwide study reveals. https://www.theguardian.com/world/2019/may/20/racism-on-the-rise-since-brexit-vote-nationwide-study-reveals (accessed 27 november 2022)

Bottero, Wendy. 2004. Class Identities and the identity of class. *Sociology* 38(5). 985–1003. https://doi.org/10.1177/0038038504047182

Bourdieu, Pierre. 1975. The specificity of the scientific field and the social conditions of the progress of reason. *Social Science Information* 14(6). 19–47.

Bourdieu, Pierre. 1977a. *Outline of a theory of practice*. Cambridge: Cambridge University Press.

Bourdieu, Pierre. 1977b. The Economics of Linguistic Exchanges. *Social Science Information* 16(6). 645–668. https://doi.org/10.1177/053901847701600601

Bourdieu, Pierre. 1984. *Distinction. A Social Critique of the judgement of Taste*. London. Routledge.

Bourdieu, Pierre. 1986. The forms of capital. In John Richardson (ed.), *Handbook of Theory and Research for the Sociology of Education*,15–19. Westport, CT: Greenwood.
Bourdieu, Pierre. 1989. Social Space and Symbolic Power. *Sociological Theory* 7(1). 14–25.
Bourdieu, Pierre. 1990a. *In Other Words*. Stanford, CA: Stanford University Press.
Bourdieu, Pierre. 1990b. *The Logic of Practice*. Cambridge: Polity Press.
Bourdieu, Pierre & Loïc J. D. Wacquant. 1992. *An invitation to reflexive sociology*. London. Polity Press.
Bourdieu, Pierre. 1998. The essence of neoliberalism. What is neoliberalism? A programme for destroying collective structures which may impede the pure market logic. https://mondediplo.com/1998/12/08bourdieu (accessed 03 march 2017)
Bourdieu, Pierre. 2003. *Language and Symbolic Power*. Cambridge: Polity Press.
Breeze, Ruth. 2011. Critical Discourse Analysis and its Critics. *Pragmatics* 21(4). 493–525.
Briseño-Senosiain, Liliana, Laura Solares-Robles & Laura Suárez de la Torre (eds.). 1986. *Obras completas. Obra histórica I, México y sus revoluciones. Volumen IV* [Complete Works. Historical Works I. Mexico and its revolutions]. México: Instituto Mora/CONACULTA.
Brown, C. 2007. Reimagining International Society and Global Community. In David Held & Anthony McGrew (eds.), G*lobalisation Theory. Approaches and Controversies*, 171–189. Cambridge: Polity Press.
Brown, Wendy. 2005 *Edgework: Critical Essays on Knowledge and Politics*. Princeton, NJ: Princeton University Press.
Brubaker, Rogers. 2000. Accidental Diasporas and External "Homelands" in Central and Eastern Europe: Past and Present. *IHS Political Science Series* 71, October 2000.
Brubaker, Rogers. 2005. The 'diaspora' diaspora. *Ethnic and Racial Studies* 28(1). 1–19.
Brubaker, Rogers. *Grounds for Difference*. Cambridge MA: Harvard University Press.
Bruner, Jerome. 1990. *Acts of Meaning*. Cambridge MA: Harvard University Press.
Bruner, Jerome. 1991. The narrative Construction of Reality. *Critical Inquiry* 18(1). 1–21.
Bucholtz, Mary & Kira Hall. 2005. Identity in interaction: a sociolinguistic approach. *Discourse Studies* 7(4–5). 585–614.
Bucholtz, Mary &Kira Hall. 2009. Locating Identity in Language. In Dominic Watt & Carmen Llamas (eds.), *Sociolinguistics: Language and Identities*,18–28. Edinburgh: Edinburgh University Press.
Bucholtz, Mary. 2014. The Feminist Foundations of Language, Gender, and Sexuality Research. In Susan Ehrlich, Miriam Meyerhoff & Janet Holmes (eds.), *The Handbook of Language, Gender, and Sexuality*, Second Edition, 23–47. UK: JohnWiley & Sons.
Butler, Judith. 1990. *Gender Trouble: Feminism and the Subversion of Identity*. New York: Routledge.
Butler, Judith. 2000. Restaging the Universal: Hegemony and the Limits of Formalism. In Judith Butler, Ernesto Laclau & Slavoj Žižek (eds.), *Contingency, Hegemony, Universality. Contemporary Dialogues on the Left*,11–43. London: Verso.
Butler, Judith. 2002. *Gender trouble. Feminism and the Subversion of Identity*. Tenth Anniversary Edition. London: Routledge.
Calvert, Peter. 1982. *The concept of class. An historical introduction*. London. Hutchinson and Co.
Calvi, Maria Vittoria. 2011. El español como lengua inmigrada en Italia. *Lengua y migración* 3(I). 9–32.
Cameron, Deborah. 2014. Gender and Language ideologies. In Susan Ehrlich, Miriam Meyerhoff & Janet Holmes (eds.), *The Handbook of Language, Gender, and Sexuality*, Second Edition, 281–296. UK: JohnWiley & Sons.
Card, David. 1990. The Impact of the Mariel Boatlift on the Miami Labor Market. *Industrial and Labor Relations Review* 43(2). 245–257. https://doi.org/10.2307/2523702
Cardoso, Fernando Henrique & Enzo Faletto. 1979. *Dependency and Development in Latin America*. Translated by Marjory Mattingly Urquidi. Berkeley: University of California Press.

Carroll, William &Collin Carson. 2006. Neoliberalism, Capitalist Class Formation and the Global Network of Corporations and Policy Groups. In Dieter Plehwe, Bernhard J.A. Walpen & Gisela Neunhöffer (eds.), *Neoliberal hegemony: A global critique*, 51–69. London: Routledge.

Carter, Ronald. 1999. Standard Grammars, Spoken Grammars: Some Educational Implications. In Tony Bex & Richard, J. Watts (eds.), *Standard English: The Widening Debate*, 149–167. London: Routledge.

Carvajal, D. (2017). As Colombia Emerges from Decades of War, Migration Challenges Mount. https://www.migrationpolicy.org/article/colombia-emerges-decades-war-migration-challenges-mount (accessed 05 may 2022)

Castillo Fernandez, Didimo & Adrian Sotelo Valencia. 2013. Outsourcing and the new labor precariousness in Latin America. *Latin American Perspectives* 40(5).14–26.

Cassarino, Jean-Pierre. 2004. Theorising Return Migration. The Conceptual Approach to Return Migration Revisited. *International Journal of Multicultural Societies* 6(2). 253–279.

Castles, Stephen. 2002. Migration and Community Formation under Conditions of Globalization. *International Migration Review* 36(4).1143–1168.

Castles, Sthephen & Mark. J. Miller. 2009. *The Age of Migration. International Population Movements in the Modern World.* Fourth edition. UK: Palgrave McMillan.

Castles, Stephen. 2010. Understanding global migration: a social transformation perspective. *Journal of Ethnic and Migration Studies* 36(10). 1565–1586.

Celis Ospina, Juan Carlos. 2012. *La subcontratación laboral en América Latina: Miradas multidimensionales* [outsourcing in Latin America: multidimensional approaches]. Colombia: CLACSO.

Chasteen, John Charles. 2001. *Born in Blood and Fire. A Concise History of Latin America.* London: W.W Norton & Company.

Chesire, Jenny. 2002. Who we are and where we're going: Language and identities in the new Europe. In Paul Gubbins & Mike Holt (eds.), *Beyond boundaries. Language and identity in contemporary Europe*, 19–34. Clevedon: Multilingual Matters.

Chisti, Muzaffar & Jessica Bolter. 2021. Court-Ordered Relaunch of Remain in Mexico Policy Tweaks Predecessor Program, but Faces Similar Challenges. Migration Policy Institute.https://www.migrationpolicy.org/article/court-order-relaunch-remain-in-mexico (Accessed 02 december 2021)

Chinoy, Ely. 2012. *La sociedad. Una Introducción a la sociología* [Society. An introducction to sociology]. México. Fondo de Cultura Económica.

Chomsky, Noam. 2017. *Requiem for the American Dream. The 10 Principles of concentration of wealth and power.* London: Seven Stories Press.

Cisneros, J. David. 2008. Contaminated Communities: The Metaphor of "Immigrant as Pollutant" in Media Representations of Immigration. *Rhetoric & Public Affairs* 11(4). 569–601.

Census Bureu. 2021. 2020 Census Statistics Highlight Local Population Changes and Nation's Racial and Ethnic Diversity. https://www.census.gov/newsroom/press-releases/2021/population-changes-nations-diversity.html (accessed 20 may 2022)

Clarke, John. 2008. Living with/in and without neo-liberalism. *Focaal* 2008(51), 135–147.

Clifford, James. 1994. Diasporas. *Cultural Anthropology* 9(3).302–38

Clyne, Michael. 2005. *Australia's Language potential.* Sydney: UNSW Press.

Coalition of Latin Americans in the UK (CLAUK). 2015. Recognition. http://www.clauk.org.uk/recognition/ (accesed 25 may 2015)

Cock, J. Camilo. 2011. Latin American commercial spaces and the formation of ethnic publics in London: The case of the elephant and castle. In Cathy McIlwaine (ed.), *Cross-Border Migration among Latin Americans: European Perspectives and Beyond*,175–196. New York: Palgrave Macmillan.

Codó, Eva. 2013. Trade Unions and NGOs under neoliberalism: Between Regimenting Migrants and Subverting the State. In Alexandre Duchêne, Melissa Moyer & Celia Roberts (eds.), *Language, Migration and Social Inequalities. A Critical Sociolinguistic Perspective on Institutions and Work*, 25–55. Bristol. Multilingual Matters.

Cohen, Deborah. 2006. From Peasant to Worker: Migration, Masculinity, and the Making of Mexican Workers in the US. *International Labor and Working-Class History* 69(1), 81–103. doi:10.1017/S0147547906000056

Cohen, Robin. 1997 *Global Diasporas: An Introduction*. London: UCL Press.

Cohen, Robin. 2008. *Global Diasporas: An Introduction*. Second Edition. London: Routledge.

Cooke, Melanie &James Simpson. 2012. Discourses about linguistic diversity. In Marilyn Jones, Adrian Blackledge & Angela Creese (eds.), *The Routledge Handbook of Multilingualism*, 116–130. London: Routledge.

Corus, Canan & Bige Saatcioglu. 2015. An intersectionality framework for transformative services research. *The Service Industries Journal* 35(7–8). 415–429

Coupland, Nikolas. 2003. Introduction: Sociolinguistics and globalisation. *Journal of Sociolinguistics* 7 (4). 465–472

Coupland, Nikolas. 2010. *The Handbook of Language and Globalization*. Singapore: Blackwell Publishing.

Courtis, Corina. 2011. Marcos Institucionales Normativos y de Políticas sobre Migración Internacional en Argentina, Chile y Ecuador [Normative institutional frames and International migration Policy in Argentina, Chile and Ecuador]. In Jorge Martínez Pizarro (ed.), *Migración Internacional en America Latina y el Caribe-Nuevas Tendencias, Nuevos Enfoques* [International migration in Latin America and the Caribbean-New trends, new approaches], 99–206. Santiago de Chile: CEPAL.

Coutin, Susan Bibler. 2000. *Legalizing moves: Salvadoran immigrants' struggle for US residency*. USA: University Michigan Press.

Crenshaw, Kimberle. 1989. Demarginalizing the intersection of race and sex: a Black feminist critique of antidiscrimination doctrine, feminist theory, and antiracist politics. *University of Chicago Legal Forum* 1(8). 139–167.

Crenshaw, Kimberle. 1991. Mapping the margins: intersectionality, identity politics, and violence against women of color. *Stanford Law Review* 43(6). 1241–99.

Creese, Gillian & Brandy Wiebe. 2012. Survival employment: gender and deskilling among African immigrants in Canada. *International Migration* 50(5). 59–76.

Creese, Angela, Adrian Blackledge & Jaspreet Kaur Takhi. 2014. The ideal 'native speaker' teacher: negotiating authenticity and legitimacy in the language classroom. *The Modern Language Journal* 98(4). 937–951.

Crawford, James. 2000. *At War with Diversity. Language Policy in an Age of Diversity*. Clevedon: Multilingual Matters.

Cruz-Manjarrez, Adriana. 2016. Transnacionalismo y migración de retorno en una comunidad Zapoteca [Transnationalism and return migration in a Zapotec community]. In Elaine Levine, Silvia Nuñez & Monica Verea (eds.), *Nuevas Experiencas de la Migración de Retorno [New experiences in return migration]*, 205–226. Mexico: UNAM.

Czarniawska, Barbara. 2004. *Narratives in Social Science Research*. London: Sage Publications.

Danielson, Michael, S. 2013. *Documented Failures: The Consequences of Immigration Policy on the U.S-Mexico Border*. Nogales: Kino Border Initiative.

Dauvergne, Catherine. 2008. *Making people Illegal. What globalisation means for Migration and Law*. New York: Cambridge University Press.

Day, Gary. 2001. *Class*. London: Routledge.

De Bres, Julia. 2013. Language ideologies for constructing inclusion and exclusion: Identity and interest in the metalinguistic discourse of cross-border workers in Luxembourg. In Erzebet Barat, Patrick Studer & Jiri Nekvapil (eds.), *Ideological Conceptualizations of Language. Discourses of linguistic diversity*, 57–84. Frankfurt: Peter Lang.

De Fina, Anna & Alexandra Georgakopoulou. 2012. *Analysing Narrative. Discourse and Sociolinguistics Perspectives*. UK: Cambridge University Press. UK.

De Fina, Anna. 2015. Narrative and Identities. In Anna De Fina & Alexandra Georgakopoulou (eds.), *The Handbook of Narrative Analysis*, 351–368. UK: Wiley.

De Genova, Nicholas P. 2002. Migrant Illegality and Deportability in Everyday life. *Annual Review of Anthropology* 31(2002). 419–47.

de Haas, Heins. 2010. Migration and Development: A Theoretical Perspective. *International Migration Review* 1. 227–264.

de Haas, Heins., Castles, Stephen & Mark J. Miller. 2020. *The Age of Migration. International Population Movements in the Modern World*. Sixth Edition. London: The Guildford Press.

de Haas, Heins. 2021. A theory of migration: the aspirations capabilities framework. *Comparative Migration Studies* 9(8).1–35.

della Paolera, Gerardo., Xavier H. Duran-Amorocho & Also Musacchio. 2018. The Industrialisation of South America revisited: Evidence from Argentina, Brazil, Chile and Colombia, 1890–2010, *nber working papper series*, 24345. https://www.nber.org/system/files/working_papers/w24345/w24345.pdf (accessed 22 november 2022

de Tracy, Destutt. (1992). *Mémoire sur la faculté de penser. De la métaphysique de Kant, et dáutres textes (1798–1802)*[Memoir on the faculty of thinking. From Kant's metaphysics and other texts]. In Anne Deneys-Tunneys & Henry Deneys (eds.). Paris: Fayard.

Del Valle, José. (2007) *La lengua, ¿patria comu'n? Ideas e ideologías del español*. Madrid/ Frankfurt: Iberoamericana/Vervuert.

Denneys, Henry. 1994. 'Le Crepuscule de l' ideologie, sur le destin de la philosphie 'ideologiste' de Deestutt de Tracy [The crepuscule of ideology, on the destiny of Deestutt de Tracy's ideologist philosophy]. In Henry Denneys & Anne Denneys-Tunney (eds.), A.L.C. Destutt de Tracy et l' ideologie, *Revue de Philosophie, no Special 26/27*, Nanterre: Corpus.

Doan, Ngoc Ba. 2016. To employ or not to employ expatriate non-native speaker teachers: views from within. *Asian Englishes* 18(1). 67–79.

Doerr, Neriko Musha. 2009. Introduction. In Neriko Musha Doerr (ed.), *The native speaker concept: Ethnographic investigations of native speaker effects*, 1–12. Berlin: De Gruyter Mouton.

Dong, Jie. 2017. *The Sociolinguistics of Voice in China*. New York. Routledge.

Doña Reveco, Cristián & Amanda Levinson. 2012. Chile: A Growing Destination Country in Search of a Coherent Approach to Migration. https://www.migrationpolicy.org/article/chile-growing-destination-country-search-coherent-approach-migration Retrieved 21/06/2022 (accessed 08 july 2022)

Doña Reveco, Cristián. 2022. Chile's welcoming approach to immigrants cools as numbers Rise. Available at: https://www.migrationpolicy.org/article/chile-immigrants-rising-numbers (accesed 08 july 2022)

Drucker, Peter T. 1985. *Innovation and Entrepreneurship. Practices and Principles*. London: Heinemann.

Duchêne, Alexandre & Monica Heller. 2012. *Language in Late Capitalism. Pride and Profit*. New York: Routledge.

Duchêne, Alexandre, Melissa Moyer & Celia Roberts. 2013. *Language, Migration and Social Inequalities. A critical sociolinguistic perspective on institutions and work*. Bristol: Multilingual Matters.

Duffard Evangelista, Irene. 2016. *Del caribe haitiano a la Argentina Trayectorias de cuerpos en movilidad humana pos terremoto 2010* [From Haitian Caribbean to Argentina. Trajectories of bodies in human mobility post 2010 earthquake]. Argentina: CLACSO.

Dufoix, Stéphane. 2008. *Diaspora*. Berkeley: University of California Press.

Dustmann, Christian, Tommasso Frattini & Ian P. Preston. 2013. The Effect of Immigration along the Distribution of Wages. *Review of Economic Studies* 80(1). 145-73

Düvell, Franck, Anna Triandafyllidou & Bastian Vollmer. 2009. Ethical Issues in Irregular Migration Research in Europe. *Population, Space and Place* 16(3). 227-239.

Eagleton, Terry. 1990. *The Ideology of the Aesthetic*. Oxford: Blackwell.

ECLAC (Economic Commission for Latin America and the Caribbean). 2012. *Population, Territory and Sustainable Development*. Santiago: ECLAC-United Nations.

Eckert, Penelope & Sally McConnell-Ginet. 1992. Think practically and look locally: Language and gender as community-based practice. *Annual Review of Anthropology* 21. 461-90.

Edgerton, Jason D. & Lance W. Roberts. 2014. Cultural capital or habitus? Bourdieu and beyond in the explanation of enduring educational inequality. *Theory and Research in Education* 12(2).193-220.

Edles, Laura. 2004. Rethinking 'race', 'ethnicity' and 'culture': Is Hawai'i the 'model minority' state? *Ethnic and Racial Studies* 27(1). 37-68

Edwards, John. 2009. *Language and Identity. Key Topics in Sociolinguistics*. Cambridge: Cambridge University Press.

Eidlin, Barry. 2014. Class Formation and Class Identity: Birth, Death, and Possibilities for Renewal. *Sociology Compass* 8(8). 1045-1062.

Elbert, Rodolfo & Pablo Perez. 2018. The identity of class in Latin America: Objective class position and subjective class identification in Argentina and Chile. *Current Sociology* 66(5).1-24.

Elizaga, Juan Carlos. 1972. *Migraciones Interiores, el Proceso de Urbanización, Movilidad Social* [Internal Migration, urbanization process and social mobility]. Santiago: Centro Latinoamericano de Demografía (CELADE).

Elliot, Anthony. 2020. *Concepts of the self*. Cambridge: Polity.

Emirbayer, Mustafa & Matthew Desmond. 2012. Race and reflexivity. *Ethnic and Racial Studies* 35(4). 574-599.

Engstrom, David W.1997. *Presidential Decision Making Adrift: The Carter Administration and the Mariel Boatlift*. Lanham, Rowman and Littlefield Publisher.

Esterberg, Kristin G. 2002. *Qualitative Methods in Social Research*. USA: McGraw-Hill Higher Education.

Equality and Human Rights Commission. 2014. *The invisible Workforce: Employment Practices in the Service Sector*. https://www.equalityhumanrights.com/sites/default/files/the_invisible_workforce_full_report_08-08-14.pdf (accessed 06 february 2017]

Errington, Joseph. 2001. Ideology. In Alessandro Duranti (ed.), *Key Terms in Language and Culture*, 110-112. Malden: Blackwell.

Fairclough, Norman. 1993. Critical discourse analysis and the marketization of public discourse: the universities. *Discourse and Society* 4(2).133-68.

Fairclough, Norman &Ruth Wodak. 1997. Critical discourse analysis. In Teun van Dijk (ed.), *Discourse as Social Interaction*, 258-284. London: Sage.

Fairclough, Norman. 2003. *Analyzing Discourse. Textual Analysis for Social Research*. New York: Routledge.

Fairclough, Norman. 2010. Critical Discourse analysis. The Critical study of language (2nd edn.). London: Routledge.

Fairclough, Norman. 2016. A Dialectical-Relational Approach to Critical Discourse Analysis in Social Research. In Ruth Wodak & Michael Meyer (eds.), *Methods of Critical Discourse Studies*, 86–108. London: Sage.

Faist, Thomas. 2010. Diaspora and transnationalism: What kind of dance partners? In Thomas Faist & Rainer Bauböck (eds.), *Diaspora and Transnationalism: Concepts, Theories and Methods*, 9–34. Amsterdam: University Press.

Feline Freier, Luisa. 2015. La UE como destino. La UE en el periodo de 1998-2012. Disminución de los flujos de migrantes de ALC [The EU as destiny. The EU in the 1998-2012 period. Decrease of migration flows from Latin America]. In Rodolfo Cordero (ed.), *Dinámicas migratorias en América Latina y el Caribe (ALC), y entre ALC y la Unión Europea* [Migration dynamics in Latin America and the Caribbean (LAC), and between LAC and the European Union], 55–80. Bruselas: Organización Internacional para las Migraciones.

Fernandes, Duval & Maria da Consolação Gomes de Castro. 2014. A migração haitiana para o Brasil: resultado da pesquisa no destino [Haitian migration to Brazil: research results in a destination country]. In Jorge Peraza, Angel Camino & Lorena Bacci (eds.), *La migración haitiana hacia Brasil: Características, oportunidades y desafíos* [Haitian migration to Brazil: characteristics, opportunities and challenges],51–66. Buenos Aires: Organización Internacional para las Migraciones.

Fernández-Reino, Mariña. 2020. *Migrants and Discrimination in the UK*. https://migrationobservatory.ox.ac.uk/wp-content/uploads/2020/01/Briefing-Migrants-and-Discrimination-in-the-UK.pdf (accessed 27 november 2022)

Fitzgerald, Scott,David & David Cook-Martin. 2015. Elegir la Población: leyes de inmigración y racismo en el continente americano [Choosing the population: immigration law and racism in the american continente]. In Pablo Yenkelevich (ed.), *Inmigración y Racismo: Contribuciones a la historia de los extranjeros en México* [Immigration and racism: Contributions to the history of foreigners in Mexico], 29–58. Mexico: El Colegio de Mexico.

Fitzpatrick, Kathie & Stephen May. 2022. *Critical Ethnography and Education. Theory, Methodology, and Ethics*. New York: Routledge.

Flores Farfan, José Antonio & Anna Holzscheiter. 2011. The Power of Discourse and the Discourse of Power. In Ruth Wodak, Barbara Johnstone & Paul Kerswill (eds.), *The Sage Handbook of Sociolinguistics*, 139–152. London: Sage Publications.

Flores Mejía, Esthela. 2014. Actitudes lingüísticas en Ecuador. Una tradición normativa que subsiste. *Bergen Language and Linguistic Studies* (BeLLS) 5. 409–488.

Ford, Robert & Matthew Goodwin. 2014. Understanding UKIP: Identity, Social Change and the Left Behind. *The Political Quarterly* 85(3). 277–284.

Foster, David & Paul Bolton. 2018. Adult ESOL in England. *Briefing Paper*, 7905. http://researchbriefings.files.parliament.uk/documents/CBP-7905/CBP-7905.pdf (accessed 15 march 2019)

Foucault, Michel. 1988. Technologies of the self. In Martin, Luther, Huck Gutman & Patrick H. Hutton (eds.), *Technologies of the Self: A Seminar with Michel Foucault*, 16–49. Amherst: Univ. Mass. Press.

Foucault, Michel. 2008. *The Birth of Biopolitics: Lectures at the College de France*. 1979-1979 (Translated by G. Burchill, Ed M. Sellenart). Basingstoke: Palgrave Macmillan.

Frankenberg, Ruth. 1993. *White women, race matters: the social construction of whiteness*. Minneapolis: University of Minnesota Press.

Freeman, Mark. 2006. Life "on holiday"? *Narrative Inquiry* 16(1). 131–138.

Freeman, Mark. 2015. Narrative as a Mode of Understanding: Method, Theory, Praxis. In Anna De Fina & Alexandra Georgakopoulou (eds.), *The Handbook of Narrative Analysis*, 21–37. UK: Wiley.

Fuller, Janet M. & Jennifer Leeman. 2020. *Speaking Spanish in the US. The sociopolitics of Language*. 2nd Edition. Bristol: Multilingual Matters.

Gal, Susan. 1989. Language and Political Economy. *Annual Review of Anthropology* 18. 345–367.

Gal, Susan. 2006. Migration, minorities and multilingualism. Language Ideologies in Europe. In Clare Mar-Molinero & Patrick Stevenson (eds.), *Language Ideologies, Policies and Practices: Language and the Future of Europe*, 13–27. Basingstoke: Palgrave Macmillan.

Garcia Canclini, Nestor. 2002. *Latinoamericanos Buscando Lugar en este Siglo* [Latin Americans looking for a place in this century]. Paidos. Buenos Aires. Argentina.

Garcia, Ofelia & Li Wei. 2014. *Translanguaging: Language, Bilingualism and Education*. UK: Palgrave Macmillan.

Garrido, Rosa María & Eva Codó. 2017. Deskilling and delanguaging African migrants in Barcelona: pathways of labour market incorporation and the value of 'global' English. *Globalisation, Societies and Education* 15(1). 29–49

Georgakopoulou, Alexandra. 2006. Thinking big with small stories in narrative and identity analysis. Special Issue. Narrative-State of the Art. *Narrative Inquiry* 16(1).129–37.

Georgakopoulou, Alexandra. 2011. Teachers, students and ways of telling in classroom sites: A case of out- of- (work)place identities. In Jo Angouri & Meredith Marra (eds.), *Constructing Identities at Work*, 151–174. Basingstoke, UK: Palgrave Macmillan.

Gilbert, Alan. 2004. The Urban Revolution. In Robert N. Gwyne & Cristobal Kay (eds.), *Latin America Transformed. Globalization and Modernity*, 93–114, London: Routledge.

Gill, Nick & Anthony Good. 2019. *Asylum Determination in Europe Ethnographic Perspectives*. Switzerland: Palgrave Macmillan.

Gentile, Paola. 2017. Political Ideology and the De-professionalisation of Public Service Interpreting: The Netherlands and the United Kingdom as Case Studies. In Carmen Valero-Garces & Rebecca Tipton (eds.), *Ideology, Ethics and Policy Development in Public Service Intereperting and Translation*, 63–83. Bristol: Multilingual Matters.

Georgakopolou, Alexandra. 2011. Narrative Analysis. In Ruth Wodak, Barbara Johnstone & Paul Kerswill (eds.), *The Sage Handbook of Sociolinguistics*. pp. 396–411. London: Sage Publications.

Georgakopoulou, Alexandra. 2015. Small Stories Research. Methods, Analysis, Outreach. In Anna De Fina & Alexandra Georgakopoulou (eds), *The Handbook of Narrative Analysis*, 255–271, UK: Wiley.

Giddens, Anthony. 1973. *The class structure of advanced societies*. London: Hutchinson.

Gilroy, Paul. 2000. *Between Camps: Nations, Culture and the Allure of Race*. London: Allen Lane.

Goffman, Erving. 1951. Symbols of Class Status. *The British Journal of Sociology* 2(4). 294–304.

Goffman, Erving. 1963. *Behaviour in Public Spaces*, Glencoe, IL: Free Press.

Gómez-Galvarriato, Aurora & Graciela Márquez-Colín. 2017. Industrialization and Growth in Peru and Mexico, 1870–2010: A Long-Term Assessment. In Kevin Hjortshøj O'Rourke & Jeffrey Gale Williamson (eds.), *The Spread of Modern Industry to the Periphery since 1871*, 289–317. Oxford: Oxford University Press.

Goodley, Dan. 2004. Gerry O'Toole: a design for life. In Peter Clough, Dan Goodley, Rebecca Lawthom & Michelle Moore (eds.), *Researching Life Stories. Method, Theory and Analyses in a Biographical Age*, 3–14. London: Routledge.

Gramsci, Antonio. 1971. *Selections from the Prison Notebooks*. Translated and edited by Quintin Hoare & Geoffrey Nowell Smith. New York: International Publishers.

Gramsci, Antonio. 1992. *Prison Notebooks*. Volume I. Edited by Joseph A. Buttigieg & Translated by Joseph A. Buttigieg and Antonio Callari. New York: Columbia University Press.

Granada, Lucila, Ana. 2013. *Latin Americans in London: language, integration and ethnic identity*. Unpublished PhD thesis. Aston University.

Greenhalgh Trisha. 1998. Narrative based medicine in an evidence-based world. In Trisha Greenhalgh & Brian Hurwitz (eds.), *Narrative-based medicine: dialogue and discourse in clinical practice*, 247–265. London: BMJ Books.
Grenfell, Michael (ed.). 2011. Bourdieu: A Theory of Practice. In Michael Grenfell (ed.), *Bourdieu, Language and Linguistics*, 7–34. London: Continuum.
Greven, Thomas. 2016. *The Rise of Right-Wing Populism in Europe and the United States: A Comparative Perspective*. http://www.fesdc.org/fileadmin/user_upload/publications/RightwingPopulism.pdf (accessed 21 december 2022)
Grin, François. 2016. The Economics of English in Europe. In Thomas Ricento (ed.), *Language Policy and Political Economy. English in a Global Context*, 119–144. New York; Oxford University Press.
Grzymala-Kazlowska, Aleksandra & Jenny Phillimore. 2017. Introduction: rethinking integration. New perspectives on adaptation and settlement in the era of superdiversity. *Journal of ethnic and migration studies* 44(2). 179–196.
Guarnizo, Luis Eduardo, Alejandro Portes & William Haller. 2003. Assimilation and Transnationalism: Determinants of Transnational Political Action among Contemporary Migrants. *American Journal of Sociology* 108(6), 1211–1248
Gutiérrez, Ramón A. 2019. *Mexican Immigration to the United States*. https://oxfordre.com/americanhistory/view/10.1093/acrefore/9780199329175.001.0001/acrefore-9780199329175-e-146?print=pdf (accessed 24 november 2022]
Gzesh, Susan. 2006. Central Americans and Asylum Policy in the Reagan Era. https://www.migrationpolicy.org/article/central-americans-and-asylum-policy-reagan-era (accessed 25 november 2022)
Hall, Kira & Nilep Chad. 2015. Code-Switching, Identity and Globalization. In Deborah Tannen, Heidi E. Hamilton & Deborah Schifrin (eds.), *The Handbook of Discourse Analysis*, 597–619. UK: Blackwell Publishers.
Hall, M.M. 1992. A nation of shoppers, *Observer Magazine* 13. 16–29
Hall, Stuart. 1988. The Toad in the Garden: Thatcherism Among the Theorists. In Cary Nelson & Larry Grossberg (eds.), *Marxism and the Interpretation of Culture*, 35–74 Basingstoke: Macmillan Education.
Hall, Stuart. 1993. Cultural identity and diaspora'. In Patrick Williams & Laura Chrisman (eds.), *Colonial Discourse and Post-Colonial Theory*, 392–401. New York: Harvester Wheatsheaf.
Hammersley, Martyn. 1995. *The Politics of Social Research*. London: Sage.
Hammersley, Martyn & Paul Atkinson. 2007. *Ethnography. Principles in Practice*. Third Edition. UK: Routledge.
Hammersley, Martyn. 2013. *What is Qualitative Research?* UK: Bloomsbury.
Hancock, Ange-Marie. 2016. *Intersectionality: An intellectual history*. New York: Oxford University Press.
Harvey, David. 1989. *The Conditions of Postmodernity*. Oxford: Blackwell.
Harvey, David. 2005. *A brief history of Neoliberalism*. USA: Oxford University Press.
Haug, Sonja. 2008. Migration Networks and Migration Decision-Making. *Journal of Ethnic and Migration Studies* 34(4). 585–605
Heering, Liesbeth, Rob van der Erf & Leo van Wissen. 2004. The role of family networks and migration culture in the continuation of Moroccan emigration: a gender perspective. *Journal of Ethnic and Migration Studies* 30(2). 323–337.
Heller, Monica, Joan Pujolar & Alexandre Duchêne. 2014. Linguistic commodification in tourism. *Journal of Sociolinguistics* 18(4). 539–566.
Heller, Monica & Alexandre Duchêne. 2016. Treating language as an economic resource: discourse, data and debate. In Nikolas Coupland (ed.), *Sociolinguistics: Theoretical Debates*, 139–156, Cambridge: Cambridge University Press.

Heller, Monica & Bonnie McElhinny. 2018. *Language, Capitalism, Colonialism: Toward a Critical History*. Canada: University of Toronto Press.
Heller, Monica, Sari Pietikäinen & Joan Pujolar. 2018. *Critical Sociolinguistic Research Methods. Studying Language Issues that Matter*. London: Routledge.
Herbert Joanna & Richard Rodger. 2007. Frameworks: testimony, representation and interpretation. In Joanna Herbert & Richard Rodger (eds.), *Testimonies of the City: Identity, Community and Change in a Contemporary Urban World*, 1–19. Aldershot, Hants: Ashgate Publishing.
Herman, David. 2009. *Basic Elements of Narrative*. Oxford: Wiley-Blackwell.
Hernández-Suarez, Jose Luis. 2008. *Perspectiva de la migración México-Estados Unidos. Una interpretación desde el subdesarrollo* [Perspective of Mexico-United States migration. An interpretation from underdevlopment]. Tésis de doctorado en Economía, Universidad Autónoma de Zacatecas.
Herrera, Gioconda. 2013. Latin America: gender and migration. In Immanuel Ness & Peter Bellwood (eds.), *The Encyclopaedia of Global Human Migration*, 1–6. UK: Blackwell Publishing Ltd.
Herrick, Bruce H. 1965. *Urban Migration and Economic Development in Chile*. Cambridge, MA: MIT Press.
Heywood, Andrew. 2003. *Political Ideologies. An introduction*. Third Edition. London: Palgrave MacMillan.
Hidalgo, Margarita. 1986. Language contact, language loyalty, and language prejudice on the mexican border. *Language in Society* 15(2). 193–220.
Holborow, Marnie. 2015. *Language and Neoliberalism*. London. Routledge.
Holborow, Marnie. 2018. Language, commodification and labour: the relevance of Marx. *Language Sciences* 70. 58–67
Holliday, Adrian. 2005. *The Struggle to Teach English as an International Language*. Oxford: Oxford University Press.
Holliday, Adrian. 2013. Native speaker' teachers and cultural belief. In Stephanie Ann Houghton & Damian J. Rivers (eds.), *Native-speakerism in Japan*, 17–26. Bristol: Multilingual Matters.
Hollinger, David. 1995. *Postethnic America: Beyond Multiculturalism*. New York: Basic Books.
Holmes, Janet. 1997. Struggling beyond Labov and Waletzky. In Michael Bamberg (ed.), Oral versions of personal experience: Three decades of narrative analysis. *Special Issue of Journal of Narrative and Life History* 7(1–4). 139–146.
Hollway, Wendy & Tony Jefferson. 2005. Panic and perjury: a psychosocial exploration of agency, *British Journal of Social Psychology* 44 (2), 147–164.
Hooks, Bell. 1990. *Yearning: Race, gender and cultural politics*. Boston: Southend Press.
Hubble, Sue & Steven Kennedy. 2011. *Changes to funding for English for Speakers of Other Languages (ESOL) courses*. London: House of Commons Library. http://www.parliament.uk/briefing-papers/SN05946.pdf (accessed 26 march 2019).
Hughes, Arthur, Peter Trudgill & Dominic Watt. 2012. *English Accents and Dialects. An Introduction to Social and Regional Varieties of English in the British Isles*. London: Routledge.
Hymes, Dell. 1996. *Ethnography, Linguistics, Narrative Inequality: Toward an Understanding of Voice*. London: Taylor and Francis.
Irvine, Judith. 2012. Language Ideology. http://www.oxfordbibliographies.com/view/document/obo-9780199766567/obo-9780199766567-0012.xml (accessed 12 february 2016)
Israel, Emma & Jeanne Batalova. 2020. Mexican Immigrants in the United States. https://www.migrationpolicy.org/article/mexican-immigrants-united-states-2019 (accessed 10 july 2022).
Izquierdo, Mario, Juan F. Jimeno & Aitor Lacuesta. 2016. Spain: from massive immigration to vast emigration?' *IZA Journal of Migration* 5(10). 1–20.

Jachimowicz, Maia. 2006. Argentina: A new era of Migration and Migration Policy. Available at: https://www.migrationpolicy.org/article/argentina-new-era-migration-and-migration-policy (accessed 07 august 2021)

James, Malcolm. 2005. *Ecuadorian Identity*. Runnymede Trust. http://www.runnymedetrust.org/uploads/projects/EcuadorianIdentityCommunity.pdf. (accessed 07 may 2015)

Jefferson, Gail. 1984. On the Organization of Laughter in Talk about Troubles. In J. Maxwell Atkinson (ed.), *Structures of Social Action: Studies in Conversation Analysis*, 346–369. Cambridge: Cambridge University Press.

Jenkins, Jenny. 2009. English as a lingua franca: interpretations and attitudes. *World Englishes*, 28(2). 200–207.

Jessop, Bob. 2013. Putting neoliberalism in its time and place: a response to the debate. *Social Anthropology/Anthropologie Sociale* 21(1). 65–74.

Johnson, Mark R.D. 2006. Integration of New Migrants. In Sarah Spencer (ed.), *Refugees and Other New Migrants: A Review of the Evidence on Successful Approaches to Integration*, University of Oxford: COMPAS https://www.compas.ox.ac.uk/wp-content/uploads/ER-2006-Integration_Refugees_UK_HO.pdf (accessed 24 may 2018)

Jokisch, Brad D. 2014. Ecuador: From Mass Emigration to Return Migration? http://migrationpolicy.org/article/ecuador-mass-emigration-return-migration (accessed 02 april 2015)

Jones, Peter. 2007. Why there is no such thing as "critical discourse analysis. *Language and communication*, 27(4). 337–368.

Jordan, Bill & Marck Düvell. 2003. *Migration: The Boundaries of Equality and Justice*. Cambridge: Polity.

Jorgensen, Marianne & Louise, J. Phillips. 2002. *Discourse Analysis as Theory and Method*. London: Sage Publications.

Joseph, John E. 2004. *Language and Identity. National, Ethnic, Religious*. New York: Palgrave Macmillan.

Jule, Allyson. 2017. *A Beginner's Guide to Language and Gender*. 2nd Edition. Bristol: Multilingual Matters.

Justice Committee. 2013. *Interpreting and translation services and the applied language solutions contract*. https://publications.parliament.uk/pa/cm201213/cmselect/cmjust/645/645.pdf (accessed 12 november 2022)

Kalitzkus, Vera & Peter F. Matthiessen. 2009. Narrative-based Medicine. Potential, Pitfalls and Practice. *The Permanent Journal* 13(1). 80–86.

Kashiwazaki, Chikako & Tsuneo Akaha. 2006. Japanese Immigration Policy: Responding to Conflicting Pressures https://www.migrationpolicy.org/article/japanese-immigration-policy-responding-conflicting-pressures (accessed 12 june 2022]

Keen, Benjamin & Keith Haynes. 2013. *A History of Latin America*. Ninth Edition. USA: Wadsworth CENGAGE learning.

Kelsall, Sophie. 2015. Language Practices and Latinidad at a Latin American School in London. In Rosina Márquez Reiter & Luisa Martín Rojo (eds.), *A Sociolinguistics of diaspora: Latino practices, identities and ideologies*, 138–150. New York: Routledge.

Kennedy, Emmet. 1979. Ideology from Destutt De Tracy to Marx. *Journal of the History of Ideas* 40(3). 353–368

Kingston, Sharon, Roger Mitchell, Paul Florin & John Stevenson. 1999. Sense of Community in Neighbourhoods as a Multi-level Construct. *Journal of Community Psychology* 27(6).681–694

Kleinman, Sherryl. 1991. Fieldworkers' feelings: what we feel, who we are, how we analyze. In William B. Shaffir & Robert A. Stebbings (eds.), *Experiencing fieldwork*, 184–195. Newbury Park, CA: Sage.

Knowles, Murray & Rosamund Moon. 2006. *Introducing Metaphor*. New York: Routledge.

Kristeva, Julia. 1986. Word, dialogue and novel. In Toril Moi (ed.), *The Kristeva Reader*, 34–61. Oxford: Blackwell.

Kratochwill, H.K. 1995. Cross-Border Population movements and regional economic integration in Latin America, *IOM Latin American Migration Journal* 13(2). 3–11.

Kroskrity, Paul. 2004. Language ideologies. In Alessandro Duranti (ed.), *A Companion to Linguistic Anthropology*, 496–605. Oxford: Blackwell Publishings.

Kroskrity, Paul. 2010. Language Ideologies. Evolving Perspectives. In Jürgen Jaspers, Jan Ostman & Jef Verschueren (eds.), *Society and Language Use*, 192–211. USA: John Benjamins Publishing Company.

Kubota, Ryuko. 2009. Rethinking the superiority of the native speaker: Toward a relational understanding of power, In Neriko Musha Doerr (ed.), *The native speaker concept: Ethnographic investigations of native speaker effects*, 233–248. Berlin: De Gruyter.

Labov, William. 1966. *The social stratification of English in New York City*. Washington DC. Center for Applied Linguistics.

Labov, William. 1972. The transformation of experience in narrative syntax. In William Labov (ed.), *Language in the inner city: Studies in the Black English Vernacular*, 354–96. Philadelphia: University of Pennsylvania Press.

Labov, William &Joshua Waletsky. 1967. Narrative Analysis, oral versions of personal experience. In June Helm (ed.), *Essays on the Verbal and Visual Arts*, 12–44. USA: University of Washington Press.

Labov, William. 1997. Some further steps in narrative analysis. Oral versions of personal experience; Three decades of narrative analysis. In Michael Bamberg (ed.) *Special Issue of Journal of Narrative and Life History* 7(1–4). 395–415.

Labov, William. 2010. Where should I begin? In Deborah Schiffrin, Anna De Fina & Anastasia Nylund (eds.), *Telling Stories: Language, Narrative, and Social Life*, 7–22. USA: Georgetown University Press, 2010.

Lakoff, George & Mark Johnson. 2003. *Metaphors We live by*. Chicago: University of Chicago Press.

Lacque, Erick C. 2011. Immigration Law and Policy: Before and After September 11, 2001. *Social Sciences Journal* 10(1). 24–34

Latin American House. 2018. Regístrese para cursos de ingles [Register for English courses]. https://casalatina.org.uk/es/adult-education/ (accessed 04 april 2018)

Lefebvre, Henri. 1974. *The Production of Space*. Oxford: Blackwell.

Le Page, Robert Brock & Andrée Tabouret-Keller. 1985. *Acts of Identity. Creole –based Approaches to Language and Ethnicity*. Cambridge: Cambridge University Press.

Levitt, Peggy. 2004. Transnational Migrants: When "Home" Means More Than One Country. https://www.migrationpolicy.org/article/transnational-migrants-when-home-means-more-one-country (accessed 05 june 2017)

Linneker, Brian & Jane Wills. 2016. The London living wage and in-work poverty reduction: Impacts on employers and workers. *Environment and Planning C: Government and Policy* 34(5). 759–776.

Lippi-Green, Rosina. 2012. *English with an Accent. Language, ideology, and discrimination in the United States*. Nueva York: Routledge.

Lonergan Gwyneth. 2015. Migrant Women and Social Reproduction under austerity', *Feminist Review* 109 (2015).124–145.

Li, Yao Tai. 2017. Constituting Co-Ethnic Exploitation: The Economic and Cultural Meanings of Cash-in-Hand Jobs for Ethnic Chinese Migrants in Australia. *Critical Sociology* 43(6). 919–932

Linde, Chralotte. 1993. *Life Stories. The Creation of Coherence*. New York: Oxford University Press.

Lofland, John. 1971. *Analyzing Social Seetings: A guide to Qualitative Observation and Analysis*. Belmont, CA: Wadsworth.

Lohrman, R. 1987. Irregular migration: A rising issue in developing countries. *International Migration* 25(3). 253–266.

Lucia, Anntoinette D. & Richard Lepsinger. 1999. *The Art and science of competency models: Pinpointing Critical success factors in an organization*. San Francisco: Jossey-Bass/Pfeiffer.

Lukácks, Georg. 1971. *History and Class consciousness*, translated by Rodney Livingstone. Cambridge MA: MIT Press.

Lundström, Catrin. 2014. *White Migrations. Gender, Whiteness and Privilege in Transnational Migration*. UK: Palgrave MacMillan.

Machin, David & Andrea Mayr. 2012. *How to do Critical Discourse Analysis*. London: Sage.

MacKenzie, Robert & Chris Forde. 2009. The rhetoric of the 'good worker' versus the realities of employers' use and the experiences of migrant workers. *Work Employment and Society* 23(1). 142–159.

MacMaster, Neil. 2001. *Racism in Europe*. London: Palgrave.

Mahler, Sarah. J. 1995. *American Dreaming. Immigrant Life on the Margins*. UK: Princeton University Press.

Marger, Martin, N. 1997. *Race and Ethnic Relations: Global Perspectives*, 4th edn. Belmont: Wadsworth.

Marini, Francesco. 2013. Immigrants and transnational engagement in the diaspora: Ghanaian associations in Italy and the UK, African and Black Diaspora. *An International Journal* 6(2).131–144.

Latonero, Mark & Paula Kift. 2018. On Digital Passages and Borders: Refugees and the New Infrastructure for Movement and Control. *Social Media and Society* 2018 1.11.

Márquez Reiter, Rosina &Luisa Martín Rojo. 2015. The Dynamics of (Im)Mobility. (In)Transient Capitals and Linguistic Ideologies among Latin American Migrants in London and Madrid. In Rosina Márquez Reiter & Luisa Martín Rojo (eds.), *A Sociolinguistics of Diaspora: Latino Practices, Identities and Ideologies, 83–110*. New York: Routledge.

Márquez Reiter, Rosina &Adriana Patiño-Santos. 2017. The Discursive Construction of Moral Agents among Successful Economic Migrants in Elephant & Castle, London. *Tilburg Papers in Culture Studies*, 194. 1–39.

Martin, Phillip. L. 1993. *Trade and Migration: Nafta and Agriculture*. Washington, D.C.: Institute for International Economics.

Martin, Phillip L. & J. Edward Taylor. 1996. The Anatomy of a migration hump. In J. Edward Taylor (ed.), *Development Strategy, Employment and Migration: Insights from Models*, 43–62. Paris: OECD Development Centre.

Martin, Phillip. L. 2013. *The Global Challenge of Managing Migration*. Population Bulletin. http://www.prb.org/pdf13/global-migration.pdf. (accessed 19 june 2015)

Martin Rojo, Luisa (ed). 2002. *Asimilar o Integrar. Dilemas ante el Multilingüismo en las Aulas* [Assimilate or integrate. Dilemmas before multilingualism in classrooms]. Madrid: Solana e Hijos.

Martínez-Rodríguez, Marcela. 2010. El Proyecto Colonizador de México a Finales del Siglo XIX. Algunas Perspectivas Comparativas en Latinoamerica [The colonising Project of Mexico at the end of XIX century. Some comparative perspectives in Latin America]. *Secuencia (76), 101–132*.

Marx, Karl &Friedrich Engels. 1845. *The German Ideology*. In Karl Marx & Friedrich Engels 1975–2005. Vol. 5.

Marx Karl. 1973. *Grundrisse*. Translated by Martin Nicolaus. New York: Random House.

Marx, Karl & Friedrich Engels. 1988. *The German Ideology*. London: Lawrence & Wishart.

Masferrer, Claudia &Victoria Prieto. 2019. El perfil sociodemográfico del retorno migratorio reciente. Diferencias y similutes entre contextos de procedencia y de acogida en America Latina [Sociodemographic profiles of recent return migration. Differences and similarities between sending and receiving contexts in Latin America]. In Liliana Rivera-Sánchez (ed.), *¿Volver a Casa?*

Migrantes de Retorno en America Latina. Debates, tendencias y experiencias divergentes [Retun home? Return migrants in Latin America. Debates, trends and divergent experiences]. 67–126. México: El Colegio de México.

Masferrer, Claudia. 2021. *Atlas de Migración de Retorno de Estados Unidos a México* [Atlas of Return migration from the Unites States to Mexico]. Mexico: El Colegio de Mexico.

Mas-Giralt, Rosa. 2017. Onward Migration as a Coping Strategy? Latin Americans Moving from Spain to the UK Post-2008. *Population, Space and Place* 23(3). 1–12.

Massey, Douglas S. & Karen A. Pren. 2012. Unintended consequences of US migration policy: Explaining the post-1965 surge from Latin America. *Population and Development Review* 38(1). 1–29.

May, Stephen. 2001. *Language and Minority Rights*. London: Longman.

May, Stephen. 2008. *Language and Minority Rights. Ethnicity, Nationalism and the Politics of Language*. UK: Routledge.

Mazza, Jacqueline & Eleannor Sohnen. 2010. On the Other Side of the Fence: Changing Dynamics of Migration in the Americas. https://www.migrationpolicy.org/article/other-side-fence-changing-dynamics-migration-americas (accessed 02 april 2015)

McCabe, Kristen, Serena Yi-Ying Lin, Hiroyuki Tanaka & Piotr Plewa. 2009. Pay to Go: Countries Offer Cash to Immigrants Willing to Pack their Bags. https://www.migrationpolicy.org/article/pay-go-countries-offer-cash-immigrants-willing-pack-their-bags (accessed 15 may 2016)

McCarthy, Ian & Angela Anagnostou. 2004. The impact of outsourcing on the transaction costs and boundaries of manufacturing. *International Journal of Production Economics* 88(1). 61–71

McCarthy, Helen. 2016. *Latin Americans in London: Barriers to English Language Skills*. IRMO Research Briefing. http://irmo.org.uk/wpcontent/uploads/2016/06/Research-report-English-v1.pdf (accessed 15 november 2017)

McCall, Leslie. 2005. The complexity of intersectionality. *Signs* 30(3). 1771–1800.

McElhinny, Bonnie. 2003. Theorizing Gender in Sociolinguistics and Linguistic Anthropology. In Janet Holmes & Miriam Meyerhoff (eds.), *The Handbook of Language and Gender*, 21–42. UK: Blackwell.

McElhinny, Bonnie & Sara Mills. 2007. Launching studies of Gender and Language in the early 21st century. *Gender and Language* 1(1). 1–13.

McElhinny, Bonnie. 2014. Theorizing Gender in Sociolinguistics and Linguistic Anthropology: Toward Effective Interventions in Gender Inequity. In Susan Ehrlich, Miriam Meyerhoff & Janet Holmes (eds.), *The Handbook of Language, Gender, and Sexuality*, Second Edition. 21–42. UK: John Wiley & Sons.

McFarlane, Anthony. 1995. Rebellions in Late Colonial Spanish America: A Comparative Perspective. *Bulletin of Latin American Research* 14(3). 313–338.

McGregor, Joann. 2007. Joining the BBC (British Bottom Cleaners). Zimbabwean Migrants and the UK Care Industry', *Journal of Ethnic and Migration Studies* 33(5). 801–824.

McHugh, Margie & Catrina Doxsee. 2018. *English Plus Integration. Shifting the Instructional Paradigm for Immigrant Adult Learners to Support Integration Success*. Policy Brief. Migration Policy Institute. https://www.migrationpolicy.org/sites/default/files/publications/AdultEd_EnglishPlusIntegration_Final.pdf (accessed 03 february 2019)

McIlwaine, Cathy. 2007. *Living in Latin London: How Latin American Migrants Survive in the City*. London: Queen Mary University of London. http://www.geog.qmul.ac.uk/docs/staff/4400.pdf (accessed 16 april 2015)

McIlwaine, Cathy. 2008. *Negotiating gender-based violence: the paradoxes of migration for Latin American women in London*. The Leverhulme Trust. London. http://www.geog.qmul.ac.uk/docs/staff/19691.pdf (accessed 30 april 2015)

McIlwaine, Cathy. 2011. Theoretical and Empirical Perspectives on Latin American Migration across Borders. In Cathy McIlwaine (ed.), *Cross-Border Migration among Latin Americans: European Perspectives and Beyond*, 1–17. New York: Palgrave McMillan.
McIlwaine, Cathy. 2012. *The Colombian Community in London*. Queen Mary University of London. http://www.geog.qmul.ac.uk/media/geography/docs/research/latinamerican/McIlwaine-Report-on-Colombians-in-London.pdf (accessed 25 july 2015)
McIlwaine, Cathy, J. Camilo Cock & Brian Linneker. 2011. *No Longer Invisible: The Latin American Community in London*. London. https://www.qmul.ac.uk/geog/media/geography/docs/research/latinamerican/No-Longer-Invisible-report.pdf (accessed 20 november 2014).
McIlwaine, Cathy. 2014. Everyday urban violence and transnational displacement of Colombian urban migrants to London, UK. *Environment and Urbanization* 26(2). 417–426.
McIlwaine, Cathy. 2015. Legal Latins: Creating Webs and Practices of Immigration Status among Latin American Migrants in London. *Journal of Ethnic and Migration Studies*, 41(3). 493–511.
McIlwaine, Cathy & Diego Bunge. 2016. *Towards Visibility: The Latin American Community in London*. https://www.trustforlondon.org.uk/wp-content/uploads/2016/07/Towards-Visibility-full-report.pdf (accessed 25 november 2016)
McMillan. David W. & David M. Chavis. 1986. Sense of Community: A Definition and Theory. *Journal of Community Psychology* 14(1). 6–23.
Meinhof, Ulrike Hanna & Dariusz Galasinski. 2005. *The language of Belonging*. Great Britain: Palgrave MacMillan.
Meissner, Doris, David North & Demetrious Papademetriou. 1987. *Legalization of Undocumented Aliens: Lessons from Other Countries*, Washington, DC: Carnegie Endowment for International Peace.
Méroné, Schwarz Coulange & Manuel Angel Castillo. 2020. Integración de los inmigrantes haitianos de la oleada a México del 2016 [Integration of the 2016 Haitian Immigration wave to 2016 Mexico]. *Frontera Norte* 32(11). 1–23. http://dx.doi.org/10.33679/rfn.v1i1.1964
Micheli Thirión, Jordy. 2020. FDI, regional development and structural change. The Case of three states in El Bajío, Mexico. *Análisis económico* 35(90). 199–220.
Mignolo, Walter. 2005. *The idea of Latin America*. Oxford: Blackwell Publishing.
Milani, Tomasso M. 2008. Voices of endangerment: A language ideological debate on the Swedish language. In Alexandre Duchêne & Monica Heller (eds), *Advances in Sociolinguistics: Discourses of Endangerment: Ideology and Interest in the Defence of Languages*, 169–196. London: Bloomsbury Publishing.
Milani, Tomasso M. & Sally Johnson. 2010. Critical Intersections: language ideologies and media discourse. In Sally Johnson & Tomasso M. Milani (eds.), *Language Ideologies and Media Discourse: Texts, Practices, Politics*, 3–14. London: Continuum.
Millbank, Jenni. 2009. "The Ring of Truth": A Case Study of Credibility Assessment in Particular Social Group Refugee Determination. *International Journal of Refugee Law* 21(1). 1–33.
Miller, Jennifer M. 2000. Language use, Identity, and Social Interaction: Migrant Students in Australia. *Research on Language and Social interaction* 33(1). 69–100.
Miller, Elizabeth R. 2012. Agency, language learning and multilingual spaces. *Multilingua* 31(4). 441–68.
Miller, Elizabeth R. 2014. *The language of adult immigrants. Agency in the making*. Bristol: Multilingual Matters.
Milroy, James & Lesley Milroy. 1998. *Authority in Language*. 3rd edition. London: Routledge.
Milroy, Lesley. 2001. Britain and the United States: Two Nations Divided by the Same Language (and Different Language Ideologies). *Journal of Linguistic Anthropology* 10(l). 56–8.

Milroy, James & Lesley Milroy. 2005. *Authority in Language. Investigating Standard English*. UK: Routledge.
Mkhonza, Sarah. 1995. Life Histories as Social Texts of Personal Experiences in Sociolinguistic Studies: A Look at the Lives of Domestic Workers in Swaziland. In Ruthellen Josselson & Amia Lieblich (eds.), *Interpreting Experience: The Narrative Study of Lives (The Narrative Study of Lives series): Interpreting Experience*, Volume 3. 173–204. Thousand Oaks, CA: Sage.
Mocek, Reinhard. 1999. *Socialismo revolucionario y darwinismo social* [Revolutionary socialism and social darwinism]. Madrid: Akal.
Morales- Hernández, Francisco Daniel (2021). 'You know what we Latinos are like': intragroup evaluations and relations among outsourced Latin American workers in London, *Language and Intercultural Communication* 21(5). 558–571.
Moreno-Cabrera, Juan Carlos. 2008. *El nacionalismo lingüístico. Una ideología destructiva* [Linguistic nationalism. A destructive ideology]. Barcelona: Península.
Moreno-Cabrera, Juan Carlos. 2016. *La dignidad e igualdad de las lenguas. Crítica de la discriminacion lingüística* [The dignity and equality among languages. A critique of linguistic discrimination]. Madrid: Alianza Editorial.
Moreno Mena, José Ascención. 2018. Migración haitiana hacia la frontera norte de México [Haitian migration to Mexico's north border]. *Espacio Abierto 28(1). 67–85*.
Moreno-Rivero, Javier. 2020. Translation as social policy: quality management in public service interpreting and translation'. *Languages, Society and Policy*. https://doi.org/10.17863/CAM.62273
Morris, Pam (ed.). 1997. *The Bakhtin Reader: Selected Writings of Bakhtin, Medvedev, Voloshinov*. London: Hodder Arnold.
Moyer, Melissa. 2013. Language as a Resource. Migrant Agency, Positioning and Resistance in a Health Care Clinic. In Alexandre Duchêne, Melissa Moyer & Celia Roberts (eds.), *Language, Migration and Social Inequalities. A Critical Sociolinguistics Perspective on Institutions and Work*, 196–224. UK: Multilingual Matters.
Moser, Caroline O.N & Cathy McIlwaine. 2004. *Latin American Urban Violence as a Development Concern: Towards a Framework for Violence Reduction*. http://www.uquebec.ca/observgo/fichiers/75871_latin.pdf (accessed 30 april 2015)
Mouffe, Chantal. 1979. Hegemony and Ideology in Gramsci'. In Chantal Mouffe (ed.), *Gramsci and Marxist Theory*, 168–204. London: Routledge.
Munck, Ronaldo. 2012. *Contemporary Latin America*. London: Palgrave Macmillan.
Narajan, Kirin & George, Kenneth. 2001. Personal and folk narratives as cultural representations. In Jaber F. Gubrium & James A. Holstein (eds.), *Handbook of Interview Research*, 815–832. Thousand Oaks/London: SAGE Publications.
Nagel, Joane. 1994. Constructing ethnicity: creating and recreating ethnic identity and culture. *Social problems* 41(1). 152–176.
Navarrete, Federico. 2016. *Alfabeto del racismo mexicano* [Alphabet of Mexican racism]. Mexico: Malpaso.
Nieswand, Boris. 2011. *Theorising Transnational Migration: The Status Paradox of Migration*. New York: Routledge.
Oboler, Susan. 1995. *Ethnic Labels, Latino Lives. Identity and the Politics of (re)presentation in the United States*. Minneapolis: University of Minnesota Press.
Observatorio de Legislación y Política Migratoria. 2019. En frontera sur, 2,400 elementos de la Guardia; no detendrán a migrantes, asegura el gobierno [In south border, 2400 members of the national Guard; they won't stop migrants, Government promises]. https://observatoriocolef.org/

noticias/en-frontera-sur-2400-elementos-de-la-guardia-no-detendran-a-migrantes-asegura-el-gobierno/ (accessed 22 july 2022)

O'Byrne, Darren. 2002. Working Class Culture. Local community and global conditions. In John Eade (ed.), *Living the Global city. Globalisation and Local Living*, 73–89. Routledge. London. UK.

O'Hara, Charles E. & Gregory L. O'Hara. 1994. *Fundamentals of Criminal Investigation*. Springfield, IL: Thomas Books.

Oliver, Caroline. 2014. Muddied waters: Migrants' entitlements to public services and benefits. In Bridget Anderson & Michael Keith (eds.), *Migration: The COMPAS Anthology*, 24–25. Oxford: The ESRC Centre on Migration, Policy and Society (COMPAS).

O'Reilly, Karen. 2009. *Ethnography. Key Concepts*. Sage. London.

Oxford English Dictionary. 2002. *Second edition on compact disc*. Oxford: Oxford University Press.

Padgett, Deborah K. 2008. Choosing the Right Qualitative Approach(es). In Deborah K. Padgett (ed.), *Qualitative Methods in Social Work Research*, 29–44. Thousand Oaks CA: Sage.

Padilla, Batriz & João Peixoto. 2007. Latin American Immigration to Southern Europe. Available at: http://www.migrationpolicy.org/article/latin-american-immigration-southern-europe (accessed 01 april 2015]

Paffey, Darren. 2012. *Language Ideologies and the Globalization of 'standard' Spanish: Raising the Standard*. New York: Bloomsbury.

Paffey, Darren. 2020. Spanish language visibility and the 'making of presence' in the linguistic landscape. In Andrew Lynch (ed.), *The Routledge Handbook of Spanish in the Global City*, 204–233. New York: Routledge.

Pakulsky, Jan & Malcolm Waters. 1996. *The death of Class*. London. Sage Publication.

Panayi, Panikos. 2010. *An immigration History of Britain. Multicultural Racism since 1800*. UK: Pearson.

París-Pombo, María Dolores. 2017. *Violencias y Migraciones Centroamericanas en México* [Violence and Central American migrations in Mexico]. Tijuana: El Colegio de la Frontera Norte.

París Pombo, María Dolores. 2018. *Migrantes haitianos y centroamericanos en Tijuana, Baja California, 2016-2017. Políticas gubernamentales y de la Sociedad Civil* [Haitian and Central American migrants in Tijuana, Baja California, 2016–2017. Government and civil society policies] México: Comisión Nacional de Derechos Humanos/El Colegio de la Frontera Norte.

París Pombo, María Dolores, Laura Velasco-Ortiz & Camilo Contreras Delgado. 2021. Introducción. Las caravanas y otras formas de movilidad colectiva en el nuevo contexto migratorio [Introduction. Caravans and other forms of collective mobility in the new migration context]. In Camilo Contreras Delgado, María Dolores París Pombo & Laura Velasco Ortiz (eds.), *Caravanas migrantes y desplazamientos colectivos en la frontera México-Estados Unidos* [Migrant caravans and collective displacements in the Mexico-US border],9–38. México: El Colegio de la Frontera Norte

Park, Joseph S.Y. 2010. Naturalization of competence and the neoliberal subject: Success stories of English language learning in the Korean conservative press. *Journal of Linguistic Anthropology* 20(1). 22–38.

Passel, Jefrey S. & D'vera Cohn. 2010. U. S. Unauthorized Immigration Flows Are Down Sharply Since Mid-Decade, Pew Hispanic Center. Available at: https://www.pewresearch.org/hispanic/2010/09/01/us-unauthorized-immigration-flows-are-down-sharply-since-mid-decade/ (accessed 25 march 2022]

Patiño-Santos, Adriana & Rosina Marquez-Reiter. 2019. Banal interculturalism: Latin Americans in Elephant and Castle, London. *Language and Intercultural communication* 19(3). 227–241.

Patiño Santos, Adriana. 2020. Una aproximación etnográfica a las narrativas producidas en contextos de migración [an ethnographic approach to narratives produced in migration contexts]. *Iberoromania* 2020(91). 11–27

Patiño-Santos, Adriana. 2023. Snapshots of Spanish-speaking Latin American radio producers in London. In Márquez-Reiter, Rosina & Adriana Patiño-Santos (eds.), *Language Practices and Processes Among Latin Americans in Europe*, 230–250. London: Routledge.

Paton, Michael Q. 2002. *Qualitative Research and Evaluation Methods*. Thousand Oaks, CA: Sage.

Pavlenko, Anneta. 2007. Autobiographic Narratives as Data in Applied Linguistics. *Applied Linguistics* 28(2). 163–188.

Pavlenko, Anneta. 2019. Superdiversity and why it isn't. Reflections on terminological innovations and academic branding. In Schmenk, Barbara, Stephan Breidbach & Lutz Küster (eds.), *Sloganization in Language Education Discourse*, 142–168. Bristol: Multilingual Matters.

Peck, Jamie & Nik Theodore. 2007.Variegated Neoliberalism. *Progress in Human Geography* 31(6). 731–772. https://doi.org/10.1177/0309132507083505

Petrilli, Susan. 2016. Dialogue, responsibility and literary writing: Mikhail Bakhtin and his Circle. *Semiotica* 2016(213). 307–343.

Pettersen, Normand & André Durivage. 2008. *The Structured Interview, Enhancing staff selection*. Canada: Presses de l'Universite du Quebec.

Pennycook, Alastair. 2007. The myth of English as an international language. In Sinfree Makoni & Alastair Pennycook (eds.), *Disinventing and reconstituting languages*, 90–115. Clevedon: Multilingual Matters.

Pérez-Vejo, Tomás. 2015. Extranjeros Interiores y Exteriores: La Raza en la Construcción Nacional Mexicana [Interior and exterior foreigners: Race in the national construction of Mexico]. In Pablo Yankelevich (ed.), *Inmigración y Racismo. Contribuciones a la Historia de los Extranjeros en México [Immigration and racism. Contributions to the history of foreigners in Mexico]*, 89–124. México: El Colegio de México.

Phelan, John Leddy. 1968. Pan-Latinism, French intervention in Mexico (1861–7) and the genesis of the idea of Latin America. In Juan Antonio Ortega y Medina (ed.), *Conciencia y autenticidad históricas: escritos en homenaje a Edmundo O'Gorman* [Historic awareness and authenticity: writings in honor to Edmundo O'Gorman], 279–98. Mexico: UNAM.

Phillimore, Jenny & Jayne Thornhill, Zahira Latif, Marcianne Uwimana & Lisa Goodson. 2010. *Delivering in an Age of Super-Diversity: West Midlands Review of Maternity Services for Migrant Women*. Department of Health/University of Birmingham. file:///C:/Users/moral/Downloads/Delivering_in_the_age_of_super_diversity.pdf (accessed 10 november 2017)

Pilkington, Andrew. 2003. *Racial Disadvantage and Ethnic Diversity in Britain*. London: Palgrave.

Piller, Ingrid. 2001. Who, if anyone, is a native speaker? *Verband Deutscher Anglisten* 12, (2). 109–121.

Piller, Ingrid &Jinhyun Cho. 2015. Neoliberalism as language policy. In Thomas Ricento (ed.), *Language Policy and Political Economy: English in a Global Context*, 162–186. Oxford: Oxford University Press.

Piller, Ingrid. 2016. *Linguistic Diversity and Social Justice. An Introduction to Applied Linguistics*. New York: Oxford University Press.

Pinkerton, Charles, Gail Mclaughlan & John Salt.2004. *Sizing the illegally resident population in the UK*. Home office online report. http://www.homeoffice.gov.uk/rds/pdfs04/rsdolr5804.pdf (accessed 10 february 2016)

Pietikainen, Sari & Hanele Dufva. 2006. Voices in Discourses: Dialogism, Critical Discourse Analysis and Ethnic Identity. *Journal of Sociolinguistics* 10 (2). 205–224

Plewa, Piotr. 2009. Voluntary Return Programmes: Could they assuage the effects of the Economic Crisis? *Centre on Migration, Policy and Society Working Paper 75*.

Polanyi, Livia. 1995. *Telling the Americal story: A Structural and Cultural Analysis of Conversational Storytellying*. Norwood, NJ: The MIT Press.

Ponzanesi, Sandra. 2020. Digital Diasporas: Postcoloniality, Media and Affect, *Interventions* 22(8). 977–993.

Portes, Alejandro. 1997. Immigration Theory for a New Century: Some Problems and Opportunities. *The International Migration Review* 31(4). 799–825.

Portes, Alejandro & Robert L. Bach 1985. *Latin Journey: Cuban and Mexican immigrants in the United States*. Berkeley: University of California Press.

Portes, Alejandro. 1988. Social Capital: its Origins and Applications in Modern Sociology. *Annual Review of Sociology* 24(1998). 1–24.

Prasad, Monica. 2006. *The Politics of Free Markets*. Chicago, IL: University of Chicago Press.

Prat, Mary Louise. 1992. *Imperial eyes. Travel writing and Transculturation*. London. Routledge.

Proceso. 2017. Bullying y estrés en estudiantes mexicanos rebasan el promedio [Bullying and stress in mexican students above the average]. https://www.proceso.com.mx/nacional/2017/4/19/bullying-estres-en-estudiantes-mexicanos-rebasan-el-promedio-ocde-182658.html (accessed 21 november 2017)

Proceso. 2014. Me sostengo en lo dicho la corrupción es cultural [I stand by my words corruption is cultural]. https://www.proceso.com.mx/381646/me-sostengo-en-lo-dicho-la-corrupcion-es-cultural-pena

Puri, Jyoti. 2004. *Encountering Nationalism*. Oxford: Blackwell.

Putman, Robert. 1993. The Prosperous Community: Social Capital and Public Life. *American Prospect* 4. 35–42.

Putnam, Robert. 2000. *Bowling alone: the Collapse and Revival of American Community*. New York: Simon and Schuster.

Quijano, Anibal. 2014. *Cuestiones y horizontes. De la dependencia histórico-estructural a la colonialidad/descolonialidad del poder* [Questions and horizons. From historic-structural dependency to coloniality/decoloniality of power]. Buenos Aires: CLACSO.

Quijano, Anibal. 2019. Colonialidad del poder, eurocentrismo y América Latina [Coloniality of power, eurocentrism and Latin America]. *Espacio Abierto* 28(1). 255–301.

Ramirez, Carolina. 2015. It's not how it was: the Chilean diaspora's changing landscape of belonging'. In James Malcolm, Helen Kim & Victoria Redclift (eds.), *New Racial Landscapes. Contemporary Britain and the Neoliberal Conjuncture*, 92–108. London and New York: Routledge.

Ramírez-Meda, Kenia María. 2022. El reto de la atención a migrantes haitianos en Mexicali [Addressing challenges in Haitian migrants in Mexicali] https://migracion.nexos.com.mx/2022/04/el-reto-de-la-atencion-a-migrantes-haitianos-en-mexicali/#_ftnref1 (accessed 20 july 2022).

Ramos, Cristina. 2018. Onward migration from Spain to London in times of crisis: the importance of life-course junctures in secondary migrations. *Journal of Ethnic and Migration Studies* 44(11). 1841–1857

Ramos, Pérez, Arturo. 2004. *Globalización y Neoliberalismo. Ejes de la Reestructuración del Capitalismo Mundial y del Estado en el fin del Siglo XX* [Globalisation and neoliberalism. Restructuring axis of world and state capitalism by the end of the XX century]. México: Plaza Valdez.

Rampton, Ben. 1995. *Crossing: Language and Ethnicity Among Adolescents*. London: Longman.

Rampton, Ben. 2006. *Language in late modernity: Interaction in an urban school*. Cambridge; Cambridge University Press.

Rampton, Ben. 2010. Social class and Sociolinguistics. *Applied Linguistics Review* 1. 1–21.

Rassool, Naz, Kathleen Heugh, Sabiha Mansoor & Maggie Canvin. 2007. *Global Issues in Language, Education and Development: Perspectives from Postcolonial Countries*. Clevedon: Multilingual Matters

Reagan, Ronald. 1981. Inaugural Address. http://www.presidency.ucsb.edu/ws/?pid=43130 (accessed 02 february 2018)

Rehmann, Jan. 2014. *Theories of Ideology. The Powers of Alienation and Subjection*. Chicago: Haymarket Books.

Reichman, Daniel. 2013. Honduras: The Perils of Remittance Dependence and Clandestine Migration. The Online Journal of The Migration Policy Institute. https://www.migrationpolicy.org/article/honduras-perils-remittance-dependence-and-clandestine-migration (accessed 13 january 2023)

Reina, Mauricio & Sandra Zuluaga. 2012. *The Impact of Globalization on Latin America: The Case of Colombia*. Colombia: Associate Researchers Fedesarrollo Bogotá. https://umshare.miami.edu/web/wda/hemisphericpolicy/Task_Force_Papers/Reina-GlobalizationTF.pdf (accessed 01 may 2016)

Rhenals Doria, Ana Milena & Francisco Javier Flórez Bolívar. 2013. Escogiendo entre los extranjeros "indeseables": afro-antillanos, sirio-libaneses, raza e inmigración en Colombia, 1880–1937 [Choosing among undesirable foreigners: Afroantilleans, sirian-lebanese, race and immigration in Colombia, 1880–1937]. *Anuario Colombiano de Historia Social y de la Cultura* 40 (1). 243–271

Ribando, Clare. 2005. Ecuador: Political and Economic Situation and U.S. Relations. Analyst in Latin American Affairs. Foreign Affairs, Defense, and Trade Division. www.au.af.mil/au/awc/awcgate/crs/rs21687 (accessed 11 may 2015)

Ricento, Thomas., 2012. Political economy and English as a 'global' language. *Critical Multilingualism Studies* 1(1). 31–56.

Ritzer, Geoge & Paul Dean. 2014. *Globalization: A Basic Text*. Oxford. Blackwell Publishing.

Roberts, Kenneth M. 2009. Beyond Neoliberalism: Popular Responses to Social Change in Latin Americ. In John Burdick, Philip Oxhorn & Keneth Roberts (eds.), *Beyond Neoliberalism in Latin America? Societies and Politics at the Crossroads, 1–16*. USA: Palgrave MacMillan.

Rodríguez-Vignoli, Jorge & Francisco Rowe. 2018. How is internal migration reshaping metropolitan populations in Latin America? A new method and new evidence. *Population Studies* 72(2). 253–273, https://doi.org/10.1080/00324728.2017.1416155

Rodríguez-Chavez, Ernesto. 2016. *Migración Centroamericana en Tránsito Irregular por México: Nuevas Cifras y Tendencias* [Central American migration in irregular transit through Mexico: New figures and trends]. Migración en tránsito irregular por mexico 2016.pdf (accessed 11december 2021).

Roman-Velazquez, Patria. 1999. *The Making of Latin London: Salsa Music, Place and Identity*. UK. Taylor & Francis Ltd.

Roman-Velazquez, Patria (2014). Claiming a place in the global city: Urban regeneration and Latin American spaces in London.' *EPTIC, Political Economy of Technology, Information and Culture Journal* 16(1). 84–104.

Roman-Velazquez, Patria; Hill, Nicola. 2016. The case for London's Latin Quarter: retention, growth, sustainability. Loughborough University. Report. https://hdl.handle.net/2134/21844 (accessed 15 may 2017)

Román-Velázquez, Patria. 2022. Resisting gentrification, reclaiming urban spaces: Latin urbanisms in London. *Journal of Urbanism: International Research on Placemaking and Urban Sustainability* https://doi.org/10.1080/17549175.2022.2071967

Romero-Galvan, José Ruben. 2003. *La nobleza indígena en la época colonial. Privilegios económicos* [The indigenous nobility in the colonial period. Economic privileges]. Mexico: Instituto de Investigaciones Históricas, UNAM. https://historicas.unam.mx/publicaciones/publicadigital/libros/419/419_04_03_PrivilegiosEconomicos.pdf (accessed 18 november 2022)

Rosas, Ana Elizabeth. 2006. *Flexible families: Bracero Families' Lives across Cultures, Communities, and Countries, 1942–1964*. USA: University of South California Doctoral thesis.

Ryan, Louise. 2011. Migrants' social Networks and Weak Ties. Accessing Resources and Constructing Relationships Post-Migration. *The Sociological Review* 59(4). 707–724.

Ruhs, Martin & Bridget Anderson. 2010. *Who needs Migrant Workers? Labour shortages. Immigration and Public Policy*. Oxford: Oxford University Press.

Rzepnikowska, Alina. 2019. Racism and xenophobia experienced by Polish migrants in the UK before and after Brexit vote. *Journal of Ethnic and Migration Studies* 45(1). 61–77 https://doi.org/10.1080/1369183X.2018.1451308

Safran William. 1991. Diasporas in modern societies: Myths of homeland and return'. *Diaspora* 1(1). 83–99.

Salazar Anaya, Delia. 1996. *La población extranjera en México (1895 –1990)* [The foreign population in Mexico (1895–1990)]. Mexico city: Instituto Nacional de Antropología e Historia.

Sallabank, Julia. 2011. Language Endangerment. In Ruth Wodak, Barbara Johnstone & Paul Kerswill (eds.), *The Sage Handbook of Sociolinguistics*, 496–512. London: Sage Publications.

Salinas, Cristobal. 2020. "The Complexity of the "x" in Latinx: How Latinx/a/o Students Relate to, identify with, and understand the Term Latinx". *Journal of Hispanic Higher Education* 19(2). 149–168.

Samers, Michael. 2010. *Migration*. USA: Routledge.

Santa Ana, Otto. 2002. *Brown Tide Rising: Metaphors of Latinos in Contemporary American Public Discourse*. Austin: University of Texas Press.

Sapiro, Giselle (ed.). 2010. *Sociology is a Martial art: Political Writings by Pierre Bourdieu*. New York: The New Press.

Sassen, Saskia. 2002. Global Cities and Diasporic Networks: Microsites in Global Civil Society. In Marlies Glasius, Mary Kaldor & Helmut Anheier (eds.), *Global Civil Society*. 217–238. Oxford: Oxford University Press.

Sassen, Saskia. 2017. The city: A collective good? *The Brown Journal of World Affairs* 23(2). 119–126.

Savage, Michael. 2000. *Class Analysis and Social Transformation*. Oxford: Oxford University Press.

Say, Jean Baptiste. 1971 [1803]. *A Treatise on Political Economy*. New York: Augustus M. Kelly.

Schwarcz, Lilia. 1990. De festa também se vive: reflexões sobre o centenário da abolição em São Paulo, [we also celebrate: reflections upon one hundred years of abolition in Sao Paolo] *Estudos Afro-Asiaticos* 18. 13–26

Schultz, Kirsten. 2017. Atlantic Transformations and Brazil's Imperial Independence. In John Tutino (ed.), *New Countries: Capitalism, Revolutions, and Nations in the Americas, 1750–1870*, 201–230. USA: Duke University Press.

Sennet, Richard & Jonathan Cobb. 1972. *The Hidden Injuries of Class*. New York: Norton.

Sheffer, Gabriel. 2003. *Diaspora Politics: At Home Abroad*. Cambridge: Cambridge University Press.

Shin, Hyunjung & Joseph Sung-Yul Park. 2016. Researching language and neoliberalism. *Journal of Multilingual and Multicultural Development* 37(5). 443–452

Shuman Amy & Carol Bohmer. 2020. Discourse and Narrative in Legal Settings: The Political Asylum Process. In Anna De Fina & Alexandra Georgakapoulou (eds.), *Handbook of Discourse Studies*, 547–570. Cambridge: Cambridge University Press.

Sieber Joan E. 1992. *Planning Ethically Responsible Research: A Guide for Students and Internal Review Boards*. London: Sage.

Silverstein, Michael. 1998. The Uses and Utility of Ideology: A Commentary. In Bambi Schieffelin, Kathryn Woolard & Paul Kroskrity (eds.), *Language Ideologies*, 123–145. New York: Oxford University Press.

Silverstein, Michael. 1979. Language Structure and Linguistic Ideology. In Paul Clyne, Williams F. Hanks & Carol L. Hofbauer (eds.), *The Elements: A parasession on Linguistic units and Levels*, 193–248. Chicago: Chicago Linguistics Society.

Silverstein, Michael. 2003. Indexical Order and the Dialectics of Sociolinguistic Life. *Language and Communication* 23 (3–4). 193–229.

Simonsen, Roberto.C. 1957. *Historia Económica do Brasil:1500–1800* [Economic history of Brazil: 1500–1800]. Sao Paulo: Companhia Editora Nacional.

Simpson, Paul & Andrea May. 2000. *Language and Power: A Resource Book for Students*. London. Routledge.

Simpson William & John ÓRegan. 2018. Fetishism and the language commodity: a materialist critique. *Language Sciences* 70(2018). 155–166.

Sciortino, Giuseppe. 2004. Between Phantoms and necessary evils. Some critical points in the study of irregular migrations to Western Europe'. *IMIS-BEITRAGE* 24. 17–43.

Skeggs, Beverley. 1997. *Formations of class and gender: becoming respectable*. London: Sage.

Skeggs, Beverley. 2004. *Class, Self, Culture*. Great Britain: Routledge.

Slaney, Klasiena. 2012. De-professionalisation of Public Service Interpreting in the UK. http://www.linguistlounge.org/articles/de-professionalisation-of-public-service-interpreting-in-the-uk/ (accessed 06 september 2018).

Slaven, Mike & Christina Boswell. 2019. Why symbolise control? Irregular migration to the UK and symbolic policy-making in the 1960s. *Journal of Ethnic and Migration Studies* 45(9). 1477–1495. https://doi.org/10.1080/1369183X.2018.1459522

Slembrouck, Stef. 2011. Globalization Theory and Migration. In Ruth Wodak, Barbara Johnstone & Paul Kerswill (eds.), *The Sage Handbook of Sociolinguistics*, 153–165 London: Sage Publications.

Smith, J. 2005. Narrative in sociolinguistic research. In E. Keith Brown & Ron Asher (eds.), *The Encyclopedia of Language and Linguistics*, 473–476. Amsterdam: Elsevier.

Smith, Nicola. 2007. Neoliberalism. In Mark Bevir (ed.), *Encyclopaedia of Governance*. Thousand Oaks. Sage Publications.

Somerville, Will. 2016. When the Dust Settles: Migration Policy after Brexit. Migration Policy Institute. https://www.migrationpolicy.org/news/when-dust-settles-migration-policy-after-brexit (accessed 26 september 2018)

Song, Juyoung. 2010. Language ideology and identity in transnational space: globalization, migration, and bilingualism among Korean families in the USA. *International Journal of Bilingual Education and Bilingualism* 13(1). 23–42.

Spotti, Massimiliano. 2011. Ideologies of Success for Superdiverse Citizens: the Dutch Testing Regime for Integration and the Online Private Sector'. In Jan Blommaert, Ben Rampton & Massimiliano Spotti (eds.), *Language and Superdiversity – Special issue of Diversities Journal*. 13(2). 39–52. Max Plank/UNESCO.

Stack, John F. 1986. Ethnic mobilization in world politics: the primordial perspective. In John F. Stack (ed.), *The Primordial Challenge: Ethnicity in the Contemporary World*, 1–11. Westport, CT: Greenwood Press.

Stedman-Jones, Daniel. 2012. *Master of the Universe. Hayek, Friedman and the Birth of Neoliberal Politics*. UK: Princeton University Press.

Steger Manfred B. 2010. *Neoliberalism: a very short introduction*. New York; Oxford University Press.

Stiglitz, Joseph E. 2002. *Globalization and its discontents*. London: Penguin.

Stockler, Sarah. 2015. Mexican immigrants' views on the Spanish dialects in Mexico: a language attitudes study. *Lengua y migración* 7(2). 49–73

Sulmon, David &Juan Carlos Callirgos. 2019. ¿El país de todas las sangres? Etnicidad y raza en Perú [The country of all bloods? Ethnicity and race in Peru]. In Edward Telles & Regina Martínez Casas (eds.), *Pigmentocracias. color, etnicidad y raza en América Latina* [Pigmentocracy, colour, ethnicity and race in Latin America], 159–206. México: Fondo de Cultura Económica.

Summers, Chris. 2005. Interpreter shortage poses threat. http://news.bbc.co.uk/2/hi/uk_news/4416984.stm (accessed 08 november 2020)

Sveinsson, Kjartan Pall. 2007. *Bolivians in London – Challenges and Achievements of a London Community*. Runnymede Community Studies, Runnymede Trust. http://www.runnymedetrust.org/uploads/publications/pdfs/BoliviansInLondon-2007.pdf (accessed 02 march 2015)

Takenaka, Ayumi, Karsten Paerregaard & Ulla Berg. 2010. Introduction: Peruvian Migration in a Global Context. *Latin American Perspectives* 37(5). 3–11.

Taylor Sims, Kit. 1970. The Economics of Sugar and Slavery in Northeastern Brazil. *Agricultural History* 44(3). 267–280.

Telles, Edward & Regina Martínez-Casas. 2019. *Pigmentocracias. Color, Etnicidad y Raza en America Latina* [Pigmentocracy, colour, ethnicity and race in Latin America]. Mexico: Fondo de Cultura Económica.

Teunissen, Erik, Alexandra Tsaparas, Aristoula Saridaki, Maria Trigoni, Evelyn van Weel-Baumgarten, Chris van Weel, Maria van den Muijsenbergh & Christos Lionis. 2016. Reporting mental health problems of undocumented migrants in Greece: A qualitative exploration. *European Journal of General Practice* 22(2). 119–125

Thatcher, Margaret. 1987. Interview for Woman's Own ("no such thing as society"). https://www.margaretthatcher.org/document/106689 (accessed 10 february 2017]

The Migration Observatory. 2014. Health of Migrants in the UK: What Do We Know? http://www.migrationobservatory.ox.ac.uk/resources/briefings/health-of-migrants-in-the-uk-what-do-we-know/ (accessed on 02 november 2017)

The Royal Geographic Society. 2008. *UK Migration controversies. A simple guide*. https://www.rgs.org/NR/rdonlyres/4711AA55-F60A-4B16-9F30-27DEF5232C03/0/MigrationFINAL.pdf (accessed 10 february 2016)

Thompson, John. 1984. *Studies in the theory of ideology*. Berkeley: University of California Press.

Thompson, Jack & Daniel E. Martinez. 2022. Linked fate, cumulative discrimination, and panethnic identification: awareness and use of 'Latinx' among a nationally representative sample of Hispanics/Latinos. *Journal of Ethnic and Migration Studies* 48(19). 4503–4526 https://doi.org/10.1080/1369183X.2022.2081838

Timming, Andrew R. 2016. The effect of foreign accent on employability: a study of the aural dimensions of aesthetic labour in customer-facing and non-customer-facing jobs. *Work, Employment and Society* 31(3). 409–428.

Thornborrow, Joanna & Jennifer Coates. 2005. *The Sociolinguistics of Narrative*. Amsterdam: John Benjamins Publishing.

Thränhardt, Dietrich. 1996. European migration from East to West: present patterns and future directions. *New community* 22(2). 227–242.

Tölöyan, Khachig. 1996. Rethinking diaspora(s): stateless power in the transnational moment'. *Diaspora* 5(1). 3–36.

Topping, Alexandra. 2014. Universities being used as proxy border police, say academics. https://www.theguardian.com/education/2014/mar/02/universities-border-police-academics (accessed 25 november 2018)

Torrado, Susana. 1979. International Migration Policies in Latin America. *The International Migration Review* 13(3). 428–439. https://doi.org/10.2307/2545574

Triandafyllidou, Anna. 2010. Irregular Migration in Europe in the early 21st Century. In Anna Triandafyllidou (ed.), *Research in Migration and Ethnic Relations Series: Irregular Migration in Europe: Myths and Realities*, 1–21. New York: Routledge.
Trudgill, Peter. 1974. *The Social Differentiation of English in Norwich*. Cambridge: Cambridge University Press.
Tsuda, Takeyuki. 2000. Acting Brazilian in Japan: Ethnic Resistance among Return Migrants. *Ethnology* 39(1). 55–71. https://doi.org/10.2307/3773795
Turcatti, Domiziana & Carlos Vargas-Silva. 2022. I returned to being an immigrant": onward Latin American migrants and Brexit. *Ethnic and Racial Studies* 45(16). 287–307.
Twinam, Ann. 2016. *Purchasing Whiteness. Pardos, Mulattos, and the Quest for Social Mobility in the Spanish Indies*. California: Standford University Press.
Ullman, Char. 2012. My grain of sand for society": neoliberal freedom, language learning, and the circulation of ideologies of national belonging. *International Journal of Qualitative Studies in Education* 4. 453–470.
United Nations (UN). 2017. *International Migration Report*. Department of Economic and Social Affairs. http://www.un.org/en/development/desa/population/migration/publications/migrationreport/docs/MigrationReport2017_Highlights.pdf (accessed 20 july 2018]
Urciouli, Bonnie. 2008. Skills and selves in the new workplace. *American Ethnologist* 35(2). 211–228. 209
Urciouli, Bonnie & Chaise LaDousa. 2013. Language Management/Labor. *The Annual Review of Anthropology* 42. 175–190.
Viáfara López, Carlos Augusto & Mara Viveros Vogoya. 2019. Del Mestizaje Blanco al multiculturalismo triétnico. Raza y Etnicicidad en Colombia (From white mixing to triethnic multiculturalism. Race and ethnicity in Colombia]. In Edward Telles & Regina Martínez Casas (eds.), *Pigmentocracias. Color, etnicidad y raza en America Latina*, [Pigmentocracy, Colour, ethnicity and race in Latin America], 108–158. Mexico: Fondo de Cultura Económica.
van Dijk, Teun A. 1985. Semantic Discourse Analysis. In Teun A. van Dijk (ed.), *Handbook of Discourse Analysis*. Vol. 2, 103–112. London: Academic Press
van Dijk, Teun A. 1993. Principles of critical discourse analysis. *Discourse and Society* 4(2). 249–83.
Van Dijk, T. 1995. Discourse Analysis as ideology analysis. In Christina Schäffner & Anita Wenden (eds.), *Language and Peace*, 17–33. Aldershot: Dartmouth.
van Dijk, Teun A. 1997. The study of Discourse. In Teun A. van Dijk (ed.), *Discourse as Social Structure. Discourse Studies: A Multidisciplinary Approach*. Volume 1, 1–34. London: Sage.
Van Dijk, Teun A. 1998. *Ideology: A Multidisciplinary Approach*. London: Sage.
Van Dijk, Teun A. 2000. On the Analysis of Parliamentary Debates on immigration. In Martin Reisigl & Ruth Wodak (eds.), *The Semiotics of racism: Approaches in critical discourse analysis*, 85–104. Vienna: Passagen Verlag.
Van Dijk, Teun A. 2001. Multidisciplinary CDA: A Plea for Diversity. In Ruth Wodak & Michael Meyer (eds.), *Methods of Critical Discourse Studies. Introducing Qualitative Methods*, 95–120. London: Sage.
Van Dijk, Teun A. 2003. Ideology and Discourse: A Multidisciplinary Introduction. http://onlinebooks.library.upenn.edu/webbin/book/lookupid?key=olbp74712 (accesed 10 march 2016]
Van Dijk, Teun A. 2006. Politics, Ideology and Discourse. In Keith Brown (ed.), *The Encyclopedia of Language and Linguistics*. Vol. 9. 728–740. Oxford/New York: Pergamon Press,
Van Dijk, Teun A. 2013. CDA is NOT a method of critical discourse analysis. EDISO Debate- Asociación de Estudios sobre Discurso y Sociedad. www.edisoportal.org/debate/115-cda-not-method-critical-discourse-analysis (accessed 04 september 2016)

Van Dijk, Teun A. 2014. *Discourse and Knowledge. A Sociocognitive Approach*. UK: Cambridge University Press.
Van Dijk, T.A. 2016. Critical Discourse Studies: A Sociocognitive Approach. In Ruth Wodak & Michale Meyer (eds.), *Methods of Critical Discourse Studies*. Third Edition. 62–85 London: Sage.
Vertovec, Steven. 1999. Conceiving and researching transnationalism. *Ethnic and Racial Studies* 22(2). 447–62.
Vertovec, Steven. 2007. Super-Diversity and its Implications. *Ethnic and Racial Studies* 30(6). 1024–1054.
Vicente Torrado, Trinidad L. 2005. *La inmigración Latinoamericana en España* [Latin American immigration to Spain]. Expert group Meeting on International Migration and Development in Latin America and the Caribbean. Available at: http://www.un.org/esa/population/meetings/Itt MigLAC/P13_Vicente.pdf. (accessed 04 april 2015)
Villar, Juan Manuel. 1984. Argentine Experience in the Field of Illegal Immigration. *The International Migration Review* 18(3). 453–473. https://doi.org/10.1177/019791838401800305
Vollmer, Bastian. 2010. Dichotomised Discourses and Changing Landscapes: Counting the Uncountable in the UK. In Anna Triandafyllidou (ed.), *Research in Migration and Ethnic Relations Series: Irregular Migration in Europe: Myths and Realitiies*, 267–290. GB: Ashgate.
Von, Mises, Ludwig. 2007. *Human Action: A Treatise on Economics*. USA: Liberty Fund.
Wade, Peter. 2010. *Race and Ethnicity in Latin America*. Second edition. London: Pluto Press.
Wadsworth, Jonathan. 2017. *Immigration and the UK economy. Centre for Economic Performance*. London School of Economics and Political Science. http://cep.lse.ac.uk/pubs/download/ea039.pdf (accessed 05 march 2018)
Waldinger, Roger & David Fitzgerald. 2004. Transnationalism in question. *American Journal of Sociology* 109(5). 1177–1195
Walker, Charles. 2019. *La Rebelion de Tupac Amaru* [Tupac Amaru's uprising]. Segunda Edición Revisada. Lima: Instituto de Estudios Peruanos.
Warriner, Doris S. 2007. "It's just the nature of the beast": Re-imagining the literacies of schooling in adult ESL education. *Linguistics and Education* 18(3–4). 305–324.
Weiss, Anja. 2005. The transnationalization of social inequality: conceptualizing social positions on a world scale. *Current Sociology* 53(4). 707–724.
Westmarland, Louise. 2000. Taking the flak: operational policing, fear and violence. In Geraldine Lee Treweek and Stephanie Linkogle (eds.), *Danger in the Field: Risk and Ethics in Social Research*, 26–42. London: Routledge.
Wilder, Gary. 2022. *Concrete Utopianism. The Politics of Temporality and Solidarity*. New York: Fordham University Press.
Wills, Jane, Kavita Datta & Yara Evans. 2009. *Global Cities at Work: New Migrant Divisions of Labour*. London: Pluto Press.
Williams, Raymond. 1977. *Marxism and Literature*. Oxford: Oxford University Press.
Williamson, E. 2009. ESOL and community cohesion: inclusion or just exclusion under another name? http://esolsig.files.wordpress.com/2010/07/esol-and-community-cohesioninclusion-or-just-exclusion-under-another-name.docx (accessed 26 march 2019)
Wimmer, Andreas & Nina Glick Schiller. 2002. Methodological nationalism and the study of Migration. *Archives Européennes de Sociologie* 43(2). 17–40.
Wodak, Ruth. 2001. What CDA is about: a summary of its history, important concepts and its developments. In Ruth Wodak & Micahel Meyer (eds.), *Methods of Critical Discourse Studies. Introducing Qualitative Methods*, 1–13. London: Sage.

Wodak, Ruth. 2009. The semiotics of racism. A Critical Discourse-Historical Analysis. In Jan Renkema (ed.), *Discourse, of course: An overview of research in discourse studies*, 311–326. Amsterdam/ Philadelphia: John Benjamins Publishing Company.
Wodak, Ruth, Barbara Johnstone & Paul Kerswill. 2011. Introduction. In Ruth Wodak, Barbara Johnstone & Paul Kerswil (eds.), *The Sage Handbook of Sociolinguistics*, 1–8. London: Sage Publications.
Wodak, Ruth &Martin Reisigl. 2016. The Discourse-Historical Approach. In Ruth Wodak & Michael Meyer (eds.), *Methods of Critical Discourse Studies*, 23–61. London: Sage Publications.
Wodak, Ruth & Michael Meyer (eds.). 2016. *Methods of Critical Discourse Studies*. London: Sage Publications.
Woodcock, Jamie. 2014. Precarious Workers in London: New forms of organisation and the city. *City* 18(6). 776–788.
Woodward, Kath (ed). 2004. *Questioning Identity Gender: Gender, Class, Ethnicity*. London: Routledge.
Woolard, Kathryn A. 1998. Language ideology as a field of Inquiry. In Bambi Schieffelin, Kathryn Woolard & Paul V. Kroskrity (eds.), *Language ideologies: Practice and Theory*, 1–27. Oxford: Oxford University Press.
Woolard, Kathryn A. 2008. Language and identity choice in Catalonia: the interplay of contrasting ideologies of linguistic authority. In Kirsten Süselbeck, Ulrike Mühlschlegel & Peter Masson (eds.), *Lengua, nación e identidad. La regulación del plurilingüismo en España y América Latina* [Language, nation and identity. Regulating plurilingualism in Spain and Latin America], 303–323. Frankfurt am Main & Madrid: Vervuert & Iberoamericana.
Woolard, Kathryn A. 2016. *Singular and Plural. Ideologies of Linguistic Authority in the 21st Century Catalonia*. New York: Oxford University Press.
Wrenn, Mary V. & William Waller. 2017. Care and the Neoliberal Individual. *Journal of Economic Issues* 51(2). 495–502.
Wright, Erik Olin (ed.). 2005. *Approaches to class analysis*. Cambridge: Cambridge University Press.
Wright, Katie. 2011. Conceptualizing Human Well- Being from a Gender and Life Course Perspective: The Case of Peruvian Migrants in London. In Cathy McIlwaine (ed.), *Cross-Border Migration among Latin Americans. European Perspectives and Beyond*, 139–155.New York: Palgrave McMillan.
Wu, Bin & Hon Liu. 2014. Bringing class back in: class consciousness and solidarity among Chinese migrant workers in Italy and the UK. *Ethnic and Racial Studies* 37(8). 1391–1408.
Yates, Caitlyn. 2021. Haitian Migration through the Americas: A Decade in the Making. https://www.migrationpolicy.org/article/haitian-migration-through-americas (accessed 16 august 2021)
Yee Quintero, José Carlos. 2017. Caracterizando a solicitantes de asilo a Estados Unidos: el caso de los haitianos en 2016 [Characterising asylum applicants in the United States: the case of Haitians in 2016]. In Raúl Pérez-Rojas (ed.), *Vidas en vilo. Historias y testimonios de migrantes internacionales*, [Lives on a thread. Stories and testimonies of international migrants], 53–83. Tijuana: ILCSA Ediciones.
Yepez del Castillo, Isabel. 2007. Introducción. In Isabel Yepez del Castillo & Gioconda Herrera (eds.), *Nuevas Migraciones Latinoamericanas a Europa*, 19–30. Ecuador: FLACSO.
Zapata-Barrero, Ricard & Nynke de Witte. 2006. *Report prepared for the project: A European Approach to Multicultural Citizenship. Legal Political and Educational Challenges*. Department of Social and Political Science. Universitat Pompeu Fabra. http://www.upf.edu/gritim/_pdf/griip-emilie_wp2.pdf (accessed 15 april 2015).

Index

assimilation
– linguistic 163

Brixton 15
– Jalisco restaurant 16

caste system 31
– and economic power 32
CDS 89
– sociocognitive 93
Central America 39
class 58
– as capital 59
colonisation 30
Community 53

declassing 114
deportation 116
dialogism 97
diaspora 43
– and communication technologies 44
– and identities 44
– and the homeland 44
– and transnationalism 45
– as accidental 44

Elephant and Castle 6, 55
– and gentrification 9
– demonstration 6
– la bodeguita 8
entrepreneur 66
– and self responsibilisation 152
– as speculator 157
ethnicity 79
– as instrumental 80
European migration 34
– to Peru, Mexico and Colombia 35
Europeanmigration
– to Argentina 34
– to Brazil 34
– to Chile 34
exploitation 134
extraregional migration 37

gender 76
– and language use 78

habitus 60
Hispanic 42

identity 72
ideology 80
– and language 84
– camera obscura 82
– hegemony 83
– of accent 165
– of authenticity 165
– of one nation one language 186, 195
– of socioeconomic mobility 180
– of standard language 169
illegal 115
illegality 118, 197
immigrant
– and social networks 109
– as a heavy burden 103
– as a passive object 101
– as a pollutant 101
– as a vulnerable person 108
Import Substitution Industrialisation 35
Independence 33
– and oligarchy 33
interdiscursivity 97–98
intersectionality 76
intertextuality 98
intracontinental migration 36
IRMO 13
– services 14

language 73
– and identity 74
language as commodity 68
Latin America 30
– as a political project 30
Latin American 5
– and gender 5
– and onward migration 50
– cleaner 11

https://doi.org/10.1515/9783110987973-011

– kitchen 12
– migration to the UK 47
– researcher 5
latino 125
– as manager 126
life story 21, 197
– and experience 22

NAFTA 38
narrative 18
– and asylum 20
– and people's experiences 20
– as linear structure 19
– as small and big stories 20
– oral 18
neoliberalism 63

outsourcing 126, 128

quality of space 112

race 78
removal 116
residual culture 139
Return migration 42

sociolinguistics 61
spanish
– as a bond 8

The Bracero Programme 37
the good worker 130
The Latin American House 54
topos
– of culture 128, 140
transnational identity 75

viceroyalty 31
voice 97

www.ingramcontent.com/pod-product-compliance
Lightning Source LLC
Chambersburg PA
CBHW060352190426
43201CB00044B/2044